Just for the Upper Level ISEE

- **Test Prep Works materials are developed for a specific test and level, making it easier for students to focus on relevant content**

- **The Upper Level ISEE is for students applying for admission to grades 9-12 – see table at the end of this book for materials for other grades**

- **Two books are available from Test Prep Works to help students prepare for the Upper Level ISEE**

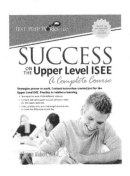

Success on the Upper Level ISEE: A Complete Course

- Strategies for each section of the test

- Reading and vocabulary drills

- In-depth math content instruction with practice sets

- 1 full-length practice test

The Best Unofficial Practice Tests for the Upper Level ISEE

- 2 additional full-length practice tests

TEST PREP WORKS, LLC.

SUCCESS

ON THE **Upper Level ISEE**

A Complete Course

Christa Abbott, M.Ed.

Published by:
Test Prep Works, LLC
PO Box 100572
Arlington, VA 22210
www.TestPrepWorks.com

For information about buying this title in bulk, or for editions with customized covers or content, please contact us at sales@testprepworks.com or (703) 944-6727.

ISEE is a registered trademark of the ERB. They have not endorsed nor are they associated with this book.

Neither the author nor the publisher of this book claims responsibility for the accuracy of this book or the outcome of students who use these materials.

ISBN 978-1-939090-32-4

Contents

About the Author

Christa Abbott has been a private test prep tutor for over a decade. She has worked with students who have been admitted to and attended some of the top independent schools in the country. Over the years, she has developed materials for each test that truly make the difference.

Christa is a graduate of Middlebury College and received her Masters in Education from the University of Virginia, a program nationally known for its excellence. Her background in education allows her to develop materials based on the latest research about how we learn so that preparation can be an effective and efficient use of time. Her materials are also designed to be developmentally appropriate for the ages of the students taking the tests. In her free time, she enjoys hiking, tennis, Scrabble, and reading. Her greatest joy is spending time with her husband and three children.

Christa continues to work with students one-on-one in the Washington, D.C., area. She also works with students internationally via Skype. If you are interested in these services, please visit www.ChristaAbbott.com.

About Test Prep Works

Test Prep Works, LLC, was founded to provide effective materials for test preparation. Its founder, Christa Abbott, spent years looking for effective materials for the private school entrance exams but came up empty-handed. The books available combined several different tests and while there are overlaps, they are not the same test. Christa found this to be very overwhelming for students and that just didn't seem necessary. Christa developed her own materials to use with students that are specific for each level of the individual tests. For the first time, these materials are available to the general public as well as other tutors. Please visit www.TestPrepWorks.com to view a complete array of offerings as well as sign up for a newsletter with recent news and developments in the world of admissions and test preparation.

Notes for Parents

What is the ISEE?

ISEE stands for Independent School Entrance Exam. It is published by the Education Records Bureau (ERB). If you have students already in independent school, you may have seen ERB scores before. You may also have heard of another independent school entrance exam – the SSAT. The schools that your student is applying to may accept either of these two tests, or they may exclusively use one test or the other. It can also depend upon which grade your child is applying for. Contact each school to which your child will apply to be sure that he or she is taking the correct test.

- Contact schools so that your child takes the right test

What level should I register my child for?

This book is designed to help students who are taking the Upper Level ISEE. If students are applying for grades 9 through 12, then they should be taking the Upper Level ISEE. If this does not describe your student, please visit www.TestPrepWorks.com to order the correct materials for the level that your student will be taking.

- Upper Level is for students applying to grades 9-12

What do I need to know about registering my child?

Students can take the ISEE up to three times during a school year – once in the fall (August-November), once in the winter (December-March), and once in the spring (April-July). Since most students take the test between October and December, it is important to plan carefully if your student wishes to take the test more than once. For schools with a traditional admissions timeline, he or she could take the test in October or November and then again in December or January. He or she could not take the test in December and then again in January because both of those dates are in the winter time period.

- Students may take the test up to three times – once in the fall (August-November), once in the winter (December-March) and once in the spring (April-July)

Registration is done through the ERB. Their website is www.erblearn.org. On this site, you can also download a copy of *What to Expect on the ISEE*. The beginning of the book gives some sample problems and the end of the book has a practice test (although it isn't quite full length). I recommend that you wait to give your student this practice test until after he or she has completed other preparations. Practice tests from the actual writers of the test are a valuable commodity, so save the practice test from *What to Expect on the ISEE*.

- Download *What to Expect on the ISEE*
- Feel free to have your student work through sample problems in the beginning of the book, but save the practice test until after your student has done other preparations

The test can be taken in paper format or online at a testing center. The paper format is given at a number of schools in a large group setting. It can also be given in a small group setting at the ERB's New York offices or at a very limited number of sites in other locations. In the most recent ISEE student guide, small group testing sites are listed for Connecticut, Florida, Massachusetts, New York, Pennsylvania, Texas, China, and South Korea. Outside of these areas, small group testing with the paper form is not available.

- Most students take the paper format at a school in a large group setting
- A very limited number of sites give the paper test in a small group setting – the list of these sites is in the *ISEE Student Guide*

The computer-based form of the test is offered at Prometric centers nationwide. The test is exactly the same as the paper format test. Students can still go back and change answers. The only difference is that the students who take the computer-based test get to type their essays while students who take the paper form have to handwrite their essays. Also, the testing centers allow you to choose the time and date that works best for your student. If you do go the testing center route, make sure that your student knows that there will be people of all ages there taking a variety of tests.

- The ISEE can be taken at a testing center on the computer
- The computer-based test offers flexibility with date/time

You must request accommodations if your child needs them. If your child has an IEP or receives accommodations in school, then start the paperwork with the ERB promptly. Don't wait until the last minute, as this can be very stress-inducing for both you and your student. If your child is going to get extended time, he or she should know that as he or she works through practice sections.

Just how important is the ISEE to the admissions process?

Every school uses the test differently. In general, the more competitive the school, the more that test scores are going to matter, but there are certainly exceptions to that rule. Reading through a school's literature is a great way to figure out whether or not a school emphasizes or deemphasizes testing. Also, call the admissions offices of the schools where your child plans to apply. Admissions officers are often quite candid about the testing profile of their admitted students.

- Talk to the schools that your child is applying to in order to get a sense of the scores that they look for

How can I help my student?

Keep your own cool. Never once has a student gotten a higher score because mom or dad freaked out. Approach this as a project. Good test taking skills can be learned. By working through the process with your child in a constructive manner, you are providing him or her with a roadmap for how to approach challenges in the future. We want a student to be confident, and we want that confidence to be earned through analysis, self-monitoring, and practice.

- Keep a positive attitude

What are the key elements of successful test preparation?

Analysis

It is important that students don't just do practice problem after practice problem without figuring out what they missed, and most importantly, WHY they missed those problems. Is there a particular type of problem that they keep missing? One issue that many students have is with categorizing problems. When you go through a problem that your student is stuck on, be sure to point out the words in the problem that pointed you in the correct direction.

- Teach your child to analyze why he or she missed a question

Self-monitoring

Students should develop a sense of their strengths and weaknesses so that they can best focus their preparation time. This book provides many practice opportunities for each section, but your child may not need that. For example, if he or she is acing the math problems, then he or she shouldn't keep spending valuable time doing more of those problems. Maybe his or her time would be better spent on vocabulary. This is a great opportunity, and your student is at the perfect age, to be learning how to prioritize.

- Help your student prioritize material to work on

Practice

While it is important that students understand WHY they are doing what they are doing, at a certain point it needs to become automatic. This is a timed test and you want the strategies to spring to mind without having to reinvent the wheel every time. Practice will make this process fast and easy. On test day, all that practice will kick in to make this a positive and affirming experience for your student.

- Teach your child to practice what he or she has learned so that it is automatic on test day

How To Use This Book

This book is designed to teach you what you need to know in order to maximize your Upper Level ISEE performance.

There are strategies for each of the four multiple-choice sections as well as advice on the essay.

This book also includes a lot of content practice. There is a complete vocabulary section and detailed instruction for the math concepts that are tested on the ISEE.

You may find that you don't need to complete all of the content instruction. It is important to prioritize your time! If vocabulary is a weakness for you, then spend your time working through the vocabulary lessons. If some of the math concepts are challenging, then you should spend your study time working through the math sections.

At the end of this book is a practice test. This will give you a good idea of how you are doing with timing and what it feels like to take a longer test. There are score charts included after the test, but please keep in mind that these are a very rough estimate. It is very, very tough to accurately determine percentiles without a huge amount of data, so we have included percentiles just as a rough guideline of how the scoring works.

After you complete the practice test in this book, complete the practice test in *What to Expect on the ISEE*. That will give you your best estimate of performance on the actual ISEE.

I have spent years studying the test and analyzing the different question types, content, and the types of answers that the test writers prefer. Now you can benefit from my hard work! I will show how to approach questions so that you can raise your score significantly.

Let's get started!

The Format of the Upper Level ISEE

You can expect to see four scored sections plus an essay. The sections are listed below in the order that they will appear on the ISEE. One great thing about the ISEE is that it has a very predictable format.

The four scored sections

- ✓ Verbal Reasoning
  - 40 total questions
  - 19 vocabulary (or synonyms) questions
  - 12 sentence completion questions with single word answer choices
  - 9 sentence completion questions with two-word answer choices
  - 20 minutes to complete

- ✓ Quantitative Reasoning
  - 37 total questions
  - 18-21 word problems
  - 14-17 quantitative comparisons
  - Not all questions require calculations
  - 35 minutes to complete

- ✓ Reading Comprehension
  - 36 total questions
  - 6 passages with 6 questions about each passage
  - 35 minutes to complete

- ✓ Mathematics Achievement
  - 47 math questions
  - Questions probably look more like questions that you see in school than Quantitative Reasoning questions do
  - 40 minutes to complete

The essay

- Prompt for students to respond to
- 30 minutes to complete
- Two lined pieces of paper to write response on
- NOT scored, but a copy of the essay is sent to schools that student applies to

Now, on to the strategies and content! The strategies covered in this book will focus on the multiple-choice sections since those are what is used to determine your score. Please also see the essay section for tips on how to write the essay.

What Students Need to Know for the ISEE – Just the Basics

Here is what you really need to know to do well on the Upper Level ISEE:

How the scoring works

On the ISEE, your score is determined by how many questions you answer correctly. No points are taken off if you answer a question incorrectly.

When to guess

On the ISEE, you want to answer absolutely everything, even if you haven't even looked at the question. You might answer the question correctly, and you won't lose any points for questions that you answer incorrectly. If you are running out of time or don't understand a question, just blindly guess – you may choose the right answer!

The percentile score

You will get a raw score for the ISEE based upon how many questions you answer correctly. This raw score will then be converted into a scaled score. Neither of these scores is what schools are really looking at. They are looking for your percentile scores.

- Percentile score is what schools are really looking at

The percentile score compares you to other students that are in your grade. For example, let's say that you are an eighth grader and you score in the 70th percentile. What this means is that out of 100 students in your grade, you have done better than 70 of them.

- Your percentile score compares you only to other students in your grade

Many students applying to independent schools are used to answering almost all of the questions correctly on a test. You will probably miss more questions on this test than you are used to missing, but because the percentile score is what schools are looking at, don't let it get to you.

- You may miss more questions than you are used to, but that is OK as long as other students your age also miss those questions

You should also look at the scoring charts in *What to Expect on the ISEE*. These charts will give you a rough idea of how many questions you need to answer correctly to achieve different percentile scores.

Students always want to know, "What is a good percentile score?" Well, that depends on the school you are applying to. The best resources are the admissions officers at the schools that you want to attend.

The Mother of All Strategies

Use the process of elimination, or "ruling out"

If you remember nothing else on test day, remember to use process of elimination. This is a multiple-choice test, and there are often answers that don't even make sense.

When you read a question, you should read all of the answer choices before selecting one. You need to keep in mind that the test will ask you to choose the answer choice that "best" answers the question. Best is a relative word, so how can you know which answer choice best answers the question if you don't read them all?

- After you read the question, read ALL of the answer choices
- Look for the "best" answer, which may just be the least wrong answer choice

After you have read all of the answer choices, rule them out in order from most wrong to least wrong. Sometimes the "best" answer choice is not a great fit, but it is better than the others. This process will also clarify your thinking so that by the time you get down to only two answer choices, you have a better idea of what makes choices right or wrong.

- Rule out in order from most wrong to least wrong

On the ISEE, you don't lose points for incorrect answers, so it can be tempting to blindly guess if you are confused. However, put a little bit of work into the question before you do that. Even if you are having trouble understanding a question, there may be one or two answer choices that don't even make sense.

- Use ruling out before you guess, even if the question leaves you totally confused

Verbal Reasoning Section – Basic Strategies

In the Verbal Reasoning section you will see two question types:

- Synonyms
- Sentence completions

On the synonym questions, you will be given one question word and then asked to choose the word that comes closest in meaning to that question word.

Synonym questions look something like this:

1. JOYOUS:

    (A) crying
    (B) happy
    (C) loud
    (D) mad

    Out of all the answer choice words, "happy" comes closest in meaning to "joyous". Choice B is correct.

The synonym questions won't all be that easy, but you get the idea.

The sentence completion questions give you a sentence with one or two dashed lines that have replaced a word or word pair. Your job is to figure out which answer choice should be inserted instead of the dashed line(s) so that the sentence makes the most sense.

On the Upper Level ISEE, there are two types of sentence completion questions. The first type has one dashed line, and the answer choices are single words. There will be 12 questions of this first type. There will also be 9 questions with sentences that have two dashes and answer choices that have two words. With these questions, the first word in the answer choice must be appropriate for the first blank in the question sentence and the second word in the answer choice must be appropriate for the second blank in the question sentence.

- There will be 12 one-blank sentence completion questions
- There will be 9 two-blank sentence completion questions

The one-blank sentence completion questions look something like this:

2. The student was afraid that she had not done well on the test, but when she got her scores back she was pleasantly -------.

(A) boisterous
(B) panicked
(C) surprised
(D) worried

In this case, the beginning of the sentence tells us that the student thinks she hasn't done well. We then have the conjunction "but" which tells us that the second part of the sentence will contradict the first, so something good must have happened. Choice C fits the bill, and it is the correct answer choice.

The two-blank sentence completion questions will look something like this:

3. Because the road is often ------- due to high water, it is better to take a slightly longer --------- than risk having to turn around.

(A) open… route
(B) obstructed… detour
(C) blocked… barrier
(D) windy… blockage

The key to this question is that both the first and second words must work in the blanks. For the first blank, we are looking for a word that is similar to "closed" since that would be the result of high water. That means that answer choices B or C could work. However, for the second word we are looking for something like "route". A detour is a route, but a barrier is not. Answer choice B is correct since "obstructed" and "detour" both work in the sentence.

These are the basic question types that you will see in the Verbal Reasoning section. They are very different, so we have different strategies for each question type.

Synonym strategies

There are several strategies that we can use on the synonyms section. Which strategy you use for an individual question is up to you. It depends on what roots you know, whether or not you have heard the word before, and your gut sense about a word.

Think of these strategies as being your toolbox. Several tools can get the job done.

Here are the strategies:

- Come up with your own word
- Use positive or negative
- Use context
- Look for roots or word parts that you know

Strategy #1: Come up with your own word

Use this strategy when you read a question and a word just pops into your head. Don't force yourself to try to come up with your own definition when you aren't sure what the word means.

- Use this strategy when the definition pops into your head

If you read a question word and a synonym pops into your head, go ahead and jot it down. It is important that you write down the word because otherwise you may try to talk yourself into an answer choice that "seems to come close." One of the biggest enemies on any standardized test is doubt. Doubt leads to talking yourself into the wrong answer choice, and physically writing down the word gives you the confidence you need when you go through the answer choices.

- Physically write down the definition – don't hold it in your head

After you write down the word, start by crossing out answer choices that are not synonyms for your word. By the time you get down to two choices, you will have a much better idea of what you are looking for.

- Cross out words that don't work

The following drill contains words that you may be able think of a definition for. You should focus on creating good habits with these questions. Even if you see the correct answer, go ahead and write down the word that you were thinking of.

What are good habits?

- Jot down the definition – this will actually save time in the long run
- Use ruling out – physically cross out answer choices that you know are incorrect

1. RAPID:

   (A) exhausted
   (B) marvelous
   (C) professional
   (D) swift

2. DAINTY:

   (A) delicate
   (B) long
   (C) surprising
   (D) warm

3. TIMID:

   (A) alive
   (B) damp
   (C) shy
   (D) upset

4. SUBDUE:

   (A) abandon
   (B) overpower
   (C) stun
   (D) wander

5. ILLUSTRATE:

   (A) demonstrate
   (B) kneel
   (C) nudge
   (D) sacrifice

(Answers to this drill are found on page 40)

Strategy #2: Use positive or negative

Sometimes you see a word, and you couldn't define that word, but you have a "gut feeling" that it is either something good or something bad. Maybe you don't know what that word means, but you know you would be mad if someone called you that!

- You have to have a "gut feeling " about a word to use this strategy

To use this strategy, when you get that feeling that a word is either positive or negative, then write in a "+" or a "−" sign next to the word. Then go to your answer choices and rule out anything that is opposite, i.e., positive when your question word is negative or negative when your question word is positive.

- Physically write a "+" or "−" after the question word

To really make this strategy work for you, you also need to rule out any words that are neutral, or neither positive nor negative. For example, let's say the question word is DISTRESS. "Distress" is clearly a negative word. So we can rule out a positive answer choice, such as "friendly," but we can also rule out a neutral word, such as "sleepy." At night, it is good to be sleepy, during the day it is not. "Sleepy" is not clearly a negative word, so it goes.

- Rule out neutral words

To summarize, here are the basic steps to using this strategy:

1. If you have a gut negative or positive feeling about a word, write a "+" or "−" next to the question word
2. Rule out any words that are opposite
3. Also rule out any NEUTRAL words
4. Pick from what is left

Here is an example of a question where you may be able to use the positive/negative strategy:

1. MALIGNANT:

   (A) courteous
   (B) harmful
   (C) nondescript
   (D) responsible

   Let's say that you know that "malignant" is bad, but you can't think of a definition. We write a "−" next to it and then rule out anything that is positive.

That means that choices A and D can go, because they are positive. Now we can also rule out neutral words, because we know that a synonym for "malignant" has to be negative. The word "nondescript" is neither positive nor negative, so choice C is out. We are left with choice B, which is correct.

On the following drill, write a "+" or "−" next to each question word. Then rule out answer choices that are opposite or neutral. Pick from what is left. Even if you aren't sure if the question word is positive or negative, take a guess! You may get more right than you would have imagined.

Drill #2

1. VIVACIOUS:

   (A) lively
   (B) musty
   (C) portable
   (D) restricted

2. AFFLUENT:

   (A) depressed
   (B) humid
   (C) resourceful
   (D) wealthy

3. BOLSTER:

   (A) express
   (B) qualify
   (C) stain
   (D) strengthen

4. ABHOR:

   (A) gobble
   (B) hate
   (C) land
   (D) pierce

5. OSTENTATIOUS:

   (A) ahead
   (B) flashy
   (C) practical
   (D) relaxed

(Answers to this drill are found on page 40)

Strategy #3: Use context – Think of where you have heard the word before

Use this strategy when you can't define a word, but you can think of a sentence or phrase where you have heard the word before.

- This strategy only works when you have heard the word before

To apply this strategy, think of a sentence or phrase where you have heard the question word before. Then try plugging the answer choices into your phrase to see which one has the same meaning within that sentence or phrase.

- Think of where you have heard the word before
- Plug question words into that sentence or phrase

Here is an example:

2.   ENDORSE:

(A)   drain
(B)   import
(C)   prowl
(D)   support

Let's say that you can't think of a definition for the word "endorse", but you have heard people say that they "endorse a candidate" for political office. Now we plug our answer choices into that phrase and see what would have the same meaning. Would it make sense to "drain a candidate"? Nope. Answer choice A is out. Would it make sense to "import a candidate" or "prowl a candidate"? No and no. Answer choices B and C are out. Finally, would it make sense to say that you "support a candidate"? Absolutely. Answer choice D is correct.

In the following drill, if you have heard the word before, then come up with a sentence or phrase and practice our strategy. If you have not heard the word before, you can't use the strategy of thinking of where you have heard the word before! Use another strategy and ruling out to answer the question anyway. You may not get every question correct, but remember, nothing ventured, nothing gained.

Keep in mind that all these words would be among the toughest on the test – the whole test will not be this hard! We just want to make sure you have practice for when the going gets tough.

Drill #3

1. FLAGRANT:

    (A) obvious
    (B) revised
    (C) standard
    (D) tough

2. INTERMITTENT:

    (A) essential
    (B) just
    (C) occasional
    (D) towering

3. FALLOW:

    (A) inactive
    (B) magnificent
    (C) private
    (D) tame

4. PENSIVE:

    (A) appealing
    (B) colossal
    (C) hospitable
    (D) thoughtful

5. BRAWNY:

    (A) awake
    (B) coarse
    (C) strong
    (D) tiny

(Answers to this drill are found on page 40)

Strategy #4: Look for roots or word parts that you know

This strategy works when you recognize that a word looks like another word that you know, or when you recognize one of the roots that you have studied in school or in this book.

If you see something familiar in the question word, underline the root or word part that you recognize. If you can think of the meaning of the root, then look for answer choices that would go with that meaning. If you can't think of a specific meaning, think of other words with that root and look for answer choices that are similar in meaning to those other words.

- Underline word parts that you recognize
- Think of the meaning of that word part
- If you can't think of a meaning for that word part, think of other words with that same word part

Here is an example of a question that uses a word with recognizable word parts:

3.   EXCLUDE:

   (A)   drift
   (B)   find
   (C)   prohibit
   (D)   send

   There are two word parts in the word "exclude" that can help us out. First, we have the prefix "ex", which means out (think of the word "exit"). Secondly, "clu" is a word root that means to shut (think of the word "include"). Using these word parts, we can see that "exclude" has something to do with shutting out. Choice C comes closest to this meaning, so it is correct.

For the following drill, try to use word parts to come up with the correct answer choices. If you can't think of what a word root, prefix, or suffix means, then think of other words that have the same root, prefix, or suffix.

Drill #4

1. MISCREANT:

   (A) burrow
   (B) lowlife
   (C) leader
   (D) scavenger

2. SUBTERRANEAN:

   (A) faded
   (B) partial
   (C) tragic
   (D) underground

3. CERTIFY:

   (A) confirm
   (B) debate
   (C) ponder
   (D) toss

4. INNATE:

   (A) awful
   (B) instinctive
   (C) narrow
   (D) tough

5. AMITY:

   (A) appearance
   (B) decay
   (C) friendship
   (D) temptation

(Answers to this drill are found on page 40)

Sentence completion strategies

We have several strategies in our toolbox for sentence completion questions.

They include:

- Underline the key idea
- Look for sentences showing contrast
- Look for sentence showing cause or sequence
- Use our strategies for synonyms when you don't know the meaning of one or more of the answer choices
- For two blank questions, look at one blank at a time if you can
- For two blank questions, think about whether the answer words should be similar to each other or different

Strategy #1: Underline the key idea

Perhaps our most powerful strategy is underlining what the sentence is about.

If you are unsure of what to underline, look for the part of the sentence that, if changed, would change what you are looking for.

- Look for the part of the sentence that, if changed, would change the word or phrase that would fit in the blank
- Underline this key word or phrase

After you underline the key word or phrase, try coming up with your own word or phrase that would fit in the blank. This will help you easily rule out answer choices that are not like your word.

- After you underline the key word/phrase, fill in your own word or phrase in the blank

Here is an example:

1. The artist spent his days ------ the walls in the cave.
2. The scientist spent his days ------ the walls in the cave.

Do you see how changing just one word changed what we would put in that blank? If the person was an artist, we might expect him to be painting the walls in the cave. If the person was a scientist, however, we might expect him to be studying the walls in the cave or analyzing the walls in the cave. In the first sentence, we would underline "artist". In the second sentence, we would underline "scientist".

Below is a drill for you to try. For this drill, you should underline the key word or phrase and then fill in a word that would work for the blank. There are no answer choices for these questions because at this point we want you to focus on the process of underlining the key word or phrase and filling in your own word.

Drill #5

1. Author Charles Dickens ------ class structure in Victorian London.

   Word to fill in the blank?

2. The company received ------ calls after they placed an ad in a widely read publication.

   Word to fill in the blank?

3. The path seemed to wander in a(n) ------ manner, twisting and turning through the woods.

   Word to fill in the blank?

4. The impulsive shopper swooped into the store and filled her cart ------.

   Word to fill in the blank?

(Answers to this drill are found on page 41)

Strategy #2: Look for sentences showing contrast

Some sentences show contrast. With these sentences, the end of the sentence changes direction from the beginning of the sentence.

These sentences often use the words "but", "although", "however", "rather", and "even though". If you see any of these words, circle them.

The first step in answering these questions is to underline the key word or phrase. We need to know what we are contrasting with. The next step is to circle the words that shows contrast, such as "but", "although", "however", and "even though".

- Underline the key word or phrase
- Circle words that show contrast, such as "but", "although", "however", "rather", and "even though"

Here is an example:

1. Although the student tried to stay interested, her expression clearly showed that she was -------.

    (A) bored
    (B) jealous
    (C) mysterious
    (D) positive

    In this question, we circle the word "although" since it shows contrast. Then we underline the word "interested" since the sentence is about the student staying interested (if we changed that word, we would change what the blank would be). Since we have the word "although," we know that we are looking for a word that contrasts with "interested". Since "bored" is the opposite of "interested," choice A is correct.

For the following drill, be sure that you:

- Underline the key word or phrase
- Circle any words that show contrast
- Fill in your own word for the blank
- Use ruling out to get to the right answer

Drill #6

1. Although poet Maya Angelou was one of the most respected and successful authors in the United States, her earlier life was marked by --------.

   (A) acclaim
   (B) boredom
   (C) harmony
   (D) penury

2. Despite the fact that the pufferfish is considered the second most poisonous vertebrate on Earth, many people consider parts of it to be a ---------.

   (A) delicacy
   (B) mistake
   (C) toxin
   (D) vessel

3. There may have been as many as 3 to 5 billion passenger pigeons in America during the mid-19th century, which makes it all the more unbelievable that the species was -------- in 1914.

   (A) changing
   (B) eliminated
   (C) growing
   (D) traded

4. Although the textbook publishers pride themselves on the ease of use of their books, many students find the text to be --------.

   (A) accessible
   (B) familiar
   (C) impenetrable
   (D) resourceful

5. People often think of China as having a large population, however, there are several regions of China that have a ----- number of inhabitants.

   (A) fluctuating
   (B) meager
   (C) spectacular
   (D) typical

6. Ansel Adams was unsuccessful as a student, but he later -------- as a photographer who travelled the American West and captured some of the most iconic images of the United States.

   (A) built
   (B) discussed
   (C) prospered
   (D) travelled

Continued on the next page

Drill #6 (continued)

7.   In contrast to the Senate where it is very rare for a candidate to run unopposed, -------- elections are much more common in the House of Representatives.

   (A)   dismal
   (B)   honorable
   (C)   late
   (D)   uncontested

(Answers to this drill are found on page 41)

Strategy #3: Look for sentences showing cause or sequence

Many sentences in the sentence completions section use the cause or sequence relationship. In these sentences, one thing leads to another. Sometimes one directly causes the other, but sometimes one just happens to come after the other.

- Look for sentences where one thing leads to another
- Think about what the effect of the given action would be

Sometimes you will see the words "because", "when", or "after" in these sentences, but there is often no one particular word that indicates cause.

- If you see words like "because", "when", or "after", you usually have a sentence showing cause or sequence
- There may be no one word that indicates this relationship in a sentence

Here is an example:

2.   Years of floods and fires left the former resort ------.

   (A)   busy
   (B)   effective
   (C)   necessary
   (D)   ravaged

To answer this question, we have to ask ourselves what years of floods and fires would lead to. While you could say that the resort would be left busy because there was a lot of cleanup work to do, the more direct answer would be that it was left ravaged. Choice D is the correct answer.

Here is a drill for you to try. Remember to look for the answer choice that shows the clearest cause or sequence relationship.

Drill #7

1. In the early 1800s there was a high demand in New England for cleared pastureland and lumber which led to the rapid -------- in the region.

    (A) deforestation
    (B) decline
    (C) growth
    (D) looting

2. John F. Kennedy's vision of a national center for performing arts was fulfilled in 1971 when the Kennedy Center ----- holding performances.

    (A) annexed
    (B) commenced
    (C) halted
    (D) limited

3. Although there was a very large crowd at the March on Washington for Jobs and Freedom in 1963, the leaders' careful planning and focus on nonviolence ensured that the event was --------.

    (A) arid
    (B) hot
    (C) peaceful
    (D) turbulent

4. The increase in the number of students forced the school district to consider ----- existing schools.

    (A) anticipating
    (B) limiting
    (C) painting
    (D) supplementing

Continued on the next page

Drill #7 (continued)

5. Because very few homes are built with basements in the Joplin, MO area, the damage caused by the tornado was particularly ------.

   (A) apathetic
   (B) catastrophic
   (C) efficient
   (D) musty

6. As the excitement over the upcoming summer break increased, the students became more and more --------.

   (A) efficient
   (B) gallant
   (C) inattentive
   (D) restrained

(Answers to this drill are found on page 41)

Strategy #4: Use our strategies for synonyms when you don't know the meaning of one or more of the answer choices

Sometimes you know what kind of word you are looking for, but the problem is that you don't know the meaning of some of the answer choices. If this is the case, ask yourself:

- Am I looking for a positive or negative word?
- Do any of the answer choices have roots or prefixes that I can use?
- Have I heard any of the answer choices used in a sentence or phrase before?

In the following drill, practice using our strategies of looking for a positive or a negative word, looking for roots or word parts that you know, or thinking of where you have heard an answer choice before. You may not be certain of the answer choice that you choose, but by using ruling out you are more likely to answer questions correctly.

Drill #8

1. The majestic mountain views often leave visitors to Yellowstone National Park feeling --------.

   (A) candid
   (B) excluded
   (C) reverent
   (D) sorrowful

2. Although it is now a commonplace literary technique, stream-of-consciousness narrative was considered quite ------ when Virginia Wolf used it in the early 20th century.

   (A) customary
   (B) novel
   (C) proper
   (D) superficial

3. The principality of Monaco is known for -------- roads that wind through the mountains with sharp turns and steep drop-offs.

   (A) acceptable
   (B) domestic
   (C) lavish
   (D) tortuous

4. Henry Thoreau took off to the woods of Concord, Massachusetts by himself in a search for --------.

   (A) accuracy
   (B) conversation
   (C) revulsion
   (D) solitude

5. The sides of the shape are not all the same size, rather they are ------.

   (A) irregular
   (B) memorable
   (C) repetitious
   (D) specific

6. When Paul Revere saw the British troops approaching, he took off with ------- to warn the other rebels as quickly as he could.

   (A) dispatch
   (B) haughtiness
   (C) laxity
   (D) silence

(Answers to this drill can be found on page 41)

Strategy #5: For two blank questions, look at one blank at a time if you can

At the end of the Verbal Reasoning section, there will be nine sentence completion questions with two blanks and two word answer choices.

Here is an example:

3.   Despite the ------- initial sales of the Model T car, it fell out of favor and was eventually --------.

    (A)   lackluster… eliminated
    (B)   mediocre … promoted
    (C)   robust… discontinued
    (D)   strong… celebrated

The first step is to decide which blank we feel more confident about. It may be easier to identify a clue for one blank than for the other. In this example, the last part of the sentence tells us that "it fell out of favor", so we can expect a negative word for that second blank. To start, we will look just at the second word of each answer choice. The words "celebrated" and "promoted" are both positive, so we can eliminate choices B and D. Now we can look at the first blank. We have the word "despite," so we know that the first part of the sentence will contrast with the second part of the sentence. That tells us that we are looking for a positive word for the first blank. If we look at the choices we have left (choices A and C), we can see that only answer choice C has a positive word for that first blank. Answer choice C is correct.

To review, the basic procedure for answering two blank questions is:

1. Decide which blank you are more confident about.
2. Rule out any answer choices with words that do not work for that blank.
3. Look only at the remaining answer choices for the other blank.

For the following drill, practice the correct process. Look at the blanks one at a time as you answer each question.

Drill #9

1. Some mushrooms are not actually ------, but because their appearance ------ that of a species that is toxic, they are often left alone by foragers.

   (A) fungus... lingers
   (B) healthy... imitates
   (C) harmful... refutes
   (D) poisonous... mimics

2. Many studies have shown that students who show ---------- and do not easily ----------- when confronted with difficult problems are more likely to succeed than students who exhibit intelligence alone.

   (A) banter... capitulate
   (B) inhibition... withhold
   (C) malice... lament
   (D) perseverance... relent

3. When George Koppelman and Daniel Weschler claimed that they had found Shakespeare's dictionary, the process to -------- it was ----------- and time consuming.

   (A) authenticate... elaborate
   (B) illustrate... definite
   (C) reproduce... cursory
   (D) shuffle... dainty

4. The mistake that many economists make is to focus on ----------- events instead of the ----------- changes that sometimes go unnoticed but have huge impacts on the economy.

   (A) adaptable... unreliable
   (B) flawed... exciting
   (C) monumental... microscopic
   (D) tragic... horrific

5. Winslow Homer was ----------- by his mother to become a painter and his works reflect the artistic talent that he -------- from her.

   (A) disdained... stole
   (B) encouraged.... inherited
   (C) ignored... borrowed
   (D) reassured... overlooked

(Answers to this drill are found on page 41)

Strategy #6: For two-blank questions, decide whether the answer words should be similar to each other or opposite from each other

Occasionally, we will have a two-blank question where one blank is the clue for the other blank.

For example, let's say the question is:

1. People who know Gertrude describe her as someone who is --------- and often--------.

In this case, the first blank could be something good or bad. Maybe she is generous or maybe she is mean- we have no other clues in the sentence. However, the word "and" tells us that the two words must be similar. The correct answer would be the answer choice with two words that are similar. In order to make this question work, the test writers will only give you one answer choice with similar answer choices.

The important thing to remember is that if the only clue we have is that the words are similar or opposite, then they can't be unrelated.

- If the two words are similar or opposite, you can also rule out any answer choices with unrelated words

For the following drill, think about the whether the words are similar or opposite. Remember to rule out any answer choices with unrelated words.

Drill #10

1. Unlike the ------- colors of impressionist paintings, the work of Andy Warhol featured a ------- palette.

   (A) standard... common
   (B) unusual... different
   (C) bright... blurry
   (D) muted... bold

2. Despite her reputation for being --------, many of Caroline's friends knew her as a very -------- person.

   (A) brusque... welcoming
   (B) flattering... homely
   (C) powerful... influential
   (D) serene... calm

3. If the architects had been more ------- with their instructions, then they could have avoided some of the confusion that arose from the ------- pages of instructions.

   (A) creative...disorganized
   (B) expressive...well-written
   (C) systematic... chaotic
   (D) terse... abbreviated

4. Because the number of students in a school can -------- from year to year, the number of staff needed is --------.

   (A) converge... limited
   (B) fluctuate... variable
   (C) languish... surging
   (D) radiate... obsolete

5. Although the grocery store had a reputation for ------- prices, an analysis of several stores revealed that their prices were actually -------.

   (A) high... expensive
   (B) modest... justifiable
   (C) outrageous... reasonable
   (D) unpredictable... common

(Answers to this drill are found on page 41)

Now you have the skills that you need to do well on the Verbal Reasoning section of the ISEE! An important part of improving your Verbal Reasoning score is also studying vocabulary. Be sure to spend time with the following vocabulary section.

Answers to Synonym Drills

Drill #1

1. D
2. A
3. C
4. B
5. A

Drill #2

1. A
2. D
3. D
4. B
5. B

Drill #3

1. A
2. C
3. A
4. D
5. C

Drill #4

1. B
2. D
3. A
4. B
5. C

Answers to Sentence Completion Drills

Drill #5

1. Underline "author", fill in in a word like "describes"
2. Underline "widely read", fill in a word like "many"
3. Underline "twisting and turning", fill in a word like "indirect"
4. Underline "impulsive", fill in a word like "quickly"

Drill #6

1. D
2. A
3. B
4. C
5. B
6. C
7. D

Drill #7

1. A
2. B
3. C
4. D
5. B
6. C

Drill #8

1. C
2. B
3. D
4. D
5. A
6. A

Drill #9

1. D
2. D
3. A
4. C
5. B

Drill #10

1. D
2. A
3. C
4. B
5. C

Vocabulary Review

A key component of increasing your Verbal Reasoning score is improving your vocabulary. Following are ten lessons that will help you do just that.

Each lesson has twenty new words for you to learn. There are good words, there are bad words, and there are even words with roots. Exciting, eh?

After you learn the words, complete the activities for each lesson. The best way to learn new words is to think of them in categories and to evaluate how the words relate to one another. The activities will help you do this.

The activities also give you practice with synonyms and sentence completions. You will be working on strategy while you are learning new words – think of it as a two for one!

If there are words that you have trouble remembering as you work through the lessons, go ahead and make flashcards for them. Continue to review these flashcards until the words stick. There may also be words that you run across in the synonyms or sentence completion practice that you do not know the meaning of. Make flashcards for these words as well.

After each lesson are the answers. Be sure to check your work. It is important that you keep studying the words from previous lessons – you will be seeing them again. In the activities, any word that has been introduced is fair game, even if it was from an earlier lesson.

After the lessons, there are also three word lists. These word lists are labeled "challenging", "more challenging", and "most challenging." The harder the words are, the less likely they are to show up on the test, but if you already know the easier words then you will need to study the harder words to make progress. These three word lists include one-word synonyms, since that is how they are tested on the synonym questions in the Verbal Reasoning section of the ISEE. For further clarification, you can see example sentences using these words by visiting:

www.testprepworks.com/student/download

Lesson One

Words to learn

Below are the twenty words used in Lesson One; refer back to this list as needed as you move through the lesson.

Marina: dock
Trivial: unimportant
Terrain: ground
Apathetic: disinterested
Calamity: disaster

Devastate: destroy
Sentient: aware
Mariner: sailor
Grapple: struggle
Inter: bury

Cognizant: informed
Ameliorate: improve
Prosperity: good fortune
Aloof: withdrawn
Perceptive: sensitive

Adversity: misfortune
Subterranean: underground
Crucial: important
Submarine: underwater
Oblivious: unaware

Word List Practice

Use the words from the list above to complete the following activities.

1. List three words that describe a person who doesn't know or doesn't care.
   a.
   b.
   c.

2. List three words that could describe a person who knows what is going on.
   a.
   b.
   c.

3. List three words that have a decidedly negative meaning.
   a.
   b.
   c.

Roots practice

Below are three words. Write the definition for the words on the line provided. Based on their meanings, define the common root.

Marina _____

Mariner _____

Submarine _____

1. The root "mar" means:

Inter _____

Subterranean _____

Terrain _____

2. The root "terr/ter" means:

3. If "aqu/a" is the root meaning water, what do you think the word "aquamarine" means?

4. Based on the roots terr/ter and aqu/a, what do you think the word "terraqueous" means?

5. Based on the words submarine and subterranean, can you figure out the meaning of the root "sub?"

Synonyms practice

Choose the answer that comes closest in meaning to the question word given

1. CALAMITY:

   (A) disaster
   (B) heaven
   (C) prosperity
   (D) terrain

2. DEVASTATE:

   (A) believe
   (B) destroy
   (C) grapple
   (D) inter

3. AMELIORATE:

   (A) devastate
   (B) finish
   (C) gesture
   (D) improve

4. GRAPPLE:

   (A) blend
   (B) incorporate
   (C) struggle
   (D) transfer

5. PERCEPTIVE:

   (A) aloof
   (B) dense
   (C) oblivious
   (D) sensitive

6. APATHETIC:

   (A) disinterested
   (B) enthusiastic
   (C) sentient
   (D) trivial

7. CRUCIAL:

   (A) devastated
   (B) important
   (C) late
   (D) subterranean

8. TERRAIN:

   (A) ground
   (B) marina
   (C) revision
   (D) walk

9. MARINA:

    (A) awareness
    (B) cabin
    (C) dock
    (D) understanding

10. INTER:

    (A) bury
    (B) devastate
    (C) envy
    (D) struggle

Sentence completion practice

Choose the answer that best completes the meaning of the sentence.

1. A love of the sea led the young boy to dream of being a --------- when he grew up.

    (A) calamity
    (B) doctor
    (C) mariner
    (D) student

2. His --------- gaze made his opponents aware that he knew about their secret weapon.

    (A) apathetic
    (B) cognizant
    (C) nonexistent
    (D) trivial

3. A young Oprah Winfrey faced much ---------- such as poverty and abusive relationships but she triumphed over it and became a stunning success.

    (A) adversity
    (B) flattery
    (C) prosperity
    (D) sincerity

4. When a hurricane is expected, the entire -------- must be removed from the water so that the waves don't ---------- it into the shoreline.

    (A) commission… push
    (B) factory… rub
    (C) marina… hurtle
    (D) submarine… protect

5. A good spy knows to focus on the seemingly-------- details that may prove to be --------clues.

    (A) aloof…. perceptive
    (B) crucial… irrelevant
    (C) exclusive… oblivious
    (D) trivial… important

Answers to Lesson One

Word list practice

1. a. apathetic
   b. aloof
   c. oblivious
2. a. sentient
   b. cognizant
   c. perceptive
3. a. calamity
   b. devastate
   c. adversity

Roots practice

1. sea
2. earth
3. color of sea water
4. formed of land and water
5. under/beneath

Synonyms practice

1. A
2. B
3. D
4. C
5. D
6. A
7. B
8. A
9. C
10. A

Sentence completion practice

1. C
2. B
3. A
4. C
5. D

Lesson Two

Words to learn

Below are the twenty words used in Lesson Two; refer back to this list as needed as you move through the lesson.

Enunciate: pronounce
Procrastinate: delay
Inscribe: write
Cleave: split
Magnitude: importance

Abashed: embarrassed
Indescribable: beyond words
Denigrate: criticize
Hew: cut
Figurative: symbolic

Grotesque: ugly
Proscribe: forbid
Corpulent: fat
Eminence: superiority
Incorporate: include

Metaphorical: figurative (not literal)
Repugnant: loathsome (nasty)
Exhilarated: elated (thrilled)
Manifest: demonstrate
Corporeal: bodily

Word list practice

Use the words from the list above to complete the following activities.

1. List three words that describe something you could do to someone.
   a.
   b.
   c.

2. If you called someone "corpulent," they might think that you are _____.

3. If you realized at school that your pants were cleaved in two, you would probably feel _____.

Roots practice

Below are three words. Write the definition for the words on the line provided. Based on their meanings, define the common root.

Inscribe _____

Proscribe _____

Indescribable _____

1. The root "scribe" means:

Corpulent _____

Incorporate _____

Corporeal _____

2. The root "corp" means:

3. Based on the meaning of "corp," what popular term for business also means "body of men?" (This is not a word from our lesson, but rather one you might know from another place.) _____

4. A doctor has to _____ many drugs before you can take them (this word is similar to one of the words in this lesson, but it is NOT that word!).

5. Based on one of the roots above, can you think of a term meaning "one who writes?"

_____

Synonyms practice

Choose the answer choice that comes closest in meaning to the question word. Keep in mind that any words that we have studied are fair game and not all of the words are from this lesson. Words may also show up in a different form (noun, verb, adjective) than they appeared in the word lists.

1. CLEAVE:

   (A) devastate
   (B) inscribe
   (C) lecture
   (D) split

2. OBLIVIOUS:

   (A) cognizant
   (B) delayed
   (C) forbidden
   (D) unaware

3. EMINENCE:

   (A) corpulence
   (B) exhilaration
   (C) superiority
   (D) uneasiness

4. METAPHORICAL:

   (A) figurative
   (B) informed
   (C) proscribed
   (D) sentient

5. PROCRASTINATE:

   (A) bury
   (B) delay
   (C) incorporate
   (D) manifest

6. ABASHED:

   (A) corporeal
   (B) devastated
   (C) embarrassed
   (D) ugly

7. ENUNCIATE:

   (A) demonstrate
   (B) inscribe
   (C) join
   (D) pronounce

8. INCORPORATE:

   (A) forbid
   (B) include
   (C) manifest
   (D) prosper

9. MAGNITUDE:

    (A) apathy
    (B) calamity
    (C) importance
    (D) need

10. SUBTERRANEAN:

    (A) underground
    (B) understated
    (C) underwater
    (D) unimportant

Sentence completion practice

Choose the answer that best completes the meaning of the sentence. Keep in mind that any words that we have studied are fair game and not all of the words are from this lesson. Words may also show up in a different form (noun, verb, adjective) than they appeared in the word lists.

1. Gargoyles, which were often featured on Gothic buildings, were small statues of creatures so hideously ugly that they were often referred as --------.

    (A) grotesque
    (B) metaphorical
    (C) subterranean
    (D) tireless

2. At a sawmill, logs must first be ------- to a standard size before they can be milled into planks of lumber to be sold.

    (A) denigrated
    (B) hewed
    (C) incorporated
    (D) proscribed

3. Many people who sky dive describe the -------- that they experience as incomparable to any other rush of emotion that they experienced.

    (A) exhilaration
    (B) prosperity
    (C) superiority
    (D) treatment

4. Many people called the film critic --------- when she referred to an actress as -------.

    (A) elated… wise
    (B) oblivious… abashed
    (C) powerful… aloof
    (D) repugnant… corpulent.

5. Psychosomatic illnesses occur when people are so convinced that they are ill that they actually ------- symptoms that are -------- even though there is not a physical cause.

    (A) ameliorate... trivial
    (B) enunciate... indescribable
    (C) manifest... corporeal
    (D) perceive... cleaved

Answers to Lesson Two

Word list practice

1. a. proscribe
    b. denigrate
    c. incorporate
2. repugnant
3. abashed

Roots practice

1. to write
2. body
3. corporation
4. prescribe
5. scribe

Synonyms practice

1. D
2. D
3. C
4. A
5. B
6. C
7. D
8. B
9. C
10. A

Sentence completion practice

1. A
2. B
3. A
4. D
5. C

Lesson Three

Words to learn

Below are the twenty words used in Lesson Three; refer back to this list as needed as you move through the lesson.

Animate: enliven (bring to life)
Boisterous: noisy
Paraphrase: summarize
Irate: angry
Rejuvenate: refresh

Surfeit: excess
Circumvent: go around
Magnanimous: generous
Vitality: energy
Fractious: bad-tempered

Ravenous: starving
Equanimity: composure (calmness)
Intimidate: frighten
Miscreant: villain
Satiated: satisfied

Vivacious: lively
Craving: hunger or desire
Incensed: enraged
Convivial: friendly
Culprit: wrongdoer

Word list practice

Use the words from the list above to complete the following activities.

1. Would you rather spend time with someone who is fractious or convivial?

2. If you were rejuvenated, you would have more _____.

3. List three words that can be related to eating and/or being hungry:
    a.
    b.
    c.

Roots practice

Below are three words. Write the definition for the words on the line provided. Based on their meanings, define the common root.

Animate _____

Equanimity _____

Magnanimous _____

1. The root "anim" means:

Vivacious _____

Vitality _____

Convivial _____

2. The root "vi/viv" means:

3. Based on the meaning of "anim," why do you think cartoons are called "animation?"

4. The root "magna" means large. What is an alternate definition of "magnanimous," using its two roots?

5. If "oviparous" means producing young in eggs, based on one of the roots above, what do you think the word "viviparous" means?

Synonyms practice

Choose the answer choice that comes closest in meaning to the question word. Keep in mind that any words that we have studied are fair game and not all of the words are from this lesson. Words may also show up in a different form (noun, verb, adjective) than they appeared in the word lists.

1. BOISTEROUS:

   (A) happy
   (B) grotesque
   (C) noisy
   (D) repugnant

2. PARAPHRASE:

   (A) enunciate
   (B) inter
   (C) release
   (D) summarize

3. IRATE:

   (A) frightened
   (B) incensed
   (C) unimportant
   (D) vivacious

4. FRACTIOUS:

   (A) bad-tempered
   (B) hardworking
   (C) magnanimous
   (D) satisfied

5. INTIMIDATE:

   (A) alleviate
   (B) criticize
   (C) frighten
   (D) grapple

6. REJUVENATE:

   (A) anger
   (B) drain
   (C) proscribe
   (D) refresh

7. SENTIENT:

   (A) cognizant
   (B) figurative
   (C) ravenous
   (D) satiated

8. CONVIVIAL:

   (A) embarrassed
   (B) friendly
   (C) magnanimous
   (D) repugnant

9. INSCRIBE:

   (A) animate
   (B) forbid
   (C) improve
   (D) write

10. DENIGRATE:

    (A) apologize
    (B) bury
    (C) criticize
    (D) resist

Sentence completion practice

Choose the answer that best completes the meaning of the sentence. Keep in mind that any words that we have studied are fair game and not all of the words are from this lesson. Words may also show up in a different form (noun, verb, adjective) than they appeared in the word lists.

1. Stonewall Jackson, a confederate general, earned his nickname by showing remarkable ------ in the midst of the chaos of the first battle at Bull Run.

   (A) adversity
   (B) equanimity
   (C) independence
   (D) nervousness

2. Andrew Carnegie made a fortune in steel and was known both for cutthroat business practices as well as --------- gifts such as public libraries and donations to many universities.

   (A) abashed
   (B) eager
   (C) magnanimous
   (D) vivacious

3. The poet Emily Dickinson was known for being withdrawn and -------, but there has been some speculation that she had actually had a medical condition that prevented her from socializing frequently.

   (A) aloof
   (B) convivial
   (C) irate
   (D) sentient

4. A ------- of inexpensive, high fat food in the United States has contributed to an epidemic of --------- citizens.

   (A) bounty…. ravenous
   (B) dearth… animated
   (C) lack… apathetic
   (D) surfeit… corpulent

5. Although George Washington was known to be at times --------, he was generally able to control his temper and be --------- when entertaining guests.

   (A) exhilarated… elated
   (B) fractious… convivial
   (C) loud… boisterous
   (D) satiated… kind

Answers to Lesson Three

Word list practice

1. convivial
2. vitality
3. a. craving
   b. ravenous
   c. satiated

Roots practice

1. life, spirit
2. life
3. cartoons bring drawings or still images to life
4. large spirit
5. producing live young

Synonyms practice

1. C
2. D
3. B
4. A
5. C
6. D
7. A
8. B
9. D
10. C

Sentence completion practice

1. B
2. C
3. A
4. D
5. B

Lesson Four

Words to learn

Below are the twenty words used in Lesson Four; refer back to this list as needed as you move through the lesson.

Pandemonium: uproar
Hierarchy: ranked system
Subsist: exist (barely get by)
Eulogy: speech in praise
Unwittingly: unknowingly

Paraphernalia: belongings
Desist: cease (stop)
Cadaverous: ghastly (ghost-like)
Imminent: impending (about to happen)
Agitator: troublemaker

Wrangle: dispute
Deciduous: falling off
Prevalent: widespread
Stagnant: sluggish (not moving)
Decadence: decline

Epiphany: insight
Accolades: praise
Serf: slave
Pilgrimage: journey
Reimburse: pay back

Word list practice

Use the words from the list above to complete the following activities.

1.   Your parents probably give you this for bringing home good grades.

2.   Trees with leaves that turn colors each fall are called deciduous. Why?

3.   A speech written for a funeral is called a(n) _____.

4.   Though often used to describe rich desserts and other food or pleasure, this word actually means something negative:

Roots practice

Below are three words. Write the definition for the words on the line provided. Based on their meanings, define the common root.

Subsist _____

Desist _____

Stagnant _____

1.   The root "sist/sta" means:

Cadaverous _____

Decadence _____

Deciduous _____

2.   The root "cad/cid" means:

3.   Based on desist, decadence, and deciduous, what do you think the root "de" means?

4.   Based on the meaning of "cadaverous," what does the word "cadaver" mean?

5.   If the root "cad" means "to fall," what did a "cadaver" fall from?

6.   What makes water "stagnant?"

Synonyms practice

Choose the answer choice that comes closest in meaning to the question word. Keep in mind that any words that we have studied are fair game and not all of the words are from this lesson. Words may also show up in a different form (noun, verb, adjective) than they appeared in the word lists.

1. MISCREANT:

    (A) culprit
    (B) leader
    (C) mariner
    (D) serf

2. STAGNANT:

    (A) craving
    (B) eminent
    (C) loathsome
    (D) sluggish

3. PILGRIMAGE:

    (A) friend
    (B) journey
    (C) terrain
    (D) villain

4. PARAPHERNALIA:

    (A) belongings
    (B) marina
    (C) pandemonium
    (D) swing

5. CADAVEROUS:

    (A) agitated
    (B) dissatisfied
    (C) ghastly
    (D) prevalent

6. IMMINENT:

    (A) deciduous
    (B) impending
    (C) magnanimous
    (D) thrilling

7. DENIGRATE:

    (A) criticize
    (B) grapple
    (C) incorporate
    (D) trek

8. UNWITTINGLY:

    (A) uneasily
    (B) ungraciously
    (C) unknowingly
    (D) unruly

9. VIVACIOUS:

    (A) approachable
    (B) lively
    (C) oblivious
    (D) perceptive

10. PREVALENT:

    (A) brittle
    (B) firm
    (C) praised
    (D) widespread

Sentence completion practice

Choose the answer that best completes the meaning of the sentence. Keep in mind that any words that we have studied are fair game and not all of the words are from this lesson. Words may also show up in a different form (noun, verb, adjective) than they appeared in the word lists.

1. Sadly, many families in poor countries have to -------- on a meager income that barely provides food and shelter.

   (A) circumvent
   (B) eulogize
   (C) subsist
   (D) venture

2. During World War I, one of the most ---------- causes of death was influenza, which killed more people than the war itself.

   (A) animated
   (B) incensed
   (C) lanky
   (D) prevalent

3. Pigs are known for having an appetite that is tough to ---------; they eat so much food that they can gain 2 to 3 pounds a day.

   (A) hew
   (B) inter
   (C) paraphrase
   (D) satiate

4. In the tunnels that run beneath the city of Paris there exists an entire --------- world that has been used for everything from growing mushrooms to hosting --------- parties.

   (A) convivial… quiet
   (B) magnanimous….fractious
   (C) subterranean… boisterous
   (D) triumphant… chaotic

5. In the --------- of the Middle Ages, the nobility and landed gentry benefitted tremendously from the back breaking work done by --------- who were unpaid and could never advance their position in society.

   (A) hierarchy… serfs
   (B) pandemonium… merchants
   (C) schools…. culprits
   (D) terrain…. mariners

Answers to Lesson Four

Word list practice

1. accolades
2. because the leaves fall off
3. eulogy
4. decadence

Roots practice

1. stand
2. to fall
3. opposite or away from
4. corpse
5. life
6. If water is standing or not moving, it becomes stagnant.

Synonyms practice

1. A
2. D
3. B
4. A
5. C
6. B
7. A
8. C
9. B
10. D

Sentence completion practice

1. C
2. D
3. D
4. C
5. A

Lesson Five

Words to learn

Below are the twenty words used in Lesson Five; refer back to this list as needed as you move through the lesson.

Pragmatic: sensible
Mercurial: temperamental (moody)
Morose: depressed
Frustrate: disappoint
Serene: calm

Carnivorous: meat-eating
Ostentatious: flashy
Insolent: disrespectful
Omniscient: all-knowing
Effervescent: bubbly

Stupendous: wonderful
Incarnation: embodiment (a spirit being born into a body)
Omnivorous: eats everything
Impetuous: impulsive
Mediocre: unexceptional

Grovel: beg
Reincarnation: rebirth
Omnipotent: all-powerful
Interminable: boring
Fraudulent: deceptive

Word list practice

Use the words from the list above to complete the following activities.

1.   Would you rather have a mediocre meal or a stupendous meal?

2.   It would be _____ for the bank to tell you that your account had $100 in it, when you had actually deposited $500.

3.   _____ people think through decisions. Those who are _____ often do not.

Roots practice

Below are three words. Write the definition for the words on the line provided. Based on their meanings, define the common root.

Carnivorous _____

Incarnation _____

Reincarnation _____

1. The root "carn" means:

Omniscient _____

Omnipotent _____

Omnivorous _____

2. The root "omni" means:

3. If an "herbivore" eats plants, what does a "carnivore" eat?

4. What, then, does an "omnivore" eat?

5. Based on the meaning of the root, for whom does an "omnibus" provide transportation?

6. Based on the meanings of "incarnation" and "reincarnation," what do you think the root "re" means?

Synonyms practice

Choose the answer choice that comes closest in meaning to the question word. Keep in mind that any words that we have studied are fair game and not all of the words are from this lesson. Words may also show up in a different form (noun, verb, adjective) than they appeared in the word lists.

1. INSOLENT:

   (A) disrespectful
   (B) furious
   (C) grotesque
   (D) serene

2. IMPETUOUS:

   (A) decadent
   (B) impulsive
   (C) smooth
   (D) unwittingly

3. MOROSE:

   (A) curious
   (B) depressed
   (C) ravenous
   (D) sleepy

4. GROVEL:

   (A) beg
   (B) circumvent
   (C) flee
   (D) wrangle

5. STUPENDOUS:

   (A) dull
   (B) frustrated
   (C) omniscient
   (D) wonderful

6. MEDIOCRE:

   (A) grand
   (B) imminent
   (C) stagnant
   (D) unexceptional

7. VIVACIOUS:

   (A) costly
   (B) interminable
   (C) lively
   (D) repugnant

8. PRAGMATIC:

   (A) kind
   (B) irate
   (C) sensible
   (D) tedious

9. FRUSTRATE:

   (A) cease
   (B) disappoint
   (C) endure
   (D) rejuvenate

10. INCENSED:

   (A) enraged
   (B) possible
   (C) quaint
   (D) trivial

Sentence completion practice

Choose the answer that best completes the meaning of the sentence. Keep in mind that any words that we have studied are fair game and not all of the words are from this lesson. Words may also show up in a different form (noun, verb, adjective) than they appeared in the word lists.

1. One of the basic principles of the Hindu religion is ----------, or the belief that after a person dies their soul or spirit will be reborn in another body.

    (A) craving
    (B) effervescence
    (C) reincarnation
    (D) vitality

2. Tomato blight can infect soil so that even if farmers remove affected plants, they still must -------- from planting tomatoes in that same area for at least a year.

    (A) desist
    (B) favor
    (C) latch
    (D) subsist

3. It is tough to live with a person who is -------- because he or she can be excited and happy one moment but angry and withdrawn the next.

    (A) fraudulent
    (B) mercurial
    (C) popular
    (D) vivacious

4. The expensive and ---------- lifestyle that was prevalent during the 1920's was followed by a period of ---------- when the money ran out.

    (A) cognizant... adversity
    (B) extravagant.... serenity
    (C) noisy... surfeit
    (D) ostentatious... decline

5. It is hard to overstate the -------- of the launch of the Soviet Union's Sputnik satellite since it changed many people's idea of what was ----------.

    (A) equanimity.... trivial
    (B) importance... inscribed
    (C) magnitude... possible
    (D) paraphernalia... pragmatic

Answers to Lesson Five

Word list practice

1. stupendous
2. fraudulent
3. pragmatic; impetuous

Roots practice

1. flesh
2. all, every
3. flesh (meat)
4. everything
5. everyone (many people)
6. back, again

Synonyms practice

1. A
2. B
3. B
4. A
5. D
6. D
7. C
8. C
9. B
10. A

Sentence completion

1. C
2. A
3. B
4. D
5. C

Lesson Six

Words to learn

Below are the twenty words used in Lesson Six; refer back to this list as needed as you move through the lesson.

Disdain: scorn
Prognosis: forecast
Bias: prejudice
Lenient: permissive
Jaded: indifferent (not easily impressed)

Philanthropy: humanitarianism (giving to people in need)
Limpid: clear
Confound: confuse
Diagnose: identify (usually a problem)
Arrogant: proud

Arduous: difficult
Philosophy: beliefs
Bellicose: belligerent (looking for a fight)
Compassion: pity
Consensus: agreement

Bibliophile: booklover
Humility: modesty
Gnostic: wise
Distort: warp
Haphazard: disorganized

Word list practice

Use the words from the list above to complete the following activities.

1. What word found in the word list is an antonym for humble (the adjective form of the word humility)?

2. Most people want their parents to be more _____ when it comes to curfews and house rules.

3. It can be hard for _____ people to reach a consensus with people that they disagree with.

4. It is easy to become confounded when instructions are _____.

5. Studying for exams like the ISEE can be a(n) _____ process.

Roots practice

Below are three words. Write the definition for the words on the line provided. Based on their meanings, define the common root.

Philanthropy _____

Philosophy _____

Bibliophile _____

1. The root "phil" means:

    Prognosis

    Diagnose

    Gnostic

2. The root "gnos" means:

3. If the root "soph" means "wise," what is a meaning of "philosophy" derived directly from its two roots?

4. Based on the meaning of "prognosis," what does someone who "prognosticates" do?

5. If the root "anthro" means "man," what is a meaning of "philanthropy" derived directly from its two roots?

Synonyms practice

Choose the answer choice that comes closest in meaning to the question word. Keep in mind that any words that we have studied are fair game and not all of the words are from this lesson. Words may also show up in a different form (noun, verb, adjective) than they appeared in the word lists.

1. HAPHAZARD:

    (A) arduous
    (B) disorganized
    (C) morose
    (D) stunted

2. AGITATOR:

    (A) bibliophile
    (B) incarnation
    (C) procrastinator
    (D) troublemaker

3. PROGNOSIS:

    (A) forecast
    (B) humility
    (C) renewal
    (D) terrain

4. ABASHED:

    (A) delayed
    (B) embarrassed
    (C) intimidated
    (D) relieved

5. COMPASSION:

    (A) bias
    (B) frustration
    (C) pity
    (D) settling

6. LIMPID:

    (A) clear
    (B) disdainful
    (C) humorous
    (D) mediocre

7. FRAUDULENT:

    (A) calm
    (B) deceptive
    (C) omnivorous
    (D) stagnant

8. BIAS:

    (A) conservation
    (B) eminence
    (C) prejudice
    (D) serenity

9. GNOSTIC:

    (A) distorted
    (B) official
    (C) wise
    (D) zealous

10. CONSENSUS:

    (A) agreement
    (B) hierarchy
    (C) procrastination
    (D) rebirth

Sentence completion practice

Choose the answer that best completes the meaning of the sentence. Keep in mind that any words that we have studied are fair game and not all of the words are from this lesson. Words may also show up in a different form (noun, verb, adjective) than they appeared in the word lists.

1. The damage caused by Hurricane Katrina was so devastating that many journalists found it almost --------.

    (A) crowded
    (B) effervescent
    (C) figurative
    (D) indescribable

2. During the industrial revolution environmental regulations were either nonexistent or extremely --------- which led to high levels of pollution being released into the atmosphere.

    (A) bellicose
    (B) lenient
    (C) perceptive
    (D) stupendous

3. The --------- task of building the Great Pyramid at Giza took 23 years and required 20,000 to 30,000 laborers.

    (A) arduous
    (B) convivial
    (C) insolent
    (D) metaphorical

4. Members of the Shaker religious group prized -------- and considered it a sin to be ----------.

    (A) apathy... jaded
    (B) compassion... piteous
    (C) humility... arrogant
    (D) philanthropy...magnanimous

5. According to legend, the ------- that Isaac Newton had when an apple fell on his head caused him to -------- the theory of gravity.

    (A) accolades… study
    (B) calamity… ignore
    (C) epiphany… develop
    (D) surfeit… reject

Answers to Lesson Six

Word list practice

1. arrogant
2. lenient
3. bellicose
4. haphazard
5. arduous

Roots practice

1. love of
2. know
3. love of wisdom
4. make predictions
5. love of man(kind)

Synonyms practice

1. B
2. D
3. A
4. B
5. C
6. A
7. B
8. C
9. C
10. A

Sentence completion practice

1. D
2. B
3. A
4. C
5. C

Lesson Seven

Words to learn

Below are the twenty words used in Lesson Seven; refer back to this list as needed as you move through the lesson.

Mediator: negotiator
Allege: claim
Deficient: lacking
Eloquent: expressive (good with words)
Exasperate: irritate

Facile: easy
Artifice: hoax (deceptive trick)
Frivolous: trivial
Ecstasy: rapture (extreme happiness)
Proletariat: workers

Mortician: undertaker (funeral home worker)
Facilitate: help
Confection: candy
Notary: public official (who verifies signatures)
Dynamic: energetic

Facsimile: copy
Psychiatrist: therapist
Absolution: forgiveness
Cursory: brief
Lobbyist: advocate

Word list practice

Use the words from the list above to complete the following activities.

1.   List the five words that describe a job or occupation:

      a.

      b.

      c.

      d.

      e.

2.   It's best not to take a _____ look at these words, but rather to spend some time with them.

Roots practice

Below are three words. Write the definition for the words on the line provided. Based on their meanings, define the common root.

      Facsimile _____

      Facile _____

      Facilitate _____

1. The root "fac" means:

      Artifice _____

      Deficient _____

      Confection _____

2. The root "fic/fect" means:

3. Give an alternate definition for "facilitate," using the root and the definition of "facile":
    to _____.

4. Based on one of the roots above, what do you think happens in a factory?

5. If the root "magni" means great, using one of the roots above, what could the definition of "magnificent" be?

6. If something is "artificial," do you think it is created by man or does it occur in nature?

Synonyms practice

Choose the answer choice that comes closest in meaning to the question word. Keep in mind that any words that we have studied are fair game and not all of the words are from this lesson. Words may also show up in a different form (noun, verb, adjective) than they appeared in the word lists.

1. FRIVOLOUS:

   (A) carnivorous
   (B) gnostic
   (C) serious
   (D) trivial

2. ELOQUENT:

   (A) expressive
   (B) firm
   (C) mercurial
   (D) rejuvenated

3. PANDEMONIUM:

   (A) hierarchy
   (B) omniscience
   (C) prognosis
   (D) uproar

4. ALLEGE:

   (A) ask
   (B) claim
   (C) distort
   (D) facilitate

5. DYNAMIC:

   (A) biased
   (B) dependent
   (C) energetic
   (D) irate

6. CURSORY:

   (A) brief
   (B) confounded
   (C) easy
   (D) wrecked

7. EXASPERATE:

   (A) cleave
   (B) irritate
   (C) reimburse
   (D) split

8. EQUANIMITY:

   (A) accolades
   (B) belligerence
   (C) composure
   (D) prosperity

9. ABSOLUTION:

    (A) decadence
    (B) forgiveness
    (C) gloom
    (D) surfeit

10. ARDUOUS:

    (A) difficult
    (B) embarrassing
    (C) powerful
    (D) rehearsed

Sentence completion practice

Choose the answer that best completes the meaning of the sentence. Keep in mind that any words that we have studied are fair game and not all of the words are from this lesson. Words may also show up in a different form (noun, verb, adjective) than they appeared in the word lists.

1. It is hard to develop --------- when two parties both vigorously defend their opposing positions.

    (A) absolution
    (B) bias
    (C) consensus
    (D) stagnation

2. Frank Abagnale was a famous fraudster whose various acts of -------- were the basis of the movie *Catch Me If You Can.*

    (A) artifice
    (B) confection
    (C) philosophy
    (D) truth

3. Bernard Quaritch was a dedicated -------- that devoted much of his life to cataloguing books produced on the early printing press.

    (A) bibliophile
    (B) lobbyist
    (C) notary
    (D) psychiatrist

4. It was pity when the lecture turned out to be-------- even though the speaker was known for being --------.

    (A) arrogant... lenient
    (B) disdainful... rude
    (C) frivolous.... cursory
    (D) interminable.... dynamic

5. In the 1900's, traditional African sculptures had a ------- impact on the work of European artists who began ------- stylized representations of the human figure.

    (A) boisterous... identifying
    (B) forgotten... circumventing
    (C) imminent... wrangling
    (D) tremendous... incorporating

Answers to Lesson Seven

Word list practice

1. a. psychiatrist
    b. mortician
    c. mediator
    d. lobbyist
    e. notary
2. cursory

Roots practice

1. to make, to do
2. to make
3. make easy
4. things are made
5. made greatly
6. made by man

Synonyms practice

1. D
2. A
3. D
4. B
5. C
6. A
7. B
8. C
9. B
10. A

Sentence completion practice

1. C
2. A
3. A
4. D
5. D

Lesson Eight

Words to learn

Below are the twenty words used in Lesson Eight; refer back to this list as needed as you move through the lesson.

Nostalgia: longing
Precocious: advanced
Elegy: funeral song
Recuperate: recover
Enhance: increase

Posterity: descendants
Excavate: dig
Precaution: carefulness
Futile: useless
Undaunted: unafraid

Litigation: legal proceeding
Prelude: introduction
Instigate: provoke (start a fight)
Curriculum: studies
Fluctuate: waver

Demoralize: depress
Posthumous: after death
Deteriorate: worsen
Posterior: rear
Curvature: arc

Word list practice

Use the words from the list above to complete the following activities.

1. If a book was published posthumously, would the author be able to read the finished edition? Why or why not?

2. Would a superhero more likely be described as demoralized or undaunted?

3. If something doesn't get better, it either stays the same or it _____.

4. It takes a long time to _____ after an illness like whooping cough.

Roots practice

Below are three words. Write the definition for the words on the line provided. Based on their meanings, define the common root.

Posterior _____

Posterity _____

Posthumous _____

1. The root "post" means:

Prelude _____

Precocious _____

Precaution _____

2. The root "pre" means:

3. How does the meaning of the root "pre" factor into the meaning of "precocious?" If someone is "precocious," they are "advanced before" what?

4. There is another word meaning "after death" that uses the root words "post" and "mort." Can you guess what it is?

5. If the root word "inter" means "between," and a prelude is an introduction, when do you think an "interlude" happens?

6. If "posterior" means at the end (or rear), what very similar word means "at the beginning?" (Hint: "ante" means "before".)

Synonyms practice

Choose the answer choice that comes closest in meaning to the question word. Keep in mind that any words that we have studied are fair game and not all of the words are from this lesson. Words may also show up in a different form (noun, verb, adjective) than they appeared in the word lists.

1. DEFICIENT:

    (A) dainty
    (B) frivolous
    (C) jaded
    (D) lacking

2. PRECOCIOUS:

    (A) advanced
    (B) dynamic
    (C) generous
    (D) modest

3. INSTIGATE:

    (A) cut
    (B) grovel
    (C) provoke
    (D) subsist

4. NOSTALGIA:

    (A) exasperation
    (B) longing
    (C) mediation
    (D) preparation

5. FACILITATE:

    (A) disdain
    (B) help
    (C) loosen
    (D) value

6. EPIPHANY:

    (A) accolade
    (B) flight
    (C) insight
    (D) prognosis

7. FLUCTUATE:

    (A) decline
    (B) glorify
    (C) paraphrase
    (D) waver

8. HUMILITY:

    (A) modesty
    (B) pragmatism
    (C) recuperation
    (D) suspicion

9. FUTILE:

(A) fierce
(B) mediocre
(C) preferable
(D) useless

10. FACSIMILE:

(A) accolades
(B) copy
(C) excess
(D) importance

Sentence completion practice

Choose the answer that best completes the meaning of the sentence. Keep in mind that any words that we have studied are fair game and not all of the words are from this lesson. Words may also show up in a different form (noun, verb, adjective) than they appeared in the word lists.

1. In New Orleans, it is common for jazz musicians to perform elaborate --------- at funerals as a way to honor the deceased.

(A) artifice
(B) elegies
(C) pandemonium
(D) vitality

2. After moving from a small town to a big city, many people become ------- and stop noticing all the noise and commotion of living in an urban area.

(A) animated
(B) confounded
(C) jaded
(D) sentient

3. Attila the Hun was a particularly --------- leader known for invading several territories and waging many battles.

(A) bellicose
(B) compassionate
(C) impetuous
(D) oblivious

4. Construction workers must take --------- when working in a historic area in order to avoid damaging potentially fragile buildings when they --------- a new foundation.

(A) consensus... enhance
(B) facsimiles... hew
(C) miscreants... reimburse
(D) precautions... excavate

5. In an effort to avoid -------, many people work with --------- in order to come up with an agreement between two parties without having to involve the court system.

(A) consensus... agitators
(B) demoralization... lobbyists
(C) litigation... mediators
(D) prelude... notaries

Answers to Lesson Eight

Word list practice

1. no, because the author would be dead
2. undaunted
3. deteriorates
4. recuperate

Roots practice

1. after, behind
2. before
3. what is normal for his or her age
4. postmortem
5. in the middle
6. anterior

Synonyms practice

1. D
2. A
3. C
4. B
5. B
6. C
7. D
8. A
9. D
10. B

Sentence completion practice

1. B
2. C
3. A
4. D
5. C

Lesson Nine

Words to learn

Below are the twenty words used in Lesson Nine; refer back to this list as needed as you move through the lesson.

Potent: powerful
Collaborate: cooperate
Retribution: punishment
Burnish: polish
Convergence: union

Stalwart: robust (strong and dependable)
Coincide: correspond (happen at the same time)
Gusto: enjoyment
Spontaneous: impulsive
Zealous: fervent (passionate)

Deflect: divert (turn away)
Fortuitous: lucky
Succinct: brief
Genuflect: kneel
Deliberate: intentional

Premeditated: planned
Voluble: talkative
Inflection: tone (of voice)
Hybrid: mixed
Resolute: determined

Word list practice

Use the words from the list above to complete the following activities.

1. When we are electing the next president, we hope that he or she is what three things from the list above?
   a.
   b.
   c.

2. If we have to watch her give a speech, however, we hope that she is not
   _____.

3. What is "mixed" about a hybrid car?

4. Is winning the lottery "fortuitous" or "deliberate?"

Roots practice

Below are three words. Write the definition for the words on the line provided. Based on their meanings, define the common root.

Deflect _____

Genuflect _____

Inflection _____

1. The root "flect" means:

Convergence _____

Coincide _____

Collaborate _____

2. The root "co/con" means:

3. What "bends" when it comes to inflection?

4. What "bends" when someone genuflects?

5. If an "incident" is an event or occurrence, what happens in a "coincidence?"

6. Using the meaning of the root "di" (apart) and the word convergence, what is a word meaning "to go in different directions from a common point?"

Synonyms practice

Choose the answer choice that comes closest in meaning to the question word. Keep in mind that any words that we have studied are fair game and not all of the words are from this lesson. Words may also show up in a different form (noun, verb, adjective) than they appeared in the word lists.

1. BURNISH:

   (A) distort
   (B) fluctuate
   (C) light
   (D) polish

2. ZEALOUS:

   (A) determined
   (B) fervent
   (C) peaceful
   (D) undaunted

3. STALWART:

   (A) deteriorating
   (B) energetic
   (C) robust
   (D) unavailable

4. GUSTO:

   (A) enjoyment
   (B) hope
   (C) nostalgia
   (D) philanthropy

5. RETRIBUTION:

   (A) curriculum
   (B) glee
   (C) punishment
   (D) twinge

6. HYBRID:

   (A) cursory
   (B) futile
   (C) mixed
   (D) potent

7. DISDAIN:

   (A) agreement
   (B) eloquence
   (C) forecast
   (D) scorn

8. CURVATURE:

   (A) arc
   (B) distortion
   (C) limit
   (D) pilgrimage

9. DIAGNOSE:

    (A) allege
    (B) identify
    (C) paraphrase
    (D) vow

10. SUCCINCT:

    (A) cursory
    (B) ecstatic
    (C) posthumous
    (D) precocious

Sentence completion practice

Choose the answer that best completes the meaning of the sentence. Keep in mind that any words that we have studied are fair game and not all of the words are from this lesson. Words may also show up in a different form (noun, verb, adjective) than they appeared in the word lists.

1. Political candidates will often bring up their opponents' misbehavior in order to -------- attention from their own misconduct.

    (A) attract
    (B) create
    (C) deflect
    (D) recuperate

2. The -------- of a temperate climate and flat ground that is easily plowed allowed the American Midwest to become one of the most important farming regions in the United States.

    (A) apathy
    (B) convergence
    (C) mediocrity
    (D) philosophy

3. In Chinese culture, it is considered --------- to receive a red envelope because it is believed to bring prosperity.

    (A) deficient
    (B) dynamic
    (C) enhanced
    (D) fortuitous

4. Because loggerhead turtles travel to many locations, communities must --------- in order to come up with a -------- plan to conserve the species.

    (A) animate… figurative
    (B) collaborate… deliberate
    (C) frustrate… zealous
    (D) instigate… lenient

5. Although the two terms are very similar, it is more flattering to be called --------- than to be called -------.

    (A)   disdainful... serene

    (B)   morose... exasperated

    (C)   spontaneous... impetuous

    (D)   zealous... voluble

Answers to Lesson Nine

Word list practice

1. a. potent
   b. stalwart
   c. resolute
2. voluble
3. power sources for the engine: gasoline and electric
4. fortuitous

Roots practice

1. to bend
2. with, together
3. a voice, or the tone of a voice
4. knees
5. two events come together
6. diverge

Synonyms practice

1. D
2. B
3. C
4. A
5. C
6. C
7. D
8. A
9. B
10. A

Sentence completion

1. C
2. B
3. D
4. B
5. C

Lesson Ten

Words to learn

Below are the twenty words used in Lesson Ten; refer back to this list as needed as you move through the lesson.

Sustenance: nourishment
Lackluster: dull
Trajectory: path
Insurgent: rebel
Genesis: origin

Antagonistic: hostile
Illustrious: celebrated
Unkempt: messy
Trite: overused
Insurrection: revolt

Contemplate: ponder (think about)
Vogue: popularity
Lustrous: shining
Resurrect: bring back
Excruciating: agonizing

Subsistence: survival
Provenance: birthplace
Duplicity: deceptiveness
Ruminate: reflect
Averse: opposing

Word list practice

Use the words from the list above to complete the following activities.

1.   List three words from above that you would like to have associated with you:
   a.
   b.
   c.

2.   List three words from above that you would NOT like to have associated with you:
   a.
   b.
   c.

3.   If a definition of "subsist" is "keep going," do you think subsistence living includes luxuries? Why or why not?

Roots practice

Below are three words. Write the definition for the words on the line provided. Based on their meanings, define the common root.

Insurgent _____

Resurrect _____

Insurrection _____

1. The root "surg/surr" means:

Lackluster _____

Lustrous _____

Illustrious _____

2. The root "lust" means:

3. Do you think supermodels prefer their hair to be "lackluster" or "lustrous?"

4. Based on the meaning of "resurrect," what do you think "resurrection" means?

5. Based on the meaning of one of the roots above, what do you think it means when the tide "surges?"

Synonyms practice

Choose the answer choice that comes closest in meaning to the question word. Keep in mind that any words that we have studied are fair game and not all of the words are from this lesson. Words may also show up in a different form (noun, verb, adjective) than they appeared in the word lists.

1. CONTEMPLATE:

    (A) demoralize
    (B) exasperate
    (C) ruminate
    (D) warp

2. RESOLUTE:

    (A) determined
    (B) genuine
    (C) lackluster
    (D) spontaneous

3. VOLUBLE:

    (A) burnished
    (B) depressed
    (C) posterior
    (D) talkative

4. FACILE:

    (A) dynamic
    (B) easy
    (C) haphazard
    (D) probable

5. DISDAIN:

    (A) artifice
    (B) forecast
    (C) nostalgia
    (D) scorn

6. ILLUSTRIOUS:

    (A) advanced
    (B) belligerent
    (C) celebrated
    (D) flexible

7. GENUFLECT:

    (A) kneel
    (B) negotiate
    (C) resurrect
    (D) supply

8. EXCRUCIATING:

    (A) agonizing
    (B) hostile
    (C) lustrous
    (D) premeditated

9. UNKEMPT:

    (A) antagonistic
    (B) messy
    (C) stalwart
    (D) stupendous

10. TRAJECTORY:

    (A) curriculum
    (B) gusto
    (C) sustenance
    (D) path

Sentence completion practice

Choose the answer that best completes the meaning of the sentence. Keep in mind that any words that we have studied are fair game and not all of the words are from this lesson. Words may also show up in a different form (noun, verb, adjective) than they appeared in the word lists.

1. If journalists use a comparison too many times, they run the risk of their writing seeming ---------.

    (A) duplicitous
    (B) hybrid
    (C) trite
    (D) wise

2. While the teacher was opposed to increasing recess time, she was not --------- to adding additional minutes to gym class time.

    (A) averse
    (B) confounded
    (C) determined
    (D) inclined

3. The ---------- of the internet happened in the 1960s when the United States Department of Defense began awarding contracts to create a system that connected universities.

    (A) conquest
    (B) genesis
    (C) nostalgia
    (D) request

4. When Russian leader Vladimir Putin sent troops into another country, he moved beyond being merely ---------- and become downright ---------.

    (A) antagonistic…bellicose
    (B) deficient… lacking
    (C) fluctuating… demoralized
    (D) lackluster… fortuitous

5. In 1993, Bill Clinton ---------- awarded several deserving African-American soldiers from World War II the Medal of Honor to recognize the --------- they should have received during their lifetimes.

(A) boisterously…quiet
(B) famously… philosophy
(C) illustriously… provenance
(D) posthumously… accolades

Answers to Lesson Ten

Word list practice

1. a. vogue
   b. illustrious
   c. lustrous
2. a. lackluster
   b. unkempt
   c. antagonistic
3. No – because you are living with just enough to keep going or just enough for existence.

Roots practice

1. rise
2. shine
3. lustrous
4. the act of being brought back to life
5. the tides rise

Synonyms practice

1. C
2. A
3. D
4. B
5. D
6. C
7. A
8. A
9. B
10. D

Sentence completion practice

1. C
2. A
3. B
4. A
5. D

Additional Word Lists

Challenging vocabulary word list

Visit www.testprepworks.com/student/download to see sample sentences with these words.

Words that make something better

allay	soothe
bolster	support
buttress	support
embellish	to beautify
rectify	to correct
ratify	approve
subside	lessen

Words with a positive meaning

benevolent	kind
deft	nimble
diligent	persevering
dogged	persistent
exuberant	enthusiastic
invincible	undefeatable
prudent	wise
reputable	respectable
ardor	passion
allure	attraction
unerring	perfect
impartial	unprejudiced
proficient	experienced
timely	well-timed

Words that make something worse

affront	offend
depreciate	lose value
defile	pollute
taint	pollute
rend	divide

Words with a negative meaning

callous	insensitive
hapless	unlucky
cynical	pessimistic
humdrum	boring
laborious	arduous
qualm	apprehension
quandary	predicament
somber	gloomy
rue	regret
skeptical	doubtful

Words with a very negative meaning

appalling	*horrific*
atrocious	*dreadful*
bane	*curse*
bedlam	*chaos*
ire	*anger*
chagrin	*disappointment*
contemptible	*despicable*
despondent	*hopeless*
disreputable	*dishonorable*
havoc	*devastation*
morbid	*gruesome*
impertinent	*insulting*

Words that refer to a gathering

bevy	*group*
consolidate	*to unite*
glean	*infer or gather*
compile	*gather*
medley	*mixture*
tabulate	*to group*

Words that bring about an ending

curtail	*cut back*
dispel	*scatter*
eradicate	*exterminate*
evasion	*avoidance*
quell	*extinguish*
revoke	*take back*
revert	*regress*

Words related to being polite

demure	*reserved*
genteel	*polite*
discretion	*judgment*

Words used for name-calling

glutton	*one who overindulges*
hovel	*shack*
parochial	*insular*
naïve	*unsophisticated*
nonchalant	*unconcerned*
portly	*stout*
provincial	*unsophisticated*
putrid	*decaying*
tawdry	*cheap*
uncouth	*awkward*

Words related to happiness

enrapture	*enchant*
enthrall	*captivate*
revel	*merriment*
superlative	*outstanding*
incandescent	*glowing*

Words related to something not real

cryptic	*mysterious*
dupe	*to trick*
fallacy	*misconception*
feign	*pretend*
furtive	*stealthy*
hoax	*fraud*
bogus	*counterfeit*

Synonyms for confusing

mystical	*mysterious*
opaque	*murky*
disconcert	*perplex*

Words related to activity

inert	*unmoving*
invigorating	*energizing*
dormant	*inactive*
listless	*spiritless*
slothful	*lazy*
wan	*feeble*

Fighting words

brandish	*wield*
incite	*encourage*
incriminate	*accuse*
parry	*to deflect*
radical	*extreme*
rebuff	*reject*
rift	*disagreement*
skirmish	*conflict*
tumult	*riot*

Words related to height

apex	*peak*
dominant	*most important*
pinnacle	*peak*
ultimate	*highest*

Words related to humor

droll	*witty*
satire	*parody*
banter	*joke*

Additional words

auditory	*related to hearing*
axiom	*a truth*
befall	*happen*
belie	*contradict*
conclusive	*definitive*
delve	*research*
dilate	*expand*
dirge	*funeral song*
duct	*channel*
emancipate	*to free*
enumerate	*to list*
feasible	*possible*
flaunt	*show off*
foible	*weakness*
germinate	*to grow*
idiom	*an expression*
imperative	*required*
inclination	*preference*
induce	*to cause*
inevitable	*unavoidable*
pensive	*reflective*
pertinent	*relevant*
plausible	*believable*
pliable	*flexible*
stolid	*unemotional*
sundry	*diverse*
tangent	*touching*
temperance	*moderation*
vigilant	*watchful*
wend	*to journey*
whet	*sharpen*

More challenging vocabulary word list

Visit www.testprepworks.com/student/download to see sample sentences with these words.

Fighting words

accost	*attack*
assail	*attack*
contend	*compete*
pugnacious	*quarrelsome*
incendiary	*inflammatory*
renegade	*dissenter*
tirade	*diatribe*
transgress	*violate*

Words related to being a good person

affable	*friendly*
judicious	*responsible*
congenial	*friendly*
scruple	*moral*
adage	*proverb*
mien	*demeanor*
mettle	*courage*

Words that describe size and length

abridge	*shorten*
amplitude	*magnitude*
brevity	*shortness*
terse	*concise*

Words related to wanting something

acquisition	*possession*
bequeath	*grant*
covet	*desire*
procure	*obtain*
pillage	*plunder*
forbearance	*self-control*

Words related to approval

condone	*approve*
consecrate	*sanctify*
sanction	*approve*

Words related to disapproval

indict	*accuse*
refute	*disprove*
unfounded	*unjustified*

Words related to making something worse

adulterated	*cheapened*
alienate	*estrange*
discredit	*tarnish*
deplete	*reduce*
relinquish	*give up*
detriment	*disadvantage*
fetter	*restrain*
impediment	*obstacle*

Words related to dislike

aversion	*disliking*
odious	*offensive*
revulsion	*disgust*

Words related to being unpleasant

condescending	*patronizing*
contemptuous	*disdainful*
disdain	*disapproval*
reproof	*criticism*
extortion	*blackmail*
ominous	*threatening*
overbearing	*domineering*
affectation	*pretension*

Words related to time

defer	*delay*
impending	*imminent*
impromptu	*unplanned*
ensuing	*following*
antiquated	*outdated*

Words indicating a lack of truth

dubious	*doubtful*
erroneous	*wrong*
fabricate	*invent*
concoct	*make up*
devious	*crafty*
ruse	*trick*
incredulous	*skeptical*
awry	*wrong*

Words indicating clarity (or a lack thereof)

ambiguous	*unclear*
contort	*to twist*
precarious	*insecure*
tentative	*uncertain*
erratic	*unpredictable*
translucent	*clear*

Words related to staying calm

pacifist	*peaceful*
placid	*calm*
sedate	*relaxed*
tranquil	*restful*
repose	*relaxation*

Words to make a dramatic point

celestial	*heavenly*
eminent	*distinguished*
emphatic	*definite*
fervent	*enthusiastic*
fervor	*enthusiasm*
immaculate	*spotless*
nullify	*invalidate*
obliterate	*destroy*
rampant	*widespread*
resplendent	*gleaming*
scourge	*plague*
vehement	*insistent*
zenith	*peak*
rabid	*extreme*

Words related to memory

commemorate	*remember*
momentous	*important*
reminiscent	*suggestive of*
memento	*souvenir*

Celebratory words

carouse	*celebrate*
exultation	*rejoicing*
jocular	*joking*
raucous	*rowdy*

Words describing physical qualities

emaciated	*scrawny*
glower	*glare*
slovenly	*unclean*
supple	*flexible*
tepid	*lukewarm*
vibrant	*energetic*
disheveled	*untidy*
derelict	*abandoned*
fallow	*inactive*
inanimate	*lifeless*
decrepit	*weakened*
dilapidated	*crumbling*

Desirable qualities

candid	*honest*
debonair	*elegant*
peerless	*unrivaled*
virtuoso	*genius*

Undesirable qualities

monotone	*droning*
complacent	*unconcerned*
deranged	*insane*
inane	*stupid*
infamous	*notorious*
fastidious	*demanding*
pompous	*arrogant*
inept	*unskilled*
gullible	*naïve*

Words describing quantity or amount

devoid	*without*
influx	*inpouring*
myriad	*many*
negligible	*paltry*
permeate	*saturate*
glut	*overfill*

Words related to putting things together

affix	*attach*
assimilate	*conform*
composite	*combined*
converse	*discuss*
discourse	*conversation*
kindred	*related*
liaison	*contact*

Words related to sadness

doleful	*sorrowful*
encumbered	*burdened*

Words that describe going off course

diffuse	*spread*
disperse	*spread*
meander	*wander*
vagrant	*wandering*

Additional words

abdicate	*resign*
abrasion	*scrape*
abstain	*refrain*
align	*straighten*
ascribe	*credit*
audit	*inspect*
bulwark	*protection*
cessation	*stopping*
deviate	*stray*
discern	*recognize*
engross	*immerse*
evoke	*to summon*
fissure	*opening*
flagrant	*obvious*
habitable	*livable*
incongruous	*incompatible*
infringe	*violate*
insinuate	*imply*
invaluable	*precious*
kinetic	*moving*
lineage	*genealogy*
palatable	*tasty*
pathos	*pity*
recourse	*reaction*
redundant	*repetitious*
renaissance	*rebirth*
replenish	*refill*
rigorous	*strict*

saunter	*stroll*
secede	*break away*
servitude	*slavery*
solace	*comfort*
squander	*waste*
stark	*bare*
subsequent	*following*
surmount	*overcome*
taut	*tense*
traverse	*to cross*
whimsical	*fanciful*

Most challenging vocabulary word list

Visit www.testprepworks.com/student/download to see sample sentences with these words.

Words describing highly capable people

adroit	*skillful*
astute	*perceptive (smart, but not necessarily book smart)*
preeminent	*superior (better than anyone else)*

Words related to kind and pleasant people

altruistic	*generous*
amicable	*friendly*
credulous	*trusting*
amenable	*willing*
deference	*respect*
laudable	*praiseworthy*

Synonyms for boring or uninteresting

banal	*unoriginal*
insipid	*bland*
mundane	*ordinary*
prosaic	*dull*
vapid	*uninteresting*

Words related to a lack of progress

debase	*devalue (to reduce the value of)*
relegate	*demote (to put in a lesser position)*
impasse	*deadlock*
impede	*obstruct*

Words describing poor treatment of others

beguile	*trick*
crass	*gross*
coerce	*to force*
connive	*conspire*
flippant	*disrespectful*
animosity	*hatred*
caustic	*bitter*
deride	*mock*
disparage	*belittle (to put down)*
harangue	*scold*

Punishment or condemnation

censure	*criticize*
chastise	*to discipline*
decry	*condemn*

Words related to an ending

culminate	*to complete*
definitive	*ultimate (final answer)*
incessant	*unending*

Words related to being broken

defunct	*nonfunctioning*
erode	*deteriorate*
fiasco	*failure*

Words related to enthusiasm

avid	*enthusiastic*
effervescence	*enthusiasm*
vociferous	*noisy*

Desirable qualities

discreet	*prudent (respectful of privacy)*
ingenuous	*honest*
intrepid	*fearless*
paragon	*a model (a perfect example)*
solicitous	*attentive*

Undesirable qualities

pungent	*strong smelling*
fetid	*smelly*
hackneyed	*stale (or overdone)*
ignominious	*disgraceful*
indolent	*lazy*
pariah	*outcast*
supercilious	*haughty (or snobby)*
petulant	*irritable*
taciturn	*uncommunicative*
volatile	*mercurial (changing frequently)*

Words indicating a lack of energy

languid	*inactive*
lethargy	*laziness*
staid	*sedated*

Words related to truth and clarity

candor	*honesty*
guile	*deception*
conjecture	*speculate (make an assumption without the facts)*
incognito	*disguised*
indeterminate	*vague*
inexplicable	*mystifying*
nebulous	*vague*
overt	*obvious*
innuendo	*insinuation*

Words indicating absolute or unchangeable

adamant	*uncompromising*
inalienable	*absolute*
incorrigible	*unchangeable*
indomitable	*unconquerable*

Words related to size or quantity

augment	*enlarge (make bigger)*
infinitesimal	*miniscule (tiny)*
prolific	*abundant*

Words describing an extravagant lifestyle

garish	*showy*
infamy	*disrepute (fame in a bad way)*
notoriety	*fame (for all the wrong reasons)*
opulent	*luxurious*
pretentious	*showy*

Words describing physical characteristics

lithe	*flexible*
pallid	*pale*
sedentary	*sitting*
stature	*height*

Words related to the spread of something

imbue	*permeate*
pervasive	*spread throughout*
inundate	*overwhelm*

Words with very negative meanings

ludicrous	*absurd*
lurid	*gruesome*
scathing	*severe*
squalid	*repulsive*
travesty	*mockery*

Words related to religion

sacrilege	*blasphemy (defying religion)*
sagacity	*wisdom*
hallowed	*holy*
heretic	*dissenter (vocal nonbeliever)*

Additional words

facetious	*not serious*
emanate	*originate (start from)*
abduct	*kidnap*
affinity	*attraction*
digression	*deviation (to go off course)*
entreat	*beg*
ethereal	*light*
exhort	*to caution*
extol	*to praise*
extricate	*liberate*
foray	*raid*
garner	*gather*
penitent	*remorseful*
prerogative	*a right*
remiss	*careless*
reticence	*reluctance*
vacillate	*to waver*
felicity	*happiness*
levity	*lightness*

Reading Comprehension Section

In the ISEE Reading Comprehension section, you are given passages and then asked questions about these passages. There are six passages, and each passage is followed by six questions. For the entire section, there is a total of thirty-six questions. You will have thirty-five minutes to complete the section. There will be only one reading section on your test.

- 6 passages
- 6 questions for each passage
- 36 total questions
- 35 minutes to complete section
- Only one reading section

You may be thinking, "I know how to read, I am good on this section." However, most people applying to independent school know how to read. In order to get around the 50th percentile score for eighth graders on the reading section, you need to answer a little more than half of the questions correctly. This means that half of the eighth graders taking this test are getting less than that.

- To get the median score for an 8th grader, you need to answer a little more than half of the questions correctly

The issue is that not every student can get a perfect score on the reading section, so the writers have to create a test where some students who know how to read are going to miss several questions.

So how do the test writers get you to answer so many questions incorrectly? First of all, the questions can be very detail-oriented. Think of this not as a reading test, but as looking for a needle in a haystack – with very little time to find it. Secondly, the questions can include answer choices with words from the passage, but those words are describing something different. Students often see these answer choices and think that if the words show up in the passage, they must be the correct answers. However, the words are describing something else. Lastly, the questions use your own brain against you! How do they do this? They include answer choices that would be a logical conclusion, but aren't mentioned in the passage, so they are wrong.

- Very detail-oriented questions
- Test writers take words from another part of the passage and put them in the incorrect answer choices
- Some answer choices are logical conclusions, but aren't mentioned in the passage so they are not correct

By making a plan and sticking to it, however, you can overcome these obstacles and beat the average score – by a lot!

In this section, first we will cover the general plan of attack and then we will get into the details that make the difference.

Reading Section Plan of Attack

Students can significantly improve their reading scores by following an easy plan:

Step 1: Plan your time.
You have just under six minutes per passage, so be sure to lay out your time before you begin.

Step 2: Prioritize passages.
Play to your strengths. Don't just answer the passages in the order that they appear.

Step 3: Go to the questions first.
Mark questions as either specific or general. You want to know what to look for as you read.

Step 4: Read the passage.
If you run across the answer to a specific question, go ahead and answer that. But do not worry if you miss an answer.

Step 5: Answer specific questions.
If there are any specific questions that you did not answer yet, go back and find the answers.

Step 6: Answer general questions.
Answer any questions that ask about the passage as a whole.

Step 7: Repeat steps 3-6 with next passage.
You've got it under control. Just keep cranking through the section until you are done.

Keep in mind that this section is not a test of how well you read. It is a test of how well you test. You need to manage your time and think about the process.

Step #1: Plan your time

Before you do anything, take thirty seconds to plan out your time. You have just under six minutes per passage, and there are six passages.

- Just under 6 minutes per passage

Look at the starting time and make a quick chart of when you should finish each passage at the top of your first page. For example, let's say you start at 9:23, then your chart should look like this:

Start –	9:23
1 –	9:28
2 –	9:34
3 –	9:40
4 –	9:46
5 –	9:52
6 –	9:58

We make a chart like this because we won't be answering the passages in the order that they appear. You don't have to follow the pacing chart exactly, but you should be close. If you finish the first passage in 3 minutes, then you are moving way too quickly. If it takes you 8 minutes to finish the first passage, then you will know that you need to speed up. We allot only 5 minutes to the first passage because you will answer the easiest passage first.

- Timing chart is a rough guideline

Drill #1

Let's say you start a reading section and the start time is 9:32. Fill in the chart below:

Start –
1 –
2 –
3 –
4 –
5 –
6 –

(Answers to this drill are found on page 139)

Step #2: Prioritize passages

Take a quick look at your passages. You can even quickly read the first sentence to get an idea of what the passage is about. If you see a passage with a topic that you have studied in school, do that first. While you do not need any background information to answer the passage questions, it is easier to understand what is going on quickly if you are familiar with the topic. If there are any passages that stick out as being really long, save those for last.

- Look for passages with a familiar topic
- Save really long passages for last

The following are the types of passages that you may see:

Narrative

These passages read like a story. The story may be true or it may be fiction. Some of the types of narratives that you may see include biographical narrative (tells a story about a historical figure), personal narrative (an author shares an experience he or she has had), or fictional narrative (a made-up story). These passages tend to have more questions that require drawing a conclusion or figuring out what is implied.

- In the form of a story
- Can be fiction or non-fiction
- Questions tend to be more about drawing conclusions and figuring out what is implied

Expository

Expository passages explain something. The goal of an expository passage is to explain, not to tell a story. You may see passages that compare and contrast, describe a historical event, or explain a scientific occurrence. The questions for these passages tend to be more detail-oriented.

- Explain something
- Questions more detail oriented

Persuasive

These passages are designed to convince the reader of something. Persuasive passages may offer an opinion, give pros and cons, or present a problem and a solution. Questions for this type of passage tend to require following an argument or deciding which evidence supports the argument.

- Convince the reader
- Questions may ask reader to follow an argument or decide which evidence supports an argument

Descriptive

The purpose of descriptive passages is to describe something so clearly that it creates a picture in the reader's mind. Questions for descriptive passages tend to test details since the passage is mainly composed of details.

- Creates a picture in your mind
- Questions are very detail-oriented

So which passage types should you answer first? That depends on what you are good at! If you are good at finding picky details, then the expository and descriptive passages might be better for you. If inferring ideas and understanding arguments is your strength, then persuasive and narrative passages may be easier for you. In general, you want to do the passages that are easiest for you first and save the toughest one for the end.

- Different people will find different passages easy or hard
- Do the passages that are easier for you first

Drill #2

You start the reading section. After a quick scan of each passage, you have to prioritize the order of answering the passages. Quickly number the passages below in the order that you would answer them.

Passage topics:

Passage about the invention of the unicycle: #_____

Essay about the importance of school nutrition: #_____

Description of the creation of the first American Flag: #_____

Passage about why we have Leap Day: #_____

Passage from a novel: #_____

Newspaper article about the Battle of the Bulge: #_____

(Answers to this drill are found on page 139)

Step #3: When you start a passage, go to questions first

It is important that you identify specific (S) and general (G) questions before you begin to read. You may come across the answer to a specific question as you read, so you also want to underline what the question is asking about for specific questions.

- Mark general questions with a "G"
- Mark specific questions with an "S"
- For specific questions, make sure you underline what the question is about if it references a particular topic

So how do you know if a question will be specific or general? Become familiar with the question types that follow.

General questions

On the ISEE, you will see the following types of questions that are general:

- Mark these question types with a "G"

Main idea questions

These questions ask you for the overall theme of the passage.

Here are some examples:

- The primary purpose of this passage is to
- Which of the following best states the passage's main idea?
- This passage is mainly concerned with

Main idea questions are definitely general questions. You should mark them with a "G" for general and remember to answer them after any specific questions.

- Mark main idea questions with a "G" for general
- Answer them at the end

Organization questions

Organization questions ask you to look for the structure of the passage and see how the parts all fit together.

Here is what they look like:

- The function of the second paragraph is to
- Which of the following would be most logical for the author to discuss next?
- Which of the following best describes the organization of the passage as a whole?

These are general questions, so mark them with a "G". These questions want you to look at the passage as a whole. To tackle these questions, write a word or two next to each paragraph that summarizes what that paragraph is about. Look at these labels to see the flow of the passage. From this, you should be able to figure out how one paragraph functions in the passage or what would make sense to discuss next. Don't worry too much about these questions, as you may see only a couple of them on the entire reading section.

- Mark organization questions with a "G"
- Answer them at the end
- Jot down a word or two next to each paragraph so that you can see the structure of the passage as a whole
- There won't be very many of these questions, so don't worry too much about them

Tone / attitude / figurative language questions

These questions ask you to identify the tone of a piece or how the writer feels about something. They might also ask you to identify the type of figurative language the author uses in order to convey his or her attitude. Types of figurative language include similes, metaphors, personification, irony, and hyperbole.

They might look like these:

- Which best expresses the author's attitude about _____?
- The tone of the passage can best be described as

These questions can be general or specific. You may have a question that asks about the tone of the entire passage, or you may have a question that refers you to a specific part of the passage.

Here is an example of a general tone / attitude question:

1.   The author's attitude about the school lunch program can best be described as

In this case, it may look specific since it refers to the school lunch program, but the entire passage may be about the school lunch program. If it doesn't have a line reference, it is probably a general question, but remember that we have to be flexible.

- If a tone or attitude question does not have a line reference, it is probably a general question
- Be flexible – you can always adjust later if you incorrectly mark it as a general question

Here is an example of a specific tone/attitude/figurative language question:

2.   In lines 5-6, the author uses which of the following to convey suspicion?

   (A) personification
   (B) hyperbole
   (C) metaphor
   (D) humor

Also, look for moderate answers on tone or attitude questions. An author is not likely to be "enraged" on the ISEE, but he or she might be "annoyed".

- Look for answers that are less extreme

Finally, this is the least common question type on the reading section. Don't let these questions cause anxiety! You may only see one of them in the entire reading section.

- Least common question type

Specific questions

There are also several common types of specific questions:

Supporting idea questions

These questions are looking for details.

Here are some examples:

- The passage states that which of the following people helped Johnny Appleseed?
- Which question is answered by the passage?
- Which statement about the spring equinox is supported by the passage?

These questions are definitely specific questions. They are looking for details from the passage that are directly stated and not asking you to pull together information from different places. For these questions, you should be able to underline the correct answer restated word-for-word in the passage.

- Mark supporting idea questions with an "S" for specific
- You should be able to underline the correct answer in the passage

Inference questions

Inference questions ask you to draw a conclusion from the text. They might ask you how two ideas or people compare, to interpret what the author states, or to predict what might happen.

Here are some examples of inference questions:

- Charles Dickens clearly believed
- According to the passage, both Susan B. Anthony and Elizabeth Cady Stanton
- In the second paragraph, the author implies
- Which of the following best characterizes bacterial growth as the passage describes it?

These are specific questions because you will find the answer in just a small portion of the passage. Mark these questions with an "S" and remember that you must be able to underline the answer.

Inference questions are one of the most common question types on the ISEE. The key to these questions is that you may not be able to underline just one sentence in the passage that contains your answer, but you should be able to underline the evidence for the correct answer.

- Mark inference questions with an "S"
- Underline the evidence in the passage for the correct answer – it may show up in more than one place, but you should be able to underline all of it
- Practice these questions – they show up a lot!

Vocabulary questions

These questions ask you to use the context of the passage to figure out what a word means.

Here are some examples:

- In line 14, the word "capable" most nearly means
- In line 25, "captivate" most nearly means to

These are specific questions because they require you to use just a small part of the passage. You cannot underline the correct answer for these questions, however. For vocabulary questions, we have a different approach. We actually find the word in the passage, cross it out, and then plug in the answer choices to see what makes sense in that sentence. It is important that you practice this strategy – vocabulary questions are one of the most common question types in the reading section. In fact, there is usually a vocabulary question for every single passage.

- Mark vocabulary questions with an "S"
- Cross out the word in the passage and then fill in answer choices to see what has the same meaning as the question word
- Get good at vocabulary questions – there is one for almost every passage!

As you can see, there are more specific questions than general questions on the ISEE Reading Comprehension section.

To practice identifying whether questions are specific or general, complete the drills that follow by identifying each question as general or specific. Time yourself on each drill to see how you improve! If you aren't completely sure of whether a question is specific or general, don't get too worried or spend a lot of time on that. The goal of this strategy is to save time in the long run, and it is easy to change your mind as you work through a passage.

Drill #3

1. This passage is primarily about

2. As used in line 7, "graciously" most nearly means

3. It can be inferred from the passage that which statement about types of grasses is true?

4. According to the passage, how long did it take to travel across the country on the first transcontinental railway?

5. The function of the third paragraph is to

Time:

(Answers to this drill are found on page 139)

Drill #4

1. Which of the following statements does the passage provide evidence for?

2. The sounds referred to in the passage were

3. According to the author, the musicians stopped playing because

4. An "emu" is probably a type of

5. The tone of this passage can best be described as

Time:

(Answers to this drill are found on page 139)

Drill #5

1. The sound that came from the floorboards can best be described as

2. It can be inferred that from the passage that earlier setters did not have windows in their homes because

3. What made the citizens call a town meeting?

4. As it is used in line 15, the word "substantial "most nearly means

5. Which of the following questions is answered by information in the passage?

Time:

(Answers to this drill are found on page 139)

Drill #6

1. Which of the following best states the main idea of the passage?

2. In line 4, John Adams use of the word "furious" is ironic for which of the following reasons?

3. How does Adam's speech reflect the idea that government is "for the people, by the people"?

4. The purpose of Adam's speech was to

5. Why does Adams use the word "mocking" in line 13?

Time:

(Answers to this drill are found on page 139)

Step #4: Read the passage

Now, you can go ahead and read the passage. If you happen to run across the answer to one of your specific questions, go ahead and answer it. If not, don't worry about it.

You have to be a little zen about looking for the answers while you read. You can spend five minutes obsessing over finding the answer for a particular question, but if you just move on, you are likely to come across the answer later.

- It's a little like love, sometimes you have to let it go and trust that it will come back to you

Step #5: Answer specific questions

After you finish reading, answer any specific questions that you have not yet answered. For these questions, think of it as a treasure hunt. The right answer is there, you just have to find it. Generally, you should be able to underline either the exact answer paraphrased in the passage or evidence for the correct answer. If you can't do that, you haven't found it yet. Keep looking. You should also think about what category the question fits into (we will work on those in just a minute).

When you are looking for the answer to a specific question, skim! Don't read every word, you have already done that. Look quickly for the words that you underlined in the question. Also, remember our strategy of ruling out.

- Skim when looking for the answers for specific questions
- Use ruling out
- For specific questions, you should be able to underline either the correct answer restated in the passage or evidence for the correct answer
- Think about the categories that questions fit into

Now, we are going to work on practicing strategies for different categories of specific questions.

Supporting idea questions

Supporting idea questions are looking for a picky detail. When you read through this type of question, you want to underline specifically what the question is asking about. For example, if the question is "How many years did it take for the transcontinental railroad to be built?", you would underline "How many years". The whole passage is probably about the transcontinental railroad, so underlining that would not help you pinpoint where to find the answer.

- Underline the detail in the question that will tell you where to find your answer, if appropriate

Some supporting ideas questions do not have a detail to underline. For example, questions such as "Which question is answered by the passage?" and "Which statement is supported by the passage?" do not have a detail in the question that we can skim for.

- Not every supporting idea question has something to underline in the question

The key to answering this type of question is to underline the correct answer restated in the passage. If you can't do that, you have not yet found the answer – keep looking!

- Correct answer can be underlined in the passage

The following is a drill for practicing this type of question. The questions refer to the passage about war bonds.

We want to be sure that you develop good habits. So what are good habits for supporting idea questions?

- Underline in the question what it is asking about (if appropriate)
- Underline the evidence for the correct answer in the passage

On the following page is a passage that can be used for all of the question type practice drills. Go ahead and tear this passage out from the book. We want you to develop good habits of underlining and marking the passages, which is hard to do if you are flipping back and forth.

Passage for Drills 7-12

1   During World War II, propaganda advertisements were commonly used in the
2 United States to both vilify the enemy and encourage patriotism. The incredible
3 expenses of the war – upwards of a few hundred billion dollars – made it necessary for
4 the government to request the assistance of everyday citizens. To help counter the
5 military's costly demands, the government created rations and initiated special
6 programs on the home front. These programs provided Americans with different
7 avenues they could take to demonstrate their support for their war.

8   One of the largest and most well-known programs was the sale of U.S. War Bonds.
9 Called "Defense Bonds" prior to the attack on Pearl Harbor, war bonds were marketed
10 as a way for Americans to invest in their country. A person might contribute $18.75 in
11 exchange for a ten-year bond. Then after the ten-year window had passed, they could
12 exchange the bond for $25 – a small increase per single bond, but a much larger sum
13 when multiple bonds were purchased together. People who couldn't afford to secure
14 the bonds outright could buy stamps to save toward the purchase of a bond. Or they
15 could save quarters in a special folio with designated slots for the right number of coins.
16 For wealthier Americans and corporations, the bonds could also be purchased in larger
17 dominations.

18   However, above and beyond any financial benefits the bonds offered Americans,
19 the main appeal was the idea of participating in a higher cause – of doing one's patriotic
20 duty to support the military in its fight against evil forces. These emotional motivations
21 were exactly what the government and advertising agencies attempted to appeal to in
22 their war bond advertisements.

23   The ads were distributed as radio commercials and appeared as spreads in
24 newspapers and magazines and on posters. Many used images of small children or
25 mothers with babies to evoke fear of what could happen to them if bonds weren't
26 bought. Pictures of soldiers were also commonly used to suggest that Americans buying
27 bonds were as much a part of the fight as soldiers wielding weapons overseas.

28   Some of the campaigns even targeted children directly by using famous cartoon
29 characters. Many famous celebrities of the time were also hired to participate in
30 national tours promoting the bonds. Movie theaters and sporting arenas offered special
31 events, with the purchase of a bond as the price of admission.

32   Such widespread efforts to urge Americans to purchase war bonds were met with
33 great success throughout the war. Not only did a majority of Americans buy war bonds,
34 but the total amount purchased by individuals and companies reached well over $100
35 billion dollars.

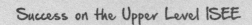

This page intentionally left blank so that passage can be removed

Please use the passage about war bonds to complete the following drill.

Drill #7

1. According to the passage, people who did not have money to buy bonds could do which of the following?

    (A)   join the army instead
    (B)   market bonds to their neighbors
    (C)   buy severely discounted bonds
    (D)   save quarters in specially designed folders

2. According to the passage, why did the American government start the war bonds program?

    (A)   in response to the attack on Pearl Harbor
    (B)   to require more Americans to participate in the war
    (C)   to finance the military during World War II
    (D)   to limit the involvement of corporations

3. The passage provides evidence for which statement?

    (A)   All Americans supported World War II.
    (B)   Advertising agencies were used to help sell war bonds.
    (C)   Children were the largest buyers of war bonds.
    (D)   War bonds are still being sold today.

(Answers to this drill are found on page 139)

Inference Questions

On the ISEE, inference questions ask you to draw conclusions from what the author has written. These questions often use the words "implies", "it can be inferred", or "the author suggests".

- If you see the words "infer", "imply", or "suggest", it is probably an inference question

The trick to these questions is that they aren't looking for some deep conclusion. They are not asking you to read into a character's motivation or determine what another person thinks or feels. That would be too hard for a multiple-choice test! The correct answer for this type of question is the answer choice that has the most evidence in the passage. Also, look for answers that are less extreme. For example, an author is more likely to suggest that an animal is a pest than to suggest that an animal should be completely eliminated.

- Look for the answer choice with the most evidence
- Look for less extreme answers

For the following drill, use the passage about war bonds to answer the questions. Remember to underline evidence for the correct answer.

- Underline evidence in the passage

1. The passage implies that using pictures of small children and mothers with babies was meant to

   (A) scare citizens about the safety of children if America did not win the war.
   (B) support soldiers in the field.
   (C) help advertising agencies make more money.
   (D) demonstrate the strength of American families.

2. The passage suggests which of the following?

   (A) war bonds were not successful
   (B) the primary purpose of war bonds was to make soldiers feel supported
   (C) war bonds were greatly supported in the entertainment industry
   (D) war bonds will be used again

(Answers to this drill are found on page 139)

Vocabulary questions

On the ISEE reading section, some questions will test whether or not you can use context to figure out the meaning of a word. The words in these questions tend to be higher-level words that you may not be familiar with.

The best way to answer these questions is to go back to the passage and cross out the word that the question asks about. Then, plug the answer choices into that space in the sentence and see which answer choice gives you the same meaning.

- Cross out word in passage
- Plug in answer choices to see what makes sense

For the following drill, use the passage about war bonds. Remember to physically cross out the word – don't just do it in your head!

1. In line 4, the word "counter" most nearly means

    (A) argue with.
    (B) compensate for.
    (C) limit.
    (D) continue.

2. In line 25, the word "evoke" most nearly means

    (A) control.
    (B) accuse.
    (C) silence.
    (D) encourage.

(Answers to this drill are found on page 139)

Step #6: Answer general questions

After answering the specific questions, you have probably read the passage multiple times. The trick for the general questions is to not get bogged down by the details, however. How do we do this? By rereading the last sentence of the entire passage before we answer general questions. This will help to clarify the main idea.

- Reread the last sentence of a passage before answering general questions

Main idea questions

Main idea questions ask you to identify what the passage is about. You can identify them because they often use the words "main" or "primarily."

- Often have the words "main" or "primarily" in them

The trick to main idea questions on the ISEE is that the incorrect answers are often details from the passage. Students see these answer choices, remember reading about that detail, and then choose that answer because it shows up in the passage. The problem is that these answers are details from the passage and not the main idea.

- Wrong answer choices are often details from the passage

For the following drill, use the war bonds passage. Remember to practice good habits.

- Reread the last sentence before answering a general question
- Don't choose a detail from the passage

Drill #10

1. The primary purpose of this passage is to

   (A) explain how bonds were marketed.
   (B) explore the differences between stocks and bonds.
   (C) examine the success of a wartime program.
   (D) describe all the ways that citizens supported soldiers during World War II.

(Answers to this drill are found on page 140)

Organization questions

Organization questions either ask about why an author has chosen to include a particular part of the passage or ask about what the author would discuss next. These questions are testing your ability to see the organization of the passage or the function of a particular section.

To answer these questions, jot down a word or two next to each paragraph that summarizes what that paragraph is about. Look for the flow and what each paragraph contributes.

- Jot down a word or two next to each paragraph
- Look at these labels to see how the pieces fit together

For the following drill, please use the passage about war bonds.

Drill #11

1. The primary purpose of the third paragraph (lines 18-22) is to

    (A) explain one motivation for buying bonds.
    (B) summarize the war bonds program.
    (C) introduce an argument.
    (D) provide the evidence contrary to the main argument.

2. Which best describes the organization of this passage?

    (A) A thesis is presented and then evidence is provided to refute it.
    (B) A concept is introduced and then further explained.
    (C) Two competing theories are presented and then evaluated.
    (D) Several viewpoints on one topic are presented.

(Answers to this drill are found on page 140)

Tone / attitude / figurative language questions

Tone or attitude questions on the ISEE ask you to draw your own conclusion about how the author approaches a topic. Is the author annoyed? Trying to be informative? Figurative language questions might ask you to identify the literary device being used or ask you to interpret the meaning of language that is not literal.

Some of these are general questions that reference the entire passage. Since these are general questions, we want to reread the last sentence before we answer them. It is also particularly important to use ruling out on these questions. Remember that we are looking for the "best" answer, which in some cases might just be the least wrong answer choice.

*   If the question asks about the passage as a whole, reread last sentence
*   Use ruling out

There are a couple of tricks to this type of question. First of all, look for moderate answers. For example, the test writers are not likely to choose a writer that is either ecstatic (extremely happy) or enraged (really, really mad). Also, don't be afraid of words that you do not know! Just because you don't know what the word "objective" means doesn't mean that it can't be the right answer.

- Look for moderate answers
- Don't avoid answer choices with words that you do not know

Finally, if it is a tone question, think about the type of passage. A fiction passage might have a tone that is lively, nervous, or excited. A non-fiction passage is more likely to have a tone that is objective, informative, or interested.

- If it is a tone question, think about what would be appropriate for fiction or non-fiction

You may also see a specific question of this type. These questions may ask about the mood of a particular part of the passage, such as the first paragraph. They may also ask you to interpret a single sentence or phrase. If a question has a line reference, it is a specific question and you need to stick just to that section of the passage.

- If there is a line reference, it is a specific question
- Look just at that section of the passage

The following drill refers to the war bonds passage.

Drill #12

1. Which best expresses the author's tone in discussing war bonds?

   (A) disrespectful
   (B) elated
   (C) conflicted
   (D) informative

2. The "ten-year window" (line 11) refers to

   (A) how long the war lasted.
   (B) part of a house.
   (C) fluctuations in price.
   (D) the time between when a bond was sold and when it was redeemed.

(Answers to this drill are found on page 140)

Step #7: Move on to your next passage and repeat!

When you complete a passage, check your time against the chart you created before starting the section, and then move on to the next passage.

- Keep track of time
- Just keep on truckin'

A note about what types of answers to look for

On the ISEE, the test writers have to make sure that not everyone gets a perfect score. As a matter of fact, they have to make sure that students who are good readers will miss several questions. The art of answering reading questions correctly often comes down to:

- On general questions, be sure not to pick a detail as an answer
- On specific questions, watch out for answer choices that take words from the passage but change them slightly so that the meaning is different

Secret #1: On general questions, be sure not to pick an answer that is a detail

The test writers need students to miss general questions. Generally, if a student sees an answer choice that was mentioned in the passage, this answer choice will be really tempting! These answer choices are wrong, however, because they are details and not the main idea. The best way to focus in on the real main idea is to reread the last sentence before answering a general question.

- Look out for answers that are details – these are the wrong answers for main idea questions
- Reread the last sentence before answering a general question

Below is a short passage followed by a general question. See if you can pick out the answers that are tricks!

Drill #13

1   In the late 1870's, King David Kalakaua sat in his palace in Honolulu reading by
2   the light of a gas lamp. At that time, there were no electric lights in Honolulu, Hawaii.
3   As a matter of fact, there were very few electric lights in the world.

4   It wasn't until 1879 that Thomas Edison invented a filament light bulb that could
5   burn for 40 hours. There were other light bulbs before this but they burned out too
6   quickly to be practical. Thomas Edison's new light bulb changed everything.

7   After reading about this new light bulb and its inventor, King Kalakaua decided
8   that he must meet this great inventor. In 1881 he had the chance. King Kalakaua was
9   on a world tour and met with Edison in New York.

10   It took five long years before a light bulb shined in the palace. On July 26, 1886, a
11   demonstration of the new electric light was held at the palace. It was a huge event with
12   a tea party thrown by two princesses. The military band played and troops marched to
13   celebrate.

14   After the exhibit, a power plant was built on the palace grounds that could power
15   more than just one light. On Friday, March 23, 1888, Princess Kaiulani threw the switch
16   and turned on the new power system. In that moment, Iolani Palace officially became
17   the first royal residence in the world to be lit by electricity. Electricity had come to the
18   Hawaiian Islands.

1.   The primary purpose of this passage is to

    (A)   describe the friendship between King Kalakaua and Thomas Edison.
    (B)   explain why Thomas Edison's lightbulb was better than the lightbulbs
         that came before it.
    (C)   relate how the Hawaiian islands came to have electricity.
    (D)   show how much King David Kalakaua cared for his people.

What is the correct answer? Which answer choices were tricks?

(Answers to this drill are found on page 140)

Secret #2: On specific questions, watch out for answer choices that have words from the passage

On the ISEE, answer choices often have words from the passage, but they might have another word or two inserted so that the meaning is different. Some answer choices also have words from the passage, but they are not the correct answer to that particular question.

- Be cautious when choosing an answer that repeats words from the passage

Here is an example. Let's say that the passage states:

John was upset when Sam got into the car with Trish.

The question may look something like:

1. Which of the following is implied by the author?

   (A) John was upset with Trish when he got into the car.
   (B) Sam and Trish were upset when John got into the car.
   (C) John and Sam were cousins.
   (D) John was not happy when Sam rode with Trish.

   Answer choices A and B use words from the passage, but do not have the same meaning as what the passage says. Choice C is just unrelated – which happens on the ISEE. Choice D restates what the passage says.

In the following drill, there is a sentence from a passage followed by a list of answer choices. You have to decide whether the answer choice has the same meaning as the passage, or whether the words have been twisted around to mean something else.

Drill #14

Passage: When the morning sun rose high above the horizon, a small boy could be spotted as he carried a bucket along the ridge of a hill in the distance.

Answer choice:	Same meaning	Twisted meaning
1. A small boy was spotted along the horizon, looking almost like a bucket on the hill.		
2. Along the ridge, a child was carrying a pail in the morning.		
3. The small boy spotted the sun rising over a ridge as he carried a bucket.		
4. Far away, it was possible to see a boy carrying a bucket as he walked along the top of a hill in the morning sun.		

(Answers to this drill are found on page 140)

We are going to finish up the reading section with three full passages.

Remember to apply what we have learned.

What are the good habits that we are looking for?

1. Mark questions "S" (specific) or "G" (general) before looking at passage.
2. Answer specific questions first.
3. Underline the correct answer in the passage for specific questions.
4. Reread the last sentence of the passage before answering general questions.
5. Rule out any answer choices that are details for general questions.

Also, be sure to time yourself. It is important that you don't stop answering questions when the six minutes is up, however, since it will take you longer at first to use our strategies. Just be aware of the time so that you know if you need to work on speeding things up.

Drill #15

Time: 6 minutes

1   The field of archaeology can often be incredibly unpredictable. An experienced archaeologist
2   may research a particular location for several years, with little to no significant findings. And a
3   random person may accidentally stumble upon an amazing archaeological discovery. Such was the
4   case with two of the most significant archaeological discoveries ever made.
5   In 1888, while tracking cattle in Colorado, two cowboys spotted something strange.
6   From their view on the edge of a canyon, they saw what looked like a living area inside the
7   walls of a cliff. After exploring further, the two men designated the ancient array of rooms as
8   Cliff Palace. It was just one of hundreds of cliff dwellings that would be discovered at the site
9   known as Mesa Verde. For hundreds of years beginning around 600 AD, the Ancient
10   Puebloans occupied the area. After initially living in villages on top of the canyons, they then
11   expanded out and built large settlements inside the canyon walls. Then suddenly, in the late
12   1200s, the Puebloans abandoned the cliff dwellings.
13   Although archaeologists are still not entirely sure why the group left the region, they
14   have developed several theories that are accepted as plausible. Some scientists support the
15   idea that disagreements, either with an outside enemy or amongst the Puebloan people
16   themselves, caused the group to disperse to areas further south. Others point to physical
17   evidence, such as logs that indicate a severe drought, to suggest that harsh environmental
18   conditions coupled with food shortages are what inspired the move. Whether or not the
19   mystery is ever solved, the breathtaking beauty and intrigue of the Mesa Verde National Park
20   still offers a unique glimpse into the lives of the ancient Pueblo people.
21   Similarly, across the globe near the city of Xi'an, China, another spectacular
22   archaeological discovery offers people a first-hand encounter with an ancient culture. It too
23   was discovered entirely by accident.
24   In 1974, workers were digging a well when they found a single clay soldier, positioned
25   as if ready to engage in battle. They called in archaeologists to the site, and upon investigating
26   further, the archaeologists were astounded to discover that the soldier was just one of
27   thousands of clay soldiers arranged in organized lines. For over two thousand years, the
28   soldiers had stood undetected, protecting the tomb of the first emperor of China, Qin Shi
29   Huang Di. According to one ancient account, more than 700,000 workers were used to build
30   the mausoleum and create the horses, chariots, and guards that protect it. After its discovery,
31   the site was quickly established as a museum, and has since become one of the most visited
32   historical sites in all of China.
33   Both of these discoveries serve to demonstrate that people may never know what lies just
34   below their feet. One can only venture a guess at what ancient mystery will be uncovered next.

Drill #15 (continued)

1. The primary purpose of this passage is to

    (A) explain how the Pueblo caves were discovered.
    (B) describe the soldiers at Xi'an.
    (C) argue that archaeologists rarely make the truly important finds.
    (D) point out that important discoveries are often made when no one is looking for them.

2. Which statement about Puebloans is most clearly supported by the passage?

    (A) They left the cliff dwellings because of fighting among themselves.
    (B) They originally lived on the plateau above the cliff dwellings.
    (C) The Puebloans frequently fought with local cowboys.
    (D) The Puebloans named the cliff dwellings the Cliff Palace.

3. According to the passage, the soldiers at Xi'an

    (A) were created to guard a grave.
    (B) were first discovered by archaeologists looking for the soldiers.
    (C) are not frequently visited.
    (D) represent the greatness of the second emperor of China.

4. In line 14, the word "plausible" is closest in meaning to

    (A) unlikely.
    (B) proven.
    (C) possible.
    (D) wonderful.

5. Which word best describes the tone of this passage?

    (A) passionate
    (B) informative
    (C) critical
    (D) disinterested

Continued on the next page

Drill #15 (continued)

6. Which best describes how this passage is organized?

   (A) An argument is presented and then evidence is provided to refute the argument.
   (B) A problem is introduced and then several solutions are offered.
   (C) A common view is challenged.
   (D) An observation is made and then a couple of examples are given to support this observation.

(Answers to this drill are found on page 140)

Be sure to check your answers and figure out WHY you missed any questions that you answered incorrectly before moving on to the next drill.

Drill #16

Time: 6 minutes

1   As you travel deep into the ocean, the water becomes progressively colder, darker, and
2   less accommodating to life. In the zone closest to the surface, the sun warms the water, and
3   aquatic life thrives; but further below, thousands of miles from the surface, impenetrable
4   darkness, high pressure, and freezing conditions threaten all forms of life. Animals found at
5   this level are able to survive in such severe environmental conditions by relying on special
6   biological adaptations.
7   For many years, it was difficult, if not impossible, for scientists to study the life forms at
8   these deep levels. Only more recently, with the development of advanced technological
9   equipment and machines, have scientists been able to travel farther into previously
10   unexplored territories to discover the menagerie of strange creatures living in the deep ocean.
11   In fact, many of the animals found in these realms have such bizarrely unique physical
12   characteristics that some people may say they more closely resemble science fiction monsters
13   than actual living species found elsewhere on Earth. For example, in order to cope with the
14   absolute darkness, some of the creatures have extremely large or bulging eyes. Many others
15   are bioluminescent.   Amongst the pitch blackness, bright blue light flashes from
16   bioluminescent animals as their bodies process chemical reactions and create light energy.
17   This luminosity is often used for protection from predators, or in some instances, as a
18   strategy to lure and deceive prey. A squid fish may emit a flash to surprise a predator and then
19   escape from it while it is distracted. Other animals are able to distract their predators by actually
20   detaching a piece of their bodies and leaving it behind. While the predators hunt after the
21   glowing piece of flesh, the trickster animal escapes the scene with the rest of its body intact.
22   Rather than escape from its predators, a hatchetfish uses light to hide in plain sight.
23   While its predators hunt from below, the hatchetfish's body creates a light that matches the
24   light from above and disguises its shadows so that it blends in with the surface of the water.
25   On the other hand, an angler fish uses its bioluminescence to lure and attack its prey. Above
26   an angler fish's mouth, an appendage protrudes from its body and emits a light that attracts
27   other fish. Once the fish approach, the angler fish launches toward them and chomps down
28   with its huge, protruding teeth.
29   Whether an animal uses its light to escape from a predator or catch its own prey, its
30   techniques are demonstrative of the incredible adaptations that are often necessary for
31   survival in extreme environments.

Drill #16 (continued)

1. According to the passage, the hatchetfish is able to use bioluminescence to camouflage itself because

    (A) predators are hunting from below the hatchetfish and therefore the hatchetfish blends in with the light from above.
    (B) the deep sea is a surprisingly well lit environment.
    (C) the hatchetfish can detach part of its body.
    (D) other deep sea creatures can not see very well.

2. The passage implies that the squid fish

    (A) does not taste good to other sea creatures.
    (B) lacks speed.
    (C) uses a flash of light to stun predators.
    (D) has enormous teeth that it uses to attack.

3. Which of the following statements is best supported by the passage?

    (A) Animals that live in the deep sea environment are often slow to adapt.
    (B) It is easier for animals to survive in the shallow zones near the shoreline.
    (C) It is dangerous for a fish to produce a flash of light in a dark environment because predators can them see the fish.
    (D) Recent technology has not changed our understanding of sea creatures.

4. The main purpose of the third paragraph (lines 11-16) is to

    (A) introduce evidence that is contrary to a previous claim.
    (B) further explain how technological improvements have improved research.
    (C) to shift focus from the shallow water area to the deep sea environment.
    (D) to reintroduce a concept and begin to provide examples.

Continued on the next page

Drill #16 (continued)

5.   In line 10, the word "menagerie" most nearly means

(A)   animal.
(B)   disturbance.
(C)   collection.
(D)   limits.

6.   The primary purpose of this passage is to

(A)   explain how different animals have changed to survive in deep water conditions.
(B)   describe technological advances in marine biology.
(C)   offer information contrary to popular opinion.
(D)   question a theory.

(Answers to this drill are found on page 140)

Be sure to check your answers and figure out WHY you missed any questions that you answered incorrectly before moving on to the next drill.

Drill #17

1   Paulo finished the concerto and flipped back through the pages to start again. Not only
2 was it the most difficult piece he had ever played, but soon it would also be the most
3 important one. Tomorrow was his audition for the orchestra and his only chance of being
4 hired was entirely dependent on his performance of the concerto. The formal rules for the
5 auditions mandated that all applicants should only be allowed 24 hours to practice their
6 audition pieces, and Paulo had just received the sheet music early yesterday morning.
7   In the past 20 hours, Paulo had played each and every note in succession at least 100
8 times. Over and over again, he cycled through the pages until his fingers were numb. But
9 this display of determination was nothing new. From the time Paulo was five years old and
10 saw a concert of the New York Symphony Orchestra on a television special, his dream was to
11 become an instrumentalist in a professional orchestra. He often imagined himself wearing a
12 crisp tuxedo with a neat bowtie, enthusiastically playing a Beethoven Symphony alongside
13 his fellow musicians. Although Paulo's parents had limited financial resources, they were
14 able to rent a violin for him and sign him up for weekly violin lessons at the local community
15 center. Despite the difficult nature of the violin, Paulo had an innate talent that was
16 immediately obvious, and any gaps in his talent were filled in by his dedication to practice.
17   After packing up his violin, Paulo went through the motions of walking the two blocks
18 to the subway station, riding the train, and then taking a seat inside the auditorium at the
19 auditions, all the while absorbed in his own thoughts. No outside stimuli could penetrate the
20 mental barrier surrounding him like a soundproof bubble.
21   In the dark of the auditorium, he sat in a row by himself awaiting his turn to perform.
22 He closed his eyes and focused on the music playing through the headphones that sat tight
23 against his ears. It was a recording of him playing the audition concerto, and in some way,
24 it was allowing him to practice the piece one last time before his critical moment before
25 the judges.
26   As soon as the music finished, he heard his name being called by the judges. This was
27 it – the moment he had been dreaming of since he was a five-year-old little boy. He released
28 a deep breath, picked up his bow, and began playing from memory. His eyes flew over the
29 notes etched in his mind and his bow moved like a boat gliding over smooth waters. Despite
30 his intense nervousness, it was actually a relief for him to know that his destiny was no longer
31 in his hands alone.

Drill 17 (continued)

1. Which statement would the author be most likely to agree with?

    (A) The chances of Paolo being chosen for the orchestra were slim.
    (B) Paolo should have started practicing his audition piece earlier.
    (C) Paolo's family could not support his ambition.
    (D) Paolo had been dedicated to becoming a performance musician for a long time.

2. In line 15, the word "innate" most nearly means

    (A) natural.
    (B) practiced.
    (C) stubborn.
    (D) lazy.

3. Paolo's attitude toward his audition can best be described as one of

    (A) defeat.
    (B) anxiety.
    (C) confidence.
    (D) disinterest.

4. In lines 19-20, "No outside stimuli could penetrate the mental barrier" can best be interpreted as meaning that

    (A) Paolo was physically separated from other people.
    (B) there were many distractions on the way to the audition.
    (C) Paolo did not let the outside world into his thoughts.
    (D) earphones prevented Paolo from hearing what was going on around him.

Continued on the next page

Drill #17 (continued)

5. The purpose of the last paragraph (lines 26-31) is to

    (A) create a sense of suspense about whether or not Paolo will be accepted into the orchestra.
    (B) summarize Paolo's audition.
    (C) explain the importance of hard work.
    (D) change subjects.

6. Which word best describes Paolo as he is described in the passage?

    (A) unfocused
    (B) determined
    (C) young
    (D) skeptical

(Answers to this drill are found on page 140)

Answers to Drills

Drill #1

Start – 9:32
1 – 9:37
2 – 9:43
3 – 9:49
4 – 9:55
5 – 10:01
6 – 10:07

Drill #2

There is no right order for everyone. It depends upon what you find interesting! If you find the passage interesting, you are likely to pick up on more of the details.

Drill #3

1. G
2. S
3. S
4. S
5. G

Drill #4

1. S
2. S
3. S
4. S
5. G

Drill #5

1. S
2. S
3. S
4. S
5. S

Drill #6

1. G
2. S
3. S or G – it depends on what the whole passage is about. Remember, we have to stay flexible when we do this.
4. G
5. S

Drill #7

1. D
2. C
3. B

Drill #8

1. A
2. C

Drill #9

1. B
2. D

Answers to Drills (continued)

Drill #10

1. C

Drill #11

1. A
2. B

Drill #12

1. D
2. D

Drill #13

1. Choice C is the correct answer choice. Choices A and B are traps.

Drill #14

1. Twisted meaning
2. Same meaning
3. Twisted meaning
4. Same meaning

Drill #15

1. D
2. B
3. A
4. C
5. B
6. D

Drill #16

1. A
2. C
3. B
4. D
5. C
6. A

Drill #17

1. D
2. A
3. B
4. C
5. A
6. B

Quantitative Reasoning and Mathematics Achievement

On the ISEE, there are two math sections. One is Quantitative Reasoning and the other is Mathematics Achievement. All questions in both sections are multiple-choice.

- Two math sections
- All multiple-choice

The first math section is the Quantitative Reasoning section. On the Upper Level ISEE, this section has word problems and quantitative comparisons. Some word problems require you to do calculations, and some do not. The word problems that do not require calculations are testing your ability to understand operations and interpret equations. The quantitative comparison questions may or may not require calculations as well. The quantitative comparison questions ask you to determine which of two quantities is greater, if the quantities are equal, or if it cannot be determined.

- Quantitative Reasoning has word problems and quantitative comparisons
- Not all problems require calculations
- 37 questions
- 35 minutes
- A little less than one minute per problem

The Mathematics Achievement section of the test will look a little more like questions that you might be asked in school. All of the problems on the Mathematics Achievement section require calculations. There are 47 questions and you will have 40 minutes to complete the section. This means that you have a bit less than a minute per problem.

- More like questions you might see in school using terms that show up on standards tests
- All of the questions require calculations
- 47 questions
- 40 minutes
- A little less than one minute per question

Since the two math sections are similar, we will study them together. Now – on to the strategies!

Quantitative Sections – Basic Strategies

On the quantitative sections, there are problems that require you to apply the concepts of numbers and operations, algebra, geometry and measurement, and data and probability. The math is really not that hard. The ISEE is more about applying what you have learned than answering complicated questions.

You will NOT be allowed to use a calculator on the ISEE. By using strategies, however, we can get to the right answers, often without using complicated calculations.

- No calculator allowed

The goal here is for you to get a general understanding of the key strategies for the math sections. Following the basic strategies are content lessons where you will get to apply these new strategies.

Drumroll, please! The strategies are:

- Estimate – this is a multiple-choice test!
- If there are variables in the answer choices, try plugging in your own numbers
- If a question asks for the value of a variable, plug in answer choices

Strategy #1: Estimate

You can spend a lot of time finding the exact right answer on this test, or you can spend time figuring out what answers couldn't possibly work and then choosing from what is left.

For example, let's say the question is:

1.   Use the pictures below to answer the question.

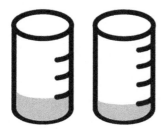

The pictures above show two jars that each hold 1 liter of liquid when they are full. They are not currently full (as shown). If the liquid from the two jars was combined, about how many liters of liquid would there be in total?

(A) $\dfrac{9}{20}$

(B) $1\dfrac{1}{5}$

(C) $1\dfrac{1}{2}$

(D) $2\dfrac{1}{4}$

We could read each jar and see that one jar has $\dfrac{1}{4}$ of a liter in it and the other jar has $\dfrac{1}{5}$ of a liter in it and then add those fractions together. However, we don't need to do that! We can clearly see that each jar is less than half full. That means that the total volume of the two combined would have to be less than a liter. Only answer choice A is less than a liter, so we can answer the question correctly without any further calculations.

One type of question that requires estimating involves determining the square roots of numbers that are not perfect squares. We can't find an exact answer since we do not have a calculator.

The trick to these questions is to find a range that the square root must fall between.

- For square root questions, find a range in order to estimate

For example, let's say we need to estimate the square root of 130.

Let's think of the numbers both higher and lower than 130 that are perfect squares and then come up with a range.

$$\sqrt{121} = 11$$

$$\sqrt{130} = ??$$

$$\sqrt{144} = 12$$

From this we can see that the square root of 130 must fall between 11 and 12.

Here is basic question for you to try:

2. Which is closest to the square root of 89?

   (A) 8

   (B) 9

   (C) 20

   (D) 45

First, let's establish a range that the answer should fall within using the perfect squares that are greater than and less than 89.

$$\sqrt{81} = 9$$

$$\sqrt{89} = ??$$

$$\sqrt{100} = 10$$

From this, we can see that the square root of 89 falls somewhere between 9 and 10. Answer choice B comes closest to this range, so it is the correct answer.

Here is a question that is a little trickier:

3.   Which is closest to $\sqrt{16 + 121}$

   (A)   11

   (B)   11.7

   (C)   15

   (D)   16.9

In order to answer this question, we first have to remember that we can NOT break apart what is under the radical since it involves addition. Since $16 + 121 = 137$, we know that we are looking to approximate $\sqrt{137}$.

$$\sqrt{121} = 11$$

$$\sqrt{137} = ?$$

$$\sqrt{144} = 12$$

We can approximate that $\sqrt{137}$ is between 11 and 12, so choice B is correct.

Here is one that does not even tell you that you must estimate a square root:

4.   Use the coordinate grid below to answer the question.

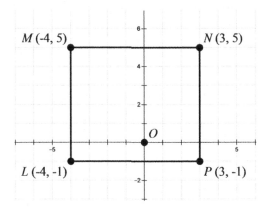

Which of the following line segments would have a length between 5 and 6?

   (A) $\overline{LO}$
   (B) $\overline{MO}$
   (C) $\overline{NO}$
   (D) $\overline{PO}$

The first part of this question is recognizing that we must apply the distance formula in order to find the distances. The distance formula is:

$$\text{distance} = \sqrt{(x_1 - x_2)^2 + (y_1 - y_2)^2}$$

(Note: This formula is derived from the Pythagorean Formula – if you opted to create triangles and use that instead you would get the same answers.)

Now let's plug in values:

$$LO = \sqrt{(-4 - 0)^2 + (-1 - 0)^2} = \sqrt{17}$$

$$MO = \sqrt{(-4 - 0)^2 + (5 - 0)^2} = \sqrt{41}$$

$$NO = \sqrt{(3 - 0)^2 + (5 - 0)^2} = \sqrt{34}$$

$$PO = \sqrt{(3 - 0)^2 + (-1 - 0)^2} = \sqrt{10}$$

Now we need to figure out which length would fall between 5 and 6. We know that $\sqrt{25} = 5$ and $\sqrt{36} = 6$. Since $\sqrt{34}$ falls between $\sqrt{25}$ and $\sqrt{36}$, answer choice C is correct.

Some questions can be ruled out down to one answer choice by estimating. It is best to first estimate and see what you can rule out, and then do the math if you need to.

- Estimate first – sometimes the answer choices are far enough apart that you don't need to do any actual math

Here is an example for you to try:

5. The graph below shows the number of sunny days in Smithville for the last 6 months.

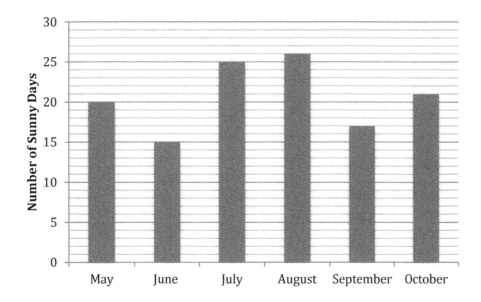

According to the graph above, what is the mean monthly number of sunny days?

(A)   15

(B)   20.67

(C)   25

(D)   26

Before we do any math, we can estimate. If we look at the graph, it looks like the average should be around 20. There are some values higher and some values lower, but we should rule out and see what remains. We can rule out choice A because it equals the lowest value of the graph (a mean is never the lowest value unless all the values are the same). Next, we can rule out choices C and D because Choice D equals the highest value and choice C is way above our estimate of 20. We are left with choice B, which is very close to our estimate. We were able to find the correct answer without doing a lot of math by estimating.

Here is another one for you to try:

6.   If a soda machine dispenses $\frac{4}{7}$ of a cup of soda in one minute, how many minutes would it take for the soda machine to dispense a full cup of soda?

(A)   0.5 minutes

(B)   1 minute

(C)   1.75 minutes

(D)   2 minutes

Before we do any math, let's think about an estimate. We know that it would take more than one minute to fill a cup since it takes a minute to fill $\frac{4}{7}$ a cup. This allows us to rule out choices A and B. Now let's think about how much of a cup could be filled in 2 minutes. We can multiply $\frac{4}{7}$ by 2 to figure out how many cups could be filled in 2 minutes. Without doing the math, we can see that $\frac{4}{7}$ is greater than one-half, so $2 \times \frac{4}{7}$ would be greater than one cup. That allows us to rule out choice D. Answer choice C is correct.

Some of the best questions to answer by estimating are questions that you give you a figure and then ask for a length.

- Can estimate for questions that give a figure and then ask for a side length

For these questions, you can compare the side lengths that you are given to the side length that is asked for and then use ruling out.

- Compare given side lengths to the side length that is asked for
- Use ruling out

Here is an example for you to try:

7.   The triangles shown below are similar.

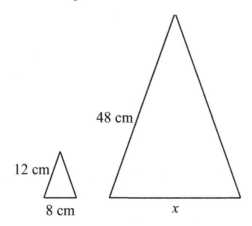

48 cm

12 cm

8 cm x

What is the value of x?

(A)   20 cm

(B)   32 cm

(C)   60 cm

(D)   72 cm

Let's answer this question by estimating. If we look at the side labeled x, we can see that it is shorter than the side that is 48 cm long. This allows us to rule out choices C and D since they are longer than 48 cm. Now let's look at the two remaining choices. If x were 20 (choice A), that side would be less than half the length of the side labeled 48 cm. Since we can see that is not true, we can rule out choice A. We are left with choice B.

Here is another one – remember to try estimating BEFORE you jump into solving:

8.   Use the trapezoid below to answer the question.

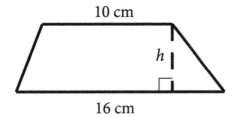

$$\text{Area of trapezoid} = \frac{(b_1 + b_2)h}{2}$$

The area of the trapezoid shown is 65 cm^2. What is the height, h?

(A)   2.5 cm

(B)   5.0 cm

(C)   11.2 cm

(D)   14.8 cm

When we first read through this question, it is very tempting to start plugging into the area equation given. Solving that equation for h would be a lot more work than just estimating, though. From the picture, we can see that the height is shorter than the side that is 10 cm. This allows us to rule out choices C and D. Now we have to decide whether the height looks like half of the length of the 10 cm side (choice B) or a quarter of the length of the 10 cm side (choice A). It looks more like half of the length of the 10 cm side, so choice B is correct. If we actually did the math, we would see that choice B is in fact correct.

You may also see a question that asks you how many digits an answer choice should have. You could do each calculation by hand, or you can estimate to answer the question more quickly.

Here is an example:

9.   Which of the following problems would have three digits in the answer?

(A) 889 ÷ 9
(B) 972 ÷ 9
(C) 12,692 ÷ 11
(D) 14,239 ÷ 11

For this question, let's use ruling out. If we look at answer choice A, in order to get a 3-digit answer, the number being divided by 9 would have to be at least 900. Since 889 is less than 900, we can rule out choice A. Choice B is a little more than 900, so we know that it would give us a 3-digit answer. If we want to be sure we have the right answer, we can keep going. If we multiply 11 by 1,000, we get 11,000. Since both choices C and D are greater than 11,000, we know that the answers in these cases would be at least 4 digits. We can eliminate choices C and D and choose choice B with confidence.

Now that you know how to estimate on the ISEE, be sure to complete the following practice drill to reinforce what you have learned.

1. Jack is making a juice cocktail. He combines $\frac{3}{4}$ cup of pineapple juice, $1\frac{1}{2}$ cups of apple juice and $\frac{1}{3}$ cup of cranberry juice. How much total juice cocktail does he now have?

    (A) $1\frac{7}{8}$

    (B) $2\frac{7}{12}$

    (C) $3\frac{5}{12}$

    (D) $3\frac{7}{12}$

2. A litter of four kittens was born. One kitten weighed 2 pounds, two kittens weighed 2.4 pounds each, and one kitten weighed 4 pounds. What was the mean weight of the four kittens?

    (A) 2 pounds

    (B) 2.4 pounds

    (C) 2.7 pounds

    (D) 4 pounds

Continued on the next page

Drill #1 (continued)

3. The triangles below are similar.

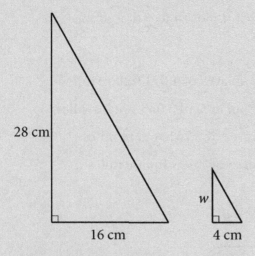

28 cm

16 cm

w

4 cm

What is the value of *w*?

(A) 7 cm

(B) 10 cm

(C) 12 cm

(D) 18 cm

4. Which is closest to $\sqrt{36 + 81}$?

(A) 9

(B) 10

(C) 10.8

(D) 15

Continued on the next page

Drill #1 (continued)

5. The area of the Gates of the Arctic National Park is about 11,756 square miles. Which National Park has an area that is closest to $\frac{2}{3}$ that of the Gates of the Arctic National Park?

    (A) Lake Clark National Park, which has an area of 4,093 square miles

    (B) Glacier Bay National Park, which has an area of 5,038 square miles

    (C) Katmai National Park, which has an area of 5,761 square miles

    (D) Denali National Park, which has an area of 7,408 square miles

6. Use the trapezoid below to answer the question.

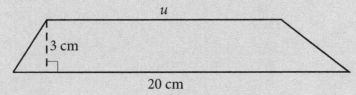

$$\text{Area of trapezoid} = \frac{(b_1 + b_2)h}{2}$$

    If the area of the trapezoid above is 51 cm^2, what is the value of u?

    (A) 7 cm

    (B) 14 cm

    (C) 18 cm

    (D) 19 cm

7. Which problem would have an answer with 4 digits?

    (A) 23×45

    (B) 99×110

    (C) 203×101

    (D) 504×20

(Answers to this drill are found on page 184)

Strategy #2: Plug in your own numbers

If you look at the answer choices and some or all of them have letters in addition to numbers, then you have variables in your answer choices. If you have variables in your answer choices, then you can always plug in for those variables. There are a few other cases where this strategy comes in handy as well.

- Look for letters in the answer choices
- This strategy also works in a few other cases

On the Upper Level ISEE, there are really two types of problems that you can plug in your own numbers for. There are straightforward questions where plugging in your own numbers just reduces the complexity of the question. There are also questions that are really testing theory. You can plug in your own numbers for both types of questions, though you sometimes have to try different numbers on the theory questions.

- For straightforward questions, you can just plug in one set of numbers
- For theory questions, you will often have to plug in more than one number in order to rule out answer choices

Here is how this strategy works:

1. Make up your own numbers for the variables.

   Just make sure they work within the problem. If the question says that x is less than 1, do not make x equal to 2! If it says that $x + y = 1$, then for heavens sake, don't make x equal to 2 and y equal to 3. Also, make sure that you write down what you are plugging in for your variables. EVERY TIME.

2. Solve the problem using your numbers.

   Write down the number that you get and circle it. This is the number you are trying to get with your answer choices when you plug in your value for the variable. For theory questions, you won't always find an answer. These problems will often include questions such as "which number would have to be an odd number?" In this case, you would circle the word "odd" because that is what you are looking for.

3. Plug the numbers that you assigned to the variables in step 1 into the answer choices, and see which answer choice matches the number that you circled.

Here are a couple examples of straightforward questions that have variables in the answer choices:

1.   If $p - r = 5$, then which of the following is equal to r?

    (A) $-p + 5$

    (B) $-p - 5$

    (C) $p + 5$

    (D) $p - 5$

This problem really wouldn't be that difficult to solve without plugging in our own numbers. However, it would be easy to forget to change all the signs when you divide by -1. To avoid making an error, we can plug in our own numbers instead. Let's make $p = 8$ and $r = 3$ (we can choose any numbers as long as $p - r = 5$). Our target is going to be 3 since the question asks for the value of r. Now we plug in 8 for p in the answer choices.

$$-p + 5 = -8 + 5 = -3$$

$$-p - 5 = -8 - 5 = -13$$

$$p + 5 = 8 + 5 = 13$$

$$p - 5 = 8 - 5 = 3$$

Answer choice D gives us our target of 3, so it is the correct answer choice.

2.   Which of the following is equivalent to $(x + 3)(x - 5)$?

    (A) $x^2 - 15$

    (B) $x^2 - 2$

    (C) $x^2 + 2x - 15$

    (D) $x^2 - 2x - 15$

Let's make x equal to 6. Choosing 6 makes our life a little easier since we will not have to deal with negative numbers by choosing a number greater than 5.

Now we will solve using our own numbers:

$$(x + 3)(x - 5) = (6 + 3)(6 - 5) = (9)(1) = 9$$

Now we plug into the answer choices. We are looking for the answer choice that is equal to 9 when we plug in 6 for x.

(A) $x^2 - 15 = 6^2 - 15 = 21$

(B) $x^2 - 2 = 6^2 - 2 = 34$

(C) $x^2 + 2x - 15 = 6^2 + 2(6) - 15 = 33$

(D) $x^2 - 2x - 15 = 6^2 - 2(6) - 15 = 9$

Since answer choice D matches our target of 9, we know that it is the correct answer. You may be saying that you could have answered the question using FOIL. You are absolutely right that you could have used that method. However, it would be much easier to make a mistake using that method, and it is helpful to know another way to solve in case you don't remember FOIL.

Some questions are actually much easier to solve with plugging in.

Here is an example:

3.   Which expression is equivalent to $\dfrac{h}{j}\left(\dfrac{j}{m} - \dfrac{h}{m}\right)$?

(A) $\dfrac{hj - 2h}{jm}$

(B) $\dfrac{hj - h^2}{j}$

(C) $\dfrac{h}{m}\left(1 - \dfrac{h}{j}\right)$

(D) $\dfrac{h}{m}\left(1 - \dfrac{1}{j}\right)$

This problem isn't as simple as just using the distributive property. If we simply distribute the $\dfrac{h}{j}$, we do not get one of the answer choices, so the question must require further rearranging. Let's plug in real numbers to see how it works.

Our first step is to choose numbers and write them down.

$h = 3$

$j = 4$

$m = 5$

Now we plug those values into the expression and solve for a target.

$$\frac{h}{j}\left(\frac{j}{m} - \frac{h}{m}\right) = \frac{3}{4}\left(\frac{4}{5} - \frac{3}{5}\right) = \frac{3}{4}\left(\frac{1}{5}\right) = \frac{3}{20}$$

Now we have our target, so we just need to plug our numbers into the answer choices and see which one matches our target:

(A) $\dfrac{hj - 2h}{jm} = \dfrac{(3)(4) - 2(3)}{(4)(5)} = \dfrac{6}{20}$

(B) $\dfrac{hj - h^2}{j} = \dfrac{(3)(4) - 3^2}{4} = \dfrac{3}{4}$

(C) $\dfrac{h}{m}\left(1 - \dfrac{h}{j}\right) = \dfrac{3}{5}\left(1 - \dfrac{3}{4}\right) = \dfrac{3}{5}\left(\dfrac{1}{4}\right) = \dfrac{3}{20}$

(D) $\dfrac{h}{m}\left(1 - \dfrac{1}{j}\right) = \dfrac{3}{5}\left(1 - \dfrac{1}{4}\right) = \dfrac{3}{5}\left(\dfrac{3}{4}\right) = \dfrac{9}{20}$

Since answer choice C matches our target of $\dfrac{3}{20}$ when we plug in our numbers, it is the correct answer choice.

Here is another one for you to try:

4.   Which expression is equivalent to $\dfrac{m}{p}\left(\dfrac{p}{r} + \dfrac{m}{r}\right)$?

(A) $\dfrac{m^2}{p^2} + \dfrac{mp}{pr^2}$

(B) $\dfrac{m}{r}\left(1 + \dfrac{m}{p}\right)$

(C) $\dfrac{p}{r}\left(1 + \dfrac{m}{p}\right)$

(D) $\dfrac{m}{p}\left(1 + \dfrac{m}{p}\right)$

We will use the same strategy of plugging in our own numbers and then solving:

$$m = 2$$

$$p = 3$$

$$r = 4$$

First, we will plug into the equation in the question to find a target number:

$$\frac{m}{p}\left(\frac{p}{r} + \frac{m}{r}\right) = \frac{2}{3}\left(\frac{3}{4} + \frac{2}{4}\right) = \frac{2}{3}\left(\frac{5}{4}\right) = \frac{10}{12} = \frac{5}{6}$$

Now we will plug in the same numbers in the answer choices and see which answer choice gives us $\frac{5}{6}$.

(A) $\dfrac{m^2}{p^2} + \dfrac{mp}{pr^2} = \dfrac{2^2}{3^2} + \dfrac{(2)(3)}{(3)(4^2)} = \dfrac{41}{72}$

(B) $\dfrac{m}{r}\left(1 + \dfrac{m}{p}\right) = \dfrac{2}{4}\left(1 + \dfrac{2}{3}\right) = \dfrac{5}{6}$

(C) $\dfrac{p}{r}\left(1 + \dfrac{m}{p}\right) = \dfrac{3}{4}\left(1 + \dfrac{2}{3}\right) = \dfrac{5}{4}$

(D) $\dfrac{m}{p}\left(1 + \dfrac{m}{p}\right) = \dfrac{2}{3}\left(1 + \dfrac{2}{3}\right) = \dfrac{10}{9}$

Answer choice B is correct.

Sometimes you have to plug in numbers and then solve for a variable. Here is an example:

5.   The area of a rectangle is M square meters. If the length of the rectangle was tripled and the width of the rectangle was reduced by one-half, what would the area of this new rectangle be in terms of M?

(A) $\dfrac{2}{3}M$

(B) $\dfrac{3}{2}M$

(C) $2M$

(D) $3M$

For this question, we will start by plugging in dimensions for the original rectangle. Let's make the width 10 and the length 10 because those are easy numbers to work with. That makes $M = 100$. If the length was tripled then the new length would be 30. If the width was reduced by one-half, then the new width would be 5. Multiply these dimensions and get that the new area is 150. Circle that number – it is our target. Now we will plug in 100 for M in the answer choices and look for 150:

(A) $\frac{2}{3}M = \frac{2}{3} \times 100 = 66\frac{2}{3}$

(B) $\frac{3}{2}M = \frac{3}{2} \times 100 = 150$

(C) $2M = 2 \times 100 = 200$

(D) $3M = 3 \times 100 = 300$

Answer choice B matches our target and is the correct answer choice.

There are also questions where you can come up with values for the variables that do not have variables in the answer choices. Some problems, in particular percent problems, are simply easier if you plug in numbers. If you are plugging in for percent problems, choose 10 or 100 as your starting number and life will just be better.

- You will not always have variables in the answer choices when you use this strategy
- If you ever think to yourself "this problem would be a whole lot easier with real numbers," then plug in real numbers
- If you are using this strategy with a percent question, plug in 10 or 100

Here is a basic example:

6. Mr. Freeman added 6 points to each of the test scores in his class. Which measure would change the least?

(A) mode
(B) mean
(C) range
(D) median

Let's make up some test scores to see how this works. Let's say the scores in the class are 2, 2, 4, 5, 6. If we added 6 to each score, our new numbers would be 8, 8, 10, 11, and 12. In the old set the mode was 2, and in the new set the mode is 8, so the mode increased by 6. In the old set the mean was a little less than 4, and in the new set the mean is a little less than 10, so the mean also increased by 6. In the old set the range was 4. In the new set the range is also 4, so there was no change in the range. In the old set the median was 4, and in the new set the median is 10, so the median increased by 6. Since only the range remained unchanged, C is the correct answer choice.

Here are a couple of percent problems to try:

7. The price of a shirt is increased 20% and then reduced 30% from that new price. The final price is what percent of the original price?

    (A) 84%
    (B) 90%
    (C) 95%
    (D) 110%

    Let's start with a shirt that costs $100. If that price is increased by 20%, then the new price would be $120. (Can you see the wisdom of choosing $100 as the starting price?) Now we need to reduce $120 by 30%. Since 10% of $120 is 12, we can multiply $3 \times 12 = 36$ to get that 30% of $120 is $36. Now we subtract $36 from $120 to get a final price of $84. Answer choice A is correct since we used $100 as our starting point and $84 is 84% of $100.

Here is one that is a little more complex:

8. A rectangular prism has a volume V. If the length of the base is increased by 10%, the width of the base is increased by 20%, and the height of the prism is increased by 30%, the volume of this new prism would be approximately what percent greater than V?

    (A) 0.72%
    (B) 72%
    (C) 600%
    (D) 6000%

    In order to avoid big numbers, let's make the dimensions of the original prism 10 by 10 by 10. That means that V is equal to 1,000. If the length of the base is increased by 10%, then the new length would be 11. If the width of the base is increased by 20% then the new width would be 12. The new height would be 13 if the old height is increased by 30%. When we multiply these new dimensions, we get $11 \times 12 \times 13 = 1,716$. Percent increase is equal to $\dfrac{final-original}{original}$, or in this case $\dfrac{1716-1000}{1000} = \dfrac{716}{1000}$. If we round off, we get $\dfrac{720}{1000}$. When you cancel a zero from the top with a zero from the bottom, you get $\dfrac{72}{100}$ or 72%. Answer choice B is correct.

Some questions that have variables in the answer choices are really testing your understanding of concepts. These questions may use the words "must be true", "CANNOT be (some math term)", and/or math terms such as "multiple", "factor", or "rational number". These questions are testing your ability to apply the rules of math, but it is often easier to see how those rules apply if you plug in your own numbers. You may also see the words "greatest" or "least" with variables in the answer choices – these questions are also usually testing your ability to apply rules.

- If the question is testing math rules, then plugging in your own numbers often makes it easier to see what they are testing
- You may see the words "must be true", "CANNOT be", math terms, and "greatest" or "least" combined with variables in the answer choices

Here are a couple of examples of questions that are easier to answer if you use real numbers rather than trying to remember "rules":

9.   If r is a factor of m and s is a factor of q, then which of the following must be true?

   (A) mq must be an even number
   (B) rs must be an even number
   (C) r must be a prime number
   (D) rs is a factor of mq

We can plug in to rule out for this question. If we plug in 9 for m and 15 for q, then we can see that it is possible to get an odd number for mq, so answer choice A should be eliminated. If we plug in 3 for r and 3 for s, then we can see that it is possible to get an odd number for rs, so choice B can be eliminated. If we look at choice C, r can really be any number, so it doesn't have to be prime. For choice D, we can plug in 3 for r, 9 for m, 3 for s, and 15 for q. We would get 9 for rs and 135 for mq. Since 9 is a factor of 135, answer choice D is correct.

10. If xy is a prime number, then which statement is always true?

   (A) x is a prime number
   (B) y is a prime number
   (C) either x or y must be 1
   (D) xy is an odd number

   In this case, if we plug in numbers, we discover that it only works if we make either x or y equal to 1. As you try plugging in different numbers for x and y, it should emerge that the only way you can get the product of the two to be prime is to have one of the numbers equal to one. If we think about this, it is the definition of a prime number that it has only itself and one as factors, but sometimes we don't make that connection so we plug in numbers to see how it works. Choice C is correct. Don't be tricked by choice D, there is one even prime number (2) so xy would not have to be odd.

Plugging in numbers also works on questions that ask you for the answer choice that is greatest or least. There are two keys to this kind of question:

1. Choose numbers that fit the problem – these questions are often testing rules about negative numbers and exponents, so pay attention to restrictions on the value of the variable.
2. You won't come up with a target, rather you will be looking for the greatest (or least) answer choice when you plug in your number.

Here are a couple of questions for you to try:

11. If $x < 0$ and x is an integer, then which of the following has the greatest value?

   (A) x
   (B) x^2
   (C) x^3
   (D) $1 - x^3$

   To answer this question, we can simply plug in a number for x. Let's make $x = -2$.

   Now we put -2 in for x in the answer choices.

(A) $x = -2$

(B) $x^2 = (-2)^2 = 4$

(C) $x^3 = (-2)^3 = -8$

(D) $1 - x^3 = 1 - (-2)^3 = 9$

From this, we can see that answer choice D would be the greatest. It is the correct answer. This question tests whether you recognize that raising a negative number to an odd exponent would give you a negative number, as well as whether you remember that subtracting a negative number actually increases the value. By plugging in our own numbers, we were able to see what the question was really testing.

12. If x is a positive integer, than which of the following is least?

(A) $(x + 1)^2$

(B) $\dfrac{x}{4}$

(C) $x^3 - \dfrac{1}{2}$

(D) $\dfrac{4}{3}\left(\dfrac{x}{x} - 1\right)$

Let's use the same method. This time x is a positive integer, so let's make $x = 2$.

(A) $(x + 1)^2 = (2 + 1)^2 = 3^2 = 9$

(B) $\dfrac{x}{4} = \dfrac{2}{4} = \dfrac{1}{2}$

(C) $x^3 - \dfrac{1}{2} = 2^3 - \dfrac{1}{2} = 8 - \dfrac{1}{2} = 7\dfrac{1}{2}$

(D) $\dfrac{4}{3}\left(\dfrac{x}{x} - 1\right) = \dfrac{4}{3}\left(\dfrac{2}{2} - 1\right) = \dfrac{4}{3}(0) = 0$

By plugging in our own numbers we can see that we would always get 0 for choice D, so that would always be the least answer choice. Choice D is correct.

Please complete the following drill by plugging in your own numbers. You might know another way to solve, but right now we want to practice this new skill of plugging in our own numbers.

Drill #2

1. If the width of a rectangle is 4 times the length, l, which of the following gives the perimeter of the rectangle?

   (A) $3l$

   (B) $5l$

   (C) $10l$

   (D) $2(4 + l)$

2. If $m - n = -3$, then which of the following is equal to n?

   (A) $3 + m$

   (B) $3 - m$

   (C) $m - 3$

   (D) $-3 - m$

3. In the first year that a school was open, its enrollment increased by 20%. The following year, the enrollment dropped by 5%. The number of students after the second year was what percent of the number of students when the school opened?

   (A) 95%

   (B) 105%

   (C) 110%

   (D) 114%

4. Which of the following is equivalent to $(x + 4)(x - 7)$?

   (A) $x^2 + 28$

   (B) $x^2 - 28$

   (C) $x^2 - 3x - 28$

   (D) $x^2 - 11x - 28$

Continued on the next page

Drill #2 (continued)

5. If $x + y = 8$ and $x - y = 2$, then what is the value of $x^2 - y^2$?

   (A) 10

   (B) 16

   (C) 20

   (D) 24

6. If $x < 0$ and x is an integer, then which has the greatest value?

   (A) x^2

   (B) $2x^2$

   (C) x^3

   (D) $-3x^3$

7. Which of the following is equivalent to $(b - 2)(b + 4)$?

   (A) $b^2 + 2b - 8$

   (B) $b^2 - 8$

   (C) $b^2 + 6b - 8$

   (D) $b^2 - 8b - 8$

8. If p is a factor of k and d is a factor of w, which statement must be true?

   (A) w is a multiple of pd

   (B) p is a multiple of kw

   (C) kw is a multiple of pd

   (D) pd is a multiple of kw

Continued on the next page

Drill #2 (continued)

9. A cube has a volume V. If each side length is decreased by 20%, the volume of this new cube would be approximately what percent of V?

   (A) 32%

   (B) 43%

   (C) 51%

   (D) 64%

10. If g is divisible by 18, which statement is NOT true?

    (A) g is divisible by both 6 and 3

    (B) g is divisible by 36

    (C) g is a composite number

    (D) g is a multiple of 9

(Answers to this drill are found on page 184)

Strategy #3: If a question asks for the value of a variable, plug in answer choices

On the ISEE, it is often easier to plug in answer choices and see what works. After all, this is a multiple-choice test, so one of those answers has to work! Keep in mind that a variable is not always a letter. The question could ask "what is the value of x," or it could ask something like "how many cars were there." In the second example, the number of cars is not a letter, but it is still a variable, or unknown quantity.

- Use this strategy when they ask for the value of a variable
- This is a multiple-choice test
- A variable is not always a letter, it is any unknown quantity

On the Upper Level ISEE, there are two types of questions that we can use the strategy of plugging in answer choices for. The first type of question is a word problem that asks for a quantity that is not represented by a letter. These questions require a little bit of work to see if an answer choice works, but you can generally get around creating an equation and then solving. This strategy allows you to choose an answer even if you cannot figure out how to properly set up an equation.

- You can often use this strategy on word problems that ask for an unknown quantity

The second type of question where you can use this strategy explicitly asks for the value of a variable that is a letter, i.e. "what is the value of x?"

These questions are generally not testing your ability to solve for a variable, but rather are testing a major concept in math. For these questions, ruling out and looking for differences in answer choices is our most important strategy.

- Questions that ask for the value of a variable that is a letter are generally testing a major concept rather than just asking you to solve for a variable
- Rule out and look for differences in answer choices for these questions

We will start with a couple of examples of word problems where working backwards from the answer choices can be helpful.

1. There are two machines that stamp envelopes. Machine A can stamp envelopes at twice the rate of Machine B. There were a total of 390 envelopes stamped in an hour. How many of those envelopes were stamped by Machine B?

   (A) 100
   (B) 130
   (C) 195
   (D) 260

   This question asks for the value of a variable (the number of envelopes stamped) so we can plug in answer choices and see what works. If we try answer choice A, we determine that if Machine B stamped 100 envelopes, then Machine A would have stamped 200 envelopes, since Machine A stamps envelops at twice the rate as Machine B. When we add these together, we get a total of 300 envelopes stamped. Since the question tells us that 390 envelopes were stamped, answer choice A is wrong. Now let's try choice B. If Machine

B stamped 130 envelopes, then Machine A would have stamped 260 envelopes. This adds up to 390 envelopes, so choice B is the correct answer.

2.   A piece of string that was 42 inches long was cut into two pieces. If one piece was 8 inches longer than the other piece, then how many inches long was the longer piece of string?

(A)   17

(B)   18

(C)   24

(D)   25

Let's use our strategy of trying out answer choices. If the longer piece of string was 17 inches, then the shorter piece would be 9 inches. This does not add up to 42 inches, so we can eliminate choice A. If the longer piece was 18 inches, then the shorter piece would be 10 inches. Again, this does not add up to 42 inches, so we can eliminate choice B. Now let's try choice C. If the longer piece was 24 inches, then the shorter piece would be 16 inches. This adds up to 40 inches, so we can eliminate choice C, but at least we know that we are closer. Only choice D remains, and if we do the math we find that if the longer piece was 25 inches, then the shorter piece would be 17 inches. If we add these together, the total length is 42 inches, so choice D is correct.

The above were examples of how this strategy can be used with word problems. We can also use this strategy for more questions that use variables to test math concepts as well.

For these questions, it is important to look at the ALL the answer choices. For example, maybe one answer choice is −2 only and another answer choice is −2 and 2. If you tried −2 and it worked, then you might be tempted to choose the first answer choice. However, maybe 2 also works, and if you didn't look at all the answer choices, then you would choose the wrong answer.

- For questions that test concepts, make sure you look at ALL the answer choices- there might be some overlap

Now let's try some of these questions that test how numbers work more than just finding an answer:

3.   If $(4.5 + 0.5)b = b$, then what must be the value of b?

(A) 5

(B) 1

(C) 0

(D) −5

If we simplify the equation, we get $5b = b$. Now we can plug in answer choices. If we plug in 5 for b we get $25 = 5$, which is not true, so we can eliminate choice A. Now let's plug in 1 for b. We get $5 = 1$, which is not true, so we can rule out choice B as well. Now let's plug in 0 for b. We get $0 = 0$, so answer choice C is correct. When you simplified to $5b = b$, you may have been able to see that the only way that this could be true was if b was equal to zero. However, the strategy gave you a way to find the correct answer if you couldn't see that.

4.   If $\frac{4+w}{w+4} = 1$, then what is the value of w?

(A) −4

(B) 0 only

(C) all real numbers

(D) all real numbers except for −4

Let's start out by plugging in answer choice A. If we plug in −4 for w, we get 0 on the bottom of a fraction, which is NOT allowed in math. (Technically, this is because any number over 0 would create an irrational number. For example, we can't have $\frac{7}{0}$ since that is essentially saying that we have seven parts out of zero, which isn't possible). We can rule out answer choice A. We can also rule out answer choice C, since −4 is a real number and it doesn't work. Now let's plug in 0 for w. This gives us $\frac{4}{4} = 1$, which is a true statement. We can't stop there, though, because choice B says that *only* 0 is a possible value. Let's try out another number to see if choice D could be correct. Let's plug in 2 for w and see what we get. $\frac{4+2}{2+4} = \frac{6}{6} = 1$, so we know that the correct answer choice is more than just 0. We can rule out choice B, and we are left with choice D as the correct answer.

5. If $\dfrac{x^2-16}{(x+8)(x-2)} = 0$, then what are possible value(s) of x?

(A) $x = 4$ only

(B) $x = -4$ and $x = 2$

(C) $x = 4$ and $x = -4$

(D) $x = 4$, $x = -4$, and $x = 2$

Let's plug in 4 for x. This gives us $\dfrac{0}{24}$, which is equal to 0, so we know that 4 works. We can't stop there, though, because more than one answer choice has 4 in it. We can rule out choice B because it doesn't include 4. Next we will try plugging in -4 for x. This gives us $\dfrac{0}{-24}$, which is equal to 0. We now know that both 4 and -4 work, so we can rule out choice A. Now we will plug in 2 for x to see if answer choice D is correct. This gives us $\dfrac{-12}{0}$, which breaks an important rule of math – we can't have a zero on the bottom of a fraction. That means that answer choice D is out, and answer choice C is the correct answer.

Plugging in answer choices is also a great strategy to use with questions that ask for the maximum value, minimum value, greatest, or least. The trick to these is to start plugging in with the largest answer if the question asks for maximum or greatest value, or the smallest answer if the question asks for minimum or least value. If this answer choice does not work, then go on to the next smallest (or largest) answer choice and work from there.

- Use this strategy on questions that ask for maximum value, greatest, minimum value, or least
- If the question asks for maximum value (or greatest), start with the largest answer choice
- If the question asks for the minimum value (or least), start with the smallest answer choice

Here are a couple of examples for you to try:

6. If $2 \leq |x + 3| \leq 7$, what is the minimum value for x?

    (A) −11
    (B) −10
    (C) −1
    (D) 4

    If we wanted to, we could solve this problem algebraically, but that sometimes gets tricky with absolute value. It is much easier to just plug in answer choices. Since the question asks for the minimum value, we will start with the answer choice that has the least value. Let's plug in −11 for x and see what we get. Since $|-11 + 3| = |-8| = 8$, $|x + 3|$ would be greater than 7 if x was equal to −11. We can eliminate answer choice A. Now let's try the next smallest answer choice, which is −10. If we plug in −10 for x, we get $|-10 + 3| = |-7| = 7$. Since this is less than or equal to 7 and greater than 2, answer choice B is correct.

7. If $y = 3x^2 + 2$ for $-3 \leq x \leq 2$, then what is the maximum value of y?

    (A) 5
    (B) 11
    (C) 14
    (D) 29

    In this case, the question is asking for the maximum value of y, so we will start by plugging in the answer choice with the greatest value, or choice D. We plug in 29 for y and then solve for x:

    $$y = 3x^2 + 2$$
    $$29 = 3x^2 + 2$$
    $$27 = 3x^2$$
    $$9 = x^2$$
    $$x = 3 \text{ or } -3$$

Since -3 falls within the acceptable range for x, answer choice D is correct. The only thing that was a little tricky was that we had to remember both the positive and negative square roots of 9.

For the following drill, try plugging in answer choices to see what works. Even if you know how to solve another way, you should practice this strategy, because there will be a time when you need it to bail you out.

Drill #3

1. If $-2 \leq x^2 - 6 \leq 10$, then what is the minimum value of x?

    (A) -6

    (B) -4

    (C) 2

    (D) 4

2. Which of the following could be the values of x and y in the equation $\frac{3}{2} \times \frac{y}{x} = 1$?

    (A) all real numbers

    (B) all real numbers except for 0

    (C) $x = 3$ and $y = 2$

    (D) $y = 3$ and $x = 2$

3. A pet store divided their mice into cages. If each cage had the same number of mice in it, and there were 6 cages, then which could be the total number of mice that the pet store has?

    (A) 11

    (B) 15

    (C) 21

    (D) 24

Continued on the next page

Drill #3 (continued)

4. What value of h makes the equation $(3.2 + 2.8)h = 6h$ true?

   (A) 0
   (B) 1
   (C) 6
   (D) all real numbers

5. If $\dfrac{x^2-36}{(x+9)(x-4)} = 0$, then what are the possible values of x?

   (A) 6 only
   (B) 6 and -6
   (C) 6, -9, and 4
   (D) 6, -6, -9, and 4

6. The sum of two numbers is 30. The larger number is 3 less than twice the smaller number. What is the smaller number?

   (A) 7
   (B) 11
   (C) 12
   (D) 17

7. If $1 \le |x + 2| \le 5$, then what is the minimum value of x?

   (A) -7
   (B) -3
   (C) -1
   (D) 1

(Answers to this drill are found on page 184)

Those are the basic strategies that you need to know for the math section. As you go through the content sections, you will learn content and the strategies that work for specific problem types.

Applying these strategies to quantitative comparison questions

On the Quantitative Reasoning section of the ISEE, you will be given questions that ask you to determine whether one quantity is greater or less than another quantity, equal to another quantity, or if the relationship between the two cannot be determined.

Here is an example:

	Column A	Column B
1.	10% of 30	25% of 20

(A) Quantity in Column A is greater.
(B) Quantity in Column B is greater.
(C) The quantities in Column A and Column B are equal.
(D) Cannot be determined from information given.

In this case, we can easily do the math. To find 10% of 30, we simply move the decimal point one place to the left and get 3 as our answer. To find 25% of 20, we can think of 25% as being equal to $\frac{1}{4}$ and we know that $\frac{1}{4}$ of 20 is 5. Since 5 is greater than 3, the quantity in Column B is larger, and answer choice B is correct.

Now that you understand the basics of how this problem type works, let's move on to the ways we can use our strategies on quantitative comparison question.

Estimating on quantitative comparison questions

Estimating is a great strategy to use on quantitative comparison questions. Since we only need to determine which quantity is larger, we often don't need to find exact answers.

Earlier, we covered the strategy of estimating for square root questions. This strategy can also be used on quantitative comparison questions that use square roots.

Here is an example for you to try:

Column A	Column B
$\sqrt{0.36}$	$\sqrt{3.6}$

2.

(A) Quantity in Column A is greater.
(B) Quantity in Column B is greater.
(C) The quantities in Column A and Column B are equal.
(D) Cannot be determined from information given.

To determine the approximate value of Column A, we can come up with a range. Since the square root of 0 is 0, and the square root of 1 is 1, we know that the value of $\sqrt{0.36}$ must fall between 0 and 1. In order to figure out the approximate value of $\sqrt{3.6}$, we need to come up with another range. Since the $\sqrt{1} = 1$ and the $\sqrt{4} = 2$, we know that $\sqrt{3.6}$ must fall between 1 and 2. Since any number in our range for Column B is always greater than any number in our range for Column A, we know that the value in Column B must be greater than the value in Column A, so answer choice B is correct.

Here is another problem for you to try that compares a whole number with a square root:

Column A	Column B
7	$\sqrt{50}$

3.

(A) Quantity in Column A is greater.
(B) Quantity in Column B is greater.
(C) The quantities in Column A and Column B are equal.
(D) Cannot be determined from information given.

To answer this question, we need to get both numbers into the same form. We can leave the 7 alone and just deal with the $\sqrt{50}$. We know that $\sqrt{49} = 7$ and that $\sqrt{64} = 8$, so $\sqrt{50}$ must be between 7 and 8. This tells us that $\sqrt{50}$ must be greater than 7, so answer choice B is correct.

We can estimate on geometry questions as well.

Here is an example:

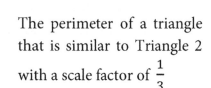

	Column A	Column B

4.   The perimeter of a triangle that is similar to Triangle 1 with a scale factor of $\frac{1}{3}$ The perimeter of a triangle that is similar to Triangle 2 with a scale factor of $\frac{1}{3}$

(A) Quantity in Column A is greater.
(B) Quantity in Column B is greater.
(C) The quantities in Column A and Column B are equal.
(D) Cannot be determined from information given.

In order to answer this question, we don't need to do any real math. We can look and see that Triangle 1 is clearly larger than Triangle 2. Therefore, since we are using the same scale factor in both cases, the triangle that is similar to Triangle 1 will be larger than the triangle that is similar to Triangle 2. Answer choice A is correct.

We can also use the strategy of estimating with problems that require us to figure out a sum.

Here is an example for you to try:

	Column A	Column B
5.	$\dfrac{1}{1+\frac{1}{3}}$	$\dfrac{1}{1+3}$

(A) Quantity in Column A is greater.
(B) Quantity in Column B is greater.
(C) The quantities in Column A and Column B are equal.
(D) Cannot be determined from information given.

To answer this question, let's round off. If we round off Column A, we get $\frac{1}{1}$, which is equal to just 1. If we do a little math with Column B, we get that $\frac{1}{1+3} = \frac{1}{4}$. Since 1 is clearly greater than $\frac{1}{4}$, we know that the quantity in Column A is larger, and answer choice A is correct.

Plugging in our own numbers on quantitative comparison questions

When there are variables in quantitative comparison questions, it is often easiest to plug in our own real numbers to see how they work.

One thing to keep in mind with quantitative comparison questions is that if we select choice A, then quantity A must ALWAYS be bigger than quantity B. If we select choice B, then quantity B must ALWAYS be larger than quantity A. If we choose C, then the two quantities must ALWAYS have the same value. Under any other scenario, we have to choose D.

- If we choose A it has to always be larger
- If we choose B it has to always be larger
- If we choose C the two quantities must always be the same
- With all other scenarios, we choose D

This tells us that when we plug in numbers, we should look for exceptions. We should plug in 1, 0, −1, and fractions to look for situations where the "normal" rules are not followed.

- Plug in 1, 0, −1, and fractions to look for exceptions

For example, let's say that we are comparing x and x^2. Normally we think of squaring a number as making it larger. However, what if we plug in 1 for x? Then x and x^2 would both be equal to 1, so we would have to select choice D.

Here is a basic example of a quantitative comparison question with variables for you to try:

$$j > 3$$
$$k > 300$$

Column A	Column B
j	k

6.

(A)   Quantity in Column A is greater.
(B)   Quantity in Column B is greater.
(C)   The quantities in Column A and Column B are equal.
(D)   Cannot be determined from information given.

At first glance, it might look like k has to be greater than j. However, if we start plugging in numbers, we can see that isn't true. Let's say we plug in 400 for j and 301 for k. Both of these numbers fit within the rules of the problem, and in this case Column A is greater. Now let's plug in 4 for j and 301 for k. In this case, Column B is greater. Since we can get more than one relationship to work, answer choice D is correct.

Here are a couple of questions that require you to think about different possibilities:

Column A	Column B
x^3	x^{200}

7.

(A)   Quantity in Column A is greater.
(B)   Quantity in Column B is greater.
(C)   The quantities in Column A and Column B are equal.
(D)   Cannot be determined from information given.

To answer this question, let's plug in numbers. If we plug in 2 for x, we get that Column B is greater. We don't actually have to do the math on column B to see that 2^{200} would be much greater than 2^3. However, if we were to plug in 1 for x, we would get that the two quantities are equal. Since we can get different answers in different scenarios, answer choice D is correct.

	Column A	Column B

8. $4(m + 2)$ $4m + (4 \times 2)$

(A) Quantity in Column A is greater.
(B) Quantity in Column B is greater.
(C) The quantities in Column A and Column B are equal.
(D) Cannot be determined from information given.

Let's start out by plugging in the number 2 for m. If we do that, we get that the quantities in Column A and Column B both equal 16. We need to make sure that is true for all numbers, however. Let's plug in 1 and see if the quantities are still the same. If we plug in 1 for m then we get 12 for both columns. Let's try 0 and -1 to see if we can find a situation where the quantities are not equal. If we plug in 0, we get 8 for both columns and if we plug in -1, we get 4 for both columns. Since we have tried the weird numbers and still get that both columns have equal value, we can select choice C.

$$\frac{2}{5} = \frac{g}{h}$$

$$g > 0$$

$$h > 0$$

	Column A	Column B

9. $\dfrac{g}{h}$ $\dfrac{g + 2}{h + 5}$

(A) Quantity in Column A is greater.
(B) Quantity in Column B is greater.
(C) The quantities in Column A and Column B are equal.
(D) Cannot be determined from information given.

When we plug in for this question we have to remember that we can't just plug in any numbers because $\frac{g}{h}$ must be equal to $\frac{2}{5}$. If we plug in 2 for g and 5 for h, then we would get $\frac{2}{5}$ for Column A and $\frac{4}{10}$ for Column B. Since $\frac{4}{10}$ reduces to $\frac{2}{5}$, Columns A and B have the same value. Now let's plug in 4 for g and 10 for h. We would get $\frac{4}{10}$ for Column A and $\frac{6}{15}$ for Column B. These both reduce to $\frac{2}{5}$ and are therefore equal. Since we have tried a couple of different combinations, we can see that Column A and Column B are always going to have the same value, so answer choice C is correct. Note that in this case we did not plug in weird numbers because we could not have made $\frac{2}{5} = \frac{g}{h}$ if we had.

Plugging in answer choices on quantitative comparison questions

Our third strategy on the math sections (plugging in answer choices) simply doesn't apply to quantitative comparison question. There are no answer choices to plug in!

Following is a drill for you to practice estimating and plugging in your own numbers on Quantitative Comparison questions.

Drill #4

Directions – Use the information in the question to compare the quantities in Columns A and B. After comparing the two quantities, choose the correct answer choice:

(A) Quantity in Column A is greater.
(B) Quantity in Column B is greater.
(C) The quantities in Column A and Column B are equal.
(D) Cannot be determined from information given.

	Column A	Column B
1.	2	$2 + x$

$$b < 3$$

	Column A	Column B
2.	$2b + 10$	$3b + 7$

	Column A	Column B
3.	$\sqrt{7.9}$	$\sqrt{0.79}$

	Column A	Column B
4.	$6g + (6 \times 3)$	$6(g + 3)$

Continued on the next page

Drill #4 (continued)

	Column A	Column B
5.	6	$\sqrt{37}$

	Column A	Column B
6.	x	x^2

$$a < b < c < 0$$

	Column A	Column B
7.	$a + c$	b

	Column A	Column B
8.	$\dfrac{1}{1+7}$	$\dfrac{1}{1+\frac{1}{7}}$

(Answers to this drill are found on page 184)

Answers to Math Strategies Drills

Drill #1

1. B
2. C
3. A
4. C
5. D
6. B
7. A

Drill #3

1. B
2. C
3. D
4. D
5. B
6. B
7. A

Drill #2

1. C
2. A
3. D
4. C
5. B
6. D
7. A
8. C
8. C
9. B

Drill #4

1. D
2. A
3. A
4. C
5. B
6. D
7. B
8. B

Math Content Sections

We have covered the basic strategies for the math sections. Now, we are going to take a look at some of the problem types that you will see on this test.

On the ISEE, sometimes the calculations to solve a problem are not that hard. However, the toughest part of a problem might be recognizing which concept is being tested and determining the best approach to use.

On the Upper Level ISEE, there are five basic categories of math questions. They are:

- Numbers & operations (including fractions, decimals, and percents)
- Algebraic concepts (working with variables)
- Geometry
- Measurement
- Data analysis & probability

Doing well on the math sections is often a matter of decision-making. You need to determine what type of problem you are working on as well as what the most efficient way to solve will be.

Each lesson will:

- Teach you the facts that you need to know
- Show you how those facts are tested
- Give you plenty of practice

That is the book's side of the bargain, but you also have to keep up your end of the deal.

As you work through the content always ask yourself:

- What makes this problem unique?
- How will I recognize this problem in the future?

You are on your way to crushing the ISEE math sections!

Numbers & Operations

The first topic that we will cover is how numbers and operations are tested on the ISEE.

- Different types of numbers
- Order of operations (PEMDAS)
- Multiples and factors
- Fractions and decimals
- Percents
- Exponents and square roots
- Matrices

Different types of numbers

On the ISEE, there are some special types of numbers that you will need to know.

They include:

- Integers and whole numbers
- Consecutive numbers
- Prime and composite numbers
- Real, imaginary, and complex numbers
- Rational and irrational numbers

Integers and whole numbers

Integers and whole numbers are very similar. Simply put, they are numbers that do not have decimals or fractions. For example, 0, 1, 2, and 3 are all integers as well as whole numbers. The difference is that integers include negative numbers. On this test, however, you aren't really required to know the difference between integers and whole numbers. You just need to know that if you are asked for an integer or a whole number, then the correct answer cannot have a fraction or decimal.

- If a question asks for an integer, then no decimals or fractions

Here are a couple of examples of questions that test the definition of "integer":

1. If $\dfrac{x}{6}$ is an integer, which could be the value of x?

   (A) 2

   (B) 3

   (C) 20

   (D) 24

   In order to answer this question, we can plug in our answer choices for x.

   (A) $\dfrac{2}{6} = \dfrac{1}{3}$

   (B) $\dfrac{3}{6} = \dfrac{1}{2}$

   (C) $\dfrac{20}{6} = 3\dfrac{2}{3}$

   (D) $\dfrac{24}{6} = 4$

   Since only choice D gives us an integer when we plug in for x, it is the correct answer choice.

2. Deanna knows that w is an integer that is less than 10 and greater than 3. Priscilla also knows that w is an integer that is greater than 5 but less than 13. If both statements about w are correct, then how many possible values are there for w?

   (A) 4

   (B) 6

   (C) 9

   (D) more than 9

   This question tells us that w is an integer, and the only integers between 3 and 10 are 4, 5, 6, 7, 8, and 9. From this set of numbers, only 6, 7, 8, and 9 are greater than 5, so there are 4 possible values. Answer choice A is correct. If you overlooked the word "integer", then you probably chose answer choice D, because if we were counting all numbers, not just integers, there would definitely be more than 9 possible values.

Consecutive numbers

Consecutive numbers are integers that are next to each other when you count. For example, 1 and 2 are consecutive numbers. In order to solve for consecutive numbers, we can set the first number equal to x, the second number equal to $x + 1$, the third number equal to $x + 2$, and so on. There are also consecutive even numbers and consecutive odd numbers. These are the numbers that would be next to each other if you counted by twos. For example, 2 and 4 are consecutive even numbers, and 1 and 3 are consecutive odd numbers. In order to solve these questions, you can set the first number equal to x, the next number equal to $x + 2$, the next number equal to $x + 4$, and so on.

- "Consecutive" means in a row
- Use $x, x + 1, x + 2$, and so on to solve for consecutive numbers
- Use $x, x + 2, x + 4$, and so on to solve for consecutive even or odd numbers

Here are a couple of examples of questions that test consecutive numbers:

The product of three consecutive even numbers is 192.

	Column A	Column B
3.	The greatest of the 3 consecutive even numbers	12

(A) Quantity in Column A is greater.
(B) Quantity in Column B is greater.
(C) The quantities in Column A and Column B are equal.
(D) Cannot be determined from information given.

To answer this question, we can plug in to see what works. If we make 12 the largest number, our consecutive even numbers would be 8, 10, and 12. The product of 8, 10, and 12 is 960, which is much larger than 192. We know the greatest of the consecutive even numbers must therefore be less than 12. Answer choice B is correct.

4. The least minus twice the greatest of three consecutive integers is 6. What is the value of the least of these integers?

    (A) -10
    (B) -6
    (C) 2
    (D) 6

Our first step is to set up expressions that represent each of the numbers. Since they are consecutive integers, we can represent them with $x, x + 1$, and $x + 2$. Now we have to translate "the least minus twice the greatest of three consecutive integers is 6" into an equation and solve:

$$x - 2(x + 2) = 6$$
$$x - 2x - 4 = 6$$
$$-x = 10$$
$$x = -10$$

Answer choice A is the correct answer.

Prime and composite numbers

Prime numbers are numbers greater than 1 that are only divisible by themselves and 1. For example, the number 7 is divisible only by itself and 1, so it is a prime number. A composite number is divisible by more than just itself and one. For example, the number six is divisible by 6, 1, 2, and 3, so it is a composite number. It is important to note that the only prime number that is even is 2. Also, the number 1 is neither prime nor composite.

- Prime numbers are evenly divisible by only themselves and 1
- Composite numbers are divisible by more than themselves and 1
- The only even prime number is 2
- The number 1 is neither prime nor composite

Here are some examples of questions that test these concepts:

5.   On a piece of paper, Cheryl wrote down the following numbers: 2, 3, 5, 7. Which term best describes these numbers?

   (A)   consecutive numbers
   (B)   odd numbers
   (C)   composite numbers
   (D)   prime numbers

   Let's use ruling out to solve this problem. Choice A might be tempting because the first two numbers in the sequence are consecutive. However, 3 and 5 are not consecutive numbers, so we can rule out choice A. We can also rule out choice B because 2 is included in the list of numbers, and 2 is not an odd number. So now we have to decide if the numbers are prime or composite. They are all only divisible by themselves and 1, so they are prime numbers. Choice D is correct.

6.   Which of the following numbers has 1 and itself as its only factors?

   (A)   2
   (B)   4
   (C)   6
   (D)   8

   This question does not use the term "prime number", but rather describes a prime number by definition. Since a number that has only itself and 1 as factors is a prime number, we know that we are looking for a prime number. The number 2 is the only even prime number, so answer choice A is correct.

Real, imaginary, and complex numbers

Numbers can be classified as either real or imaginary. Real numbers include just about every number that you can think of.

Real numbers include:

- Integers
- Rational numbers
- Irrational numbers

Real numbers DON'T include imaginary numbers:

- Square roots of negative numbers
- Infinity

Basically if it is not the square root of a negative number or infinity, then it is a real number.

With imaginary numbers, we use i to represent $\sqrt{-1}$.

- $i = \sqrt{-1}$

For example:

$$\sqrt{-36} = \sqrt{36} \times \sqrt{-1} = 6i$$

We also have to keep in mind that $i^2 = -1$, since $\sqrt{-1} \times \sqrt{-1} = -1$.

- $i^2 = -1$

Another type of number that you might see mentioned is a complex number. Complex numbers have a real number part and an imaginary number part. An example is $4 + 2i$. The important thing to note about complex numbers is that we cannot combine the real number part with the imaginary number part when we add.

- When it comes time to combine like terms, you cannot combine imaginary numbers with real numbers, but you can combine them with other imaginary numbers

For example:

$$(3 + 4i) + (5 + 6i) = 8 + 10i$$

Here are a couple examples of questions that test imaginary numbers:

7. If $z^2 + 16 = 0$, then what is the value of z?

    (A) 4

    (B) ± 4

    (C) $4i$

    (D) $\pm 4i$

To answer this question, we first have to isolate z:

$$z^2 + 16 = 0$$
$$z^2 = -16$$

Now we have to take the square root of both sides:

$$z = \sqrt{-16}$$

Since we can't take the square root of a negative numbers, we will factor the radical and then use i to represent $\sqrt{-1}$. We also have to remember that when we take the square root of a positive number, we get both a positive and a negative number.

$$z = \sqrt{-16} = \sqrt{16} \times \sqrt{-1} = \pm 4i$$

Answer choice D is correct.

8. Which of the following could NOT be the result of the product of two imaginary numbers?

    (A) an imaginary number
    (B) an integer
    (C) a composite number
    (D) a prime number

The trick to this question is that when we square i, we get -1 as an answer. Therefore, the product of two imaginary numbers cannot be an imaginary number. Answer choice A is correct.

9. What is the sum of $3 + 6i$ and $2 - 4i$?

    (A) 15
    (B) 7
    (C) $5 + 10i$
    (D) $5 + 2i$

In order to answer this question we have to combine like terms. For real numbers, we add 3 and 2, so we know that the real part of our sum must be 5.

Now we have to combine the imaginary terms. When we add $6i$ and $-4i$, we get $2i$. Answer choice D correctly combines the real and imaginary terms.

Rational and irrational numbers

A rational number is a number that can be written as a simple fraction. For example, 7 is a rational number because we can write it as $\frac{7}{1}$. The fraction $\frac{2}{3}$ is also a rational number.

An irrational number is one that cannot be written as a fraction.

Here are some examples:

- π – pi is a number that goes on and on without repeating, so it cannot be written as a fraction
- $\sqrt{2}$ – this number also has a decimal that goes on without repeating itself, and therefore can't be represented with a fraction
- $\frac{4}{0}$ – this looks like a fraction, but it isn't really because we can't have 4 pieces out of a total of 0 pieces

With rational number questions, sometimes the best approach is to plug in numbers and see how it works.

Here are a few examples of questions that test rational numbers:

10. What type of number could be the product of two irrational numbers?

   (A) a rational number only
   (B) an irrational number only
   (C) a rational or an irrational number
   (D) an imaginary number

For this question, let's think about some of our irrational numbers. Let's say that we multiply $\pi \times \pi$. We wind up with π^2, which is still an irrational number. Now let's try multiplying $\sqrt{2} \times \sqrt{2}$. We get 2, which is a rational number. Answer choice C is correct.

11. Which values of x make the expression $\dfrac{(x-2)(x-5)}{x^2-25}$ equal to 0?

    (A) $x = 2$ only

    (B) $x = 2$ and $x = 5$

    (C) $x = 2$, $x = 5$, and $x = -5$

    (D) $x = 2$ and $x = -5$

If we look at just the top of this expression, we would think that 2 and 5 are the correct values, since those are the numbers that give us 0 for the numerator. However, if we plug in 5 for x in the denominator, we get 0 for the denominator. Since that gives us an irrational number, we know that only 2 is a solution. Choice A is correct.

12. If p and q are both positive rational numbers, then which could be an irrational number?

    (A) $p + q$

    (B) $p - q$

    (C) $\dfrac{p}{q}$

    (D) $\sqrt{pq}$

Let's use ruling out for this question. If p and q are both rational, then simply adding the two together or finding their difference would not result in an irrational number. We can eliminate choices A and B. Now, let's take a look at choice C. The definition of a rational number is that it can be expressed as a fraction, so there is no way that choice C could be irrational. Now let's think about choice D. We know that $\sqrt{2}$ is an irrational number, so p and q could be 1 and 2 and we could wind up with $\sqrt{2}$ for answer choice D. It is possible for choice D to be an irrational number.

Order of operations (PEMDAS)

In school, you may have learned PEMDAS, or Please Excuse My Dear Aunt Sally. These are ways to remember the order of operations. The order of operations tells us which operations to perform first when we are simplifying an expression.

We do anything in parentheses first (P), then exponents (E), then multiplication or division moving from left to right (MD), and finally addition or subtraction moving from left to right (AS).

For example, let's say we have the following expression:

$$4 + (3 \times 5)$$

We have to do what comes in parentheses first.

$$4 + (15) = 19$$

Notice that if we simply went from left to right, we would get a very different answer – and it would be wrong.

Generally, order of operations problems on the ISEE are testing whether or not you recognize that the operation in parentheses must be done first. The math itself tends not to be too challenging.

Here are some examples for you to try:

1. Which expression is equivalent to $3 \times (2 + 1)$?

    (A) $6 + 1$
    (B) 6×1
    (C) $3 + 3$
    (D) 3×3

    For this question, we need to remember to do what is inside the parentheses first. So we first add $2 + 1$ to get 3. Now we are left with 3×3, or answer choice D.

2. Which of the following expressions has a value of 10?

    (A) $(2 \times 5) + 3 - 6$
    (B) $(2 \times 5 + 3) - 6$
    (C) $2 \times (5 + 3 - 6)$
    (D) $2 \times (5 + 3) - 6$

    In order to answer this question, we need to solve each answer choice and see which one gives us 10 as an answer:

    (A) $(2 \times 5) + 3 - 6 = 10 + 3 - 6 = 7$
    (B) $(2 \times 5 + 3) - 6 = 13 - 6 = 7$

(C) $2 \times (5 + 3 - 6) = 2 \times 2 = 4$

(D) $2 \times (5 + 3) - 6 = 2 \times 8 - 6 = 16 - 6 = 10$

We can see that only answer choice D gives us 10 as an answer, so that is the correct answer choice.

3. Which is equivalent to $4 \times (2 + 7) \div (4 + 2)$?

(A) 1

(B) 4

(C) 6

(D) 9

We have to remember to do the operations that are in parentheses first. This gives us:

$$4 \times (2 + 7) \div (4 + 2) = 4 \times 9 \div 6$$

Now we can solve from left to right:

$$4 \times 9 \div 6 = 36 \div 6 = 6$$

Answer choice C is correct.

Here is an example of how this concept can be tested as a quantitative comparison question:

Column A	Column B
$2 \times (7 + 4) \div 2$	$(2 \times 7 + 4) \div 2$

4.

(A) Quantity in Column A is greater.

(B) Quantity in Column B is greater.

(C) The quantities in Column A and Column B are equal.

(D) Cannot be determined from information given.

Although these two expressions look very similar, we know that location of parentheses can make a difference in the final answer. We need to solve each column in order to figure out which quantity is greater.

Column A:

$$2 \times (7 + 4) \div 2 = 2 \times (11) \div 2 = 22 \div 2 = 11$$

Column B:

$$(2 \times 7 + 4) \div 2 = (14 + 4) \div 2 = 18 \div 2 = 9$$

As you can see, which operation we do first makes a difference in our final answer. Since the final answer for Column A is greater than the final answer for Column B, answer choice A is correct.

Multiples and factors

Multiples are numbers that are the result of multiplying one number by a positive integer.

For example, the multiples of 4 are 4, 8, 12, 16, 20, and so on.

The least common multiple (or LCM) is the smallest number that is a multiple of two or more other numbers. To find the least common multiple, we list out the multiples of the numbers in question until we find a multiple that they all have in common.

- To find the least common multiple, list out the multiples of the numbers in question until you find a multiple that they have in common

For example, let's say we are trying to find the least common multiple of 3, 5, and 6.

Multiples of 3: 3, 6, 9, 12, 15, 18, 21, 24, 27, <u>30</u>

Multiples of 5: 5, 10, 15, 20, 25, <u>30</u>

Multiples of 6: 6, 12, 18, 24, <u>30</u>

The smallest number that is a multiple of 3, 5, and 6 is 30, so 30 is our least common multiple.

On the ISEE, we can use our strategy of ruling out since it is a multiple-choice test. Start with the answer choice with the smallest number and work your way up since we are looking for the LEAST common multiple.

- Use ruling out, starting with the smallest answer choice

Here is an example:

1. What is the least common multiple of 4, 6, and 8?

    (A) 2

    (B) 4

    (C) 24

    (D) 192

    To answer this question, let's use ruling out. Answer choice A is a number that is a factor of 4, 6, and 8, but not a multiple, so we can rule it out. Choice B is a multiple of 4, but not of 6 and 8, so we can also rule out choice B. Now we have choice C to look at, since it is the next biggest number. The numbers 4, 6, and 8 all go into 24 without a remainder, so we know that 24 is a multiple of all three numbers. Since it is the smallest answer choice that is a multiple of all three numbers, we can choose choice C.

On the Upper Level ISEE, you are likely to see questions with multiples that are much more difficult. On the Upper Level ISEE, there are often questions with multiples that use variables instead of numbers. The trick for these questions is to find the least common multiple for each part of the terms and then combine them.

- For LCM problems with variables, we first have to find the LCM for each part of the terms and then multiply those LCMs together to get our final answer

For example, let's say that we want to find the LCM of the following (and x and y are prime numbers):

$3x$

$6xy$

$9x^2$

First, we will look at the whole number part of each expression. We have 3, 6, and 9. The least common multiple of these numbers is 18.

Now we will look at the x component of each expression. We have: $x, x,$ and x^2. The smallest number that all three of these would go into is x^2. Essentially, we use the highest exponent, because the other terms have to go into that term evenly.

- To find the LCM for a variable, take the highest exponent for that variable.

Finally, we look at y. This is a little tricky, because only one of the terms has a y. However, if a variable shows up in even one of the terms, it must show up in the LCM. If it helps, think of the other terms as having a y^0, since any number raised to the power of 0 is simply 1. Since y^0 is equal to 1, it is not listed in the polynomial. This means that we really have y^0, y^1, and y^0. So our final LCM should have y^1, or simply y, in it.

- If a variable shows up in even one of the terms, it must show up in the LCM

If we combine the LCM for each part of our terms, we get that the LCM for $3x$, $6xy$, and $9x^2$ is $18x^2y$.

Here are a couple of questions for you to try:

2. What is the least common multiple of $2b^2$, $4bc^2$, and $6c^3$ if b and c are prime numbers?

   (A) $6bc$
   (B) $6b^2c^3$
   (C) $12b^2c^2$
   (D) $12b^2c^3$

   Let's first look at the whole number component of each term. The LCM of 2, 4, and 6 is 12, so we can rule out choices A and B. Now we can compare choice C with choice D. They both have b^2, so the only difference is with the c part of the terms. Since the last term in our question has c^3, our final answer must have c^3 in it. Answer choice D is correct.

3. What is the least common multiple of $6t$, $9w^2$, and $12x^3$, if t, w, and x are prime numbers?

   (A) $3twx$
   (B) $6twx$
   (C) $36tw^2x^3$
   (D) $36t^2w^2x^3$

   This one is a little trickier because none of the terms have a variable in common. Just remember that if a variable does not show up in a term, we can think of it as having that variable raised to the power of 0. We could rewrite the terms in the question as $6t^1w^0x^0, 9t^0w^2x^0, 12t^0w^0x^3$. If we look at the whole numbers in the answer choices, we can see that only choices C and D could work, since 3 and 6 are not multiples of 6, 9, and 12. Now if we look at the variables in choices C and D, we can see that the difference between the two answer choices is whether there should be a t or a t^2. Since none of the terms have t squared, we know that answer choice C is correct.

Factors are numbers that can be divided into another number with no remainder. For example, 8 can be divided by 1, 8, 2, and 4 without a remainder, so those are the factors of 8. Notice that 1 and the number itself are always factors.

- Factors are numbers that divide into another number without leaving a remainder
- 1 and the number itself are always factors of any number

The greatest common factor is the largest number that is a factor of each number in a group. Since this is a multiple-choice test, we can use ruling out again. This time, we want to start with the largest answer choice and work our way down.

- Greatest common factor is the largest number that is a factor of each number in a group
- We can use ruling out – start with the largest answer choice

Here is an example for you to try:

4.   What is the greatest common factor of 50 and 60?

    (A)   5

    (B)   10

    (C)   15

    (D)   300

Let's start with the largest answer choice, D. The number 300 is a multiple of 50 and 60, but not a factor, so we can rule it out. Let's look at choice C next. The number 15 is a factor of 60, but not of 50, so we can rule out choice C. Now let's look at the next largest answer choice. The number 10 is a factor of both 50 and 60, so it is the correct answer choice. Even though the number 5, choice A, is also a factor of both 50 and 60, it is not the greatest common factor. Answer choice B is the correct answer.

Other questions test the principles of greatest common factor (GCF) in questions that have variables.

The first step to answering these questions is to write each term as a product of its prime factors.

First we will demonstrate how to find the GCF using real numbers, and then we will apply these principles to terms with variables.

Let's say we want to figure out what the GCF is for 40 and 24.

First we will make factor trees to find the prime factorization of 40 and 24.

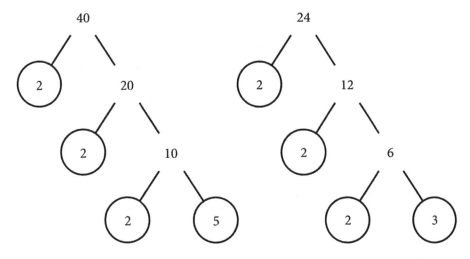

$40 = 2 \times 2 \times 2 \times 5$

$24 = 2 \times 2 \times 2 \times 3$

Now we look for the factors that they have in common and multiply those together to get the GCF.

$GCF = 2 \times 2 \times 2 = 8$

Now let's say we have to determine the GCF of $24w^2y$ and $40w^3y^2$.

We will write out the prime factorization of each:

$24w^2y = 2 \times 2 \times 2 \times 3 \times w \times w \times y$

$40w^3y^2. = 2 \times 2 \times 2 \times 5 \times w \times w \times w \times y \times y$

Now we look for the factors that they have in common and multiply those together:

$GCF = 2 \times 2 \times 2 \times w \times w \times y = 8w^2y$

Here are a couple of examples of problems that test these principles:

5. What is the greatest common factor of $15wx^2y^3$ and $20w^2x^2y$?

    (A) $5wxy$

    (B) $5wx^2y$

    (C) $300wx^2y$

    (D) $300w^3x^4y^4$

Our first step is to write out the prime factorization of each:

$$15wx^2y^3 = 5 \times 3 \times w \times x \times x \times y \times y \times y$$

$$20w^2x^2y = 5 \times 2 \times 2 \times w \times w \times x \times x \times y$$

Now we write out the factors that they have in common:

$$\text{GCF} = 5 \times w \times x \times x \times y = 5w^2xy$$

Answer choice B is correct.

6. If t is factor of both 30 and 54, then what is the largest possible value of t?

    (A) 2

    (B) 6

    (C) 15

    (D) 162

This question does not use the words "greatest common factor", but that is what it is asking us to determine. If we write out the prime factorization of each number we get $30 = 2 \times 3 \times 5$ and $54 = 2 \times 3 \times 3 \times 3$. The factors that they have in common are 2 and 3, so our greatest common factor is 6. Answer choice B is correct.

On the Upper Level ISEE, you are likely to see factor questions that have variables in them, which are much harder. Some of these questions are best answered by plugging in real numbers. We covered this question type in the strategies section, so we will just do one more question for review.

Here is an example of a question that is much easier to answer if you plug in your own numbers:

7. Some number d is a factor of w. A different number f is a factor of r. Which of the following must be true?

(A) dw is a factor of fr
(B) w is a multiple of df
(C) r is a multiple of d
(D) df is a factor of wr

Let's go ahead and plug in numbers for d, w, f, and r. We just have to remember to choose numbers where d is a factor of w and f is a factor of r.

Let's assume:

$$d = 2$$

$$w = 4$$

$$f = 3$$

$$r = 6$$

Now we will plug these numbers into our answer choices:

(A) $(2)(4)$ is a factor of $(3)(6) \rightarrow 8$ is a factor of $18 \rightarrow$ Not true!

(B) 4 is a factor of $(2)(3) \rightarrow 4$ is a factor of $6 \rightarrow$ Not true!

(C) 6 is a multiple of $2 \rightarrow$ True… in this case. However, if we plug in other numbers, we can see that it isn't always true.

(D) $(2)(3)$ is a factor of $(4)(6) \rightarrow 6$ is a factor of $24 \rightarrow$ True! If we plug in other numbers, we see that it is true in all cases.

By plugging in our own numbers, we can see that answer choice D is the correct answer.

An important fact to know is that if two numbers are prime factors of a larger number, then the product of those factors is also a factor of the larger number.

Here are a couple of questions that test this fact:

8. Use the Venn diagram below to answer the question.

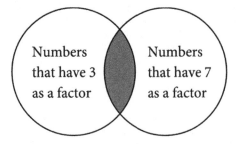

Which statement best describes the numbers that belong in the shaded region?

(A) Numbers that have 10 as a factor
(B) Numbers that have 15 as a factor
(C) Numbers that have 20 as a factor
(D) Numbers that have 21 as a factor

For this question, we have to think about which numbers would have both 7 and 3 as factors. Numbers that have the product of 7 and 3, or 21, as a factor would have both 7 and 3 as factors. Answer choice D is correct.

9. At Woods' Edge Middle School, the average class size is exactly 15 students. Which could be the total number of students at Woods' Edge?

(A) 1,335

(B) 1,450

(C) 1,520

(D) 1,634

Although this question says nothing about factors, it is really testing whether you recognize that in order to have an average class size of *exactly* 15 students, the total number of students must be divisible by 15 without a remainder. We can divide each number by 15 to see which one comes out evenly, or we can use the fact that a number must be divisible by both 3 and 5 in order to be divisible by 15. Answer choices A, B, and C are all divisible by 5, while answer choice D can be eliminated because it is not divisible by 5 (it does not end in a 0 or a 5). Now let's test to see which choice among A, B, and C is also divisible by 3. In order to test for that, we add together the digits of a number. If the sum is divisible by 3, then the number itself is also divisible by 3. Let's start with choice A. If we add together the digits, we get $1 + 3 + 3 + 5 = 12$. This number is divisible by 3, so the entire number is divisible by 3. Answer choice A is correct because 1,335 is divisible by both 3 and 5 without a remainder.

Fractions and decimals

Fractions and decimals are not a focus on the Upper Level ISEE. To cover fractions, we will just do a few of the more challenging problems. These problems are mainly designed to give you practice with the language on the test, rather than to cover the rules of fractions. If you have trouble with the math part of them (and not just interpreting what to do), be sure to review fraction rules.

Here is an example to try:

1. There are six equally sized cups that are filled with sugar that will be used for baking cookies. Hilary used $\frac{1}{2}$ of each cup, and Thomas used $\frac{1}{3}$ of each cup. How many total cups of sugar remain?

   (A) 1 cup
   (B) 1.5 cups
   (C) 3 cups
   (D) 5 cups

We can begin this problem by figuring out how much sugar was used from each cup. We need to add together the $\frac{1}{2}$ cup that Hilary used and the $\frac{1}{3}$ cup that Thomas used. In order to do this, we must first find a common denominator. This is what the math looks like:

$$\frac{1}{2} + \frac{1}{3} = \frac{3}{6} + \frac{2}{6} = \frac{5}{6}$$

Now, we can figure out how much of the total sugar was used. They used $\frac{5}{6}$ of 6 cups and the word "of" tells us to multiply:

$$\frac{5}{6} \times 6 \text{ cups} = \frac{5}{6} \times \frac{6}{1} = \frac{30}{6} = 5 \text{ cups}$$

Since 5 cups were used, only 1 cup remains. Answer choice A is correct.

Here is an example of a quantitative comparison:

	Column A	Column B
2.	$\frac{3}{5} \div \frac{1}{3}$	$\frac{3}{5} \times \frac{1}{3}$

(A) Quantity in Column A is greater.
(B) Quantity in Column B is greater.
(C) The quantities in Column A and Column B are equal.
(D) Cannot be determined from information given.

It would be easy to choose B on this question if we didn't do the math, since multiplying two numbers gives us a larger result than dividing them when working with whole numbers. However, fractions work differently. Let's go ahead and do the math.

Column A:

$$\frac{3}{5} \div \frac{1}{3} = \frac{3}{5} \times \frac{3}{1} = \frac{9}{5}$$

Column B:

$$\frac{3}{5} \times \frac{1}{3} = \frac{3}{15}$$

Answer choice A is the correct answer.

3. Use the number line below to answer the question.

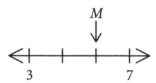

What number does point M represent on the above number line?

(A) $3\frac{2}{3}$

(B) 5

(C) $5\frac{2}{3}$

(D) 6

The trick to this question is to recognize that the number line does not count by a whole number. There are three segments between 3 and 7, and a difference of 4. We can divide 4 by 3 to see that each segment is worth $1\frac{1}{3}$. This means that the first dash after 3 represents $4\frac{1}{3}$ and the next dash represents $5\frac{2}{3}$. Answer choice C is correct.

4. Which answer choice is not equal to $\frac{1}{3}$?

(A) $0.\overline{3}$

(B) 0.333333334

(C) $\dfrac{1.5}{4.5}$

(D) $\dfrac{2.2}{6.6}$

The trick to this question is to recognize that $0.\overline{3}$ is not the same as 0.333333334. There may be a lot of threes before that four at the end, but that last digit makes the number not equal to $\frac{1}{3}$. Answer choice B is correct.

5.   In the number 2.0302, what value does the digit 3 have?

(A) $\dfrac{3}{1,000}$

(B) $\dfrac{3}{100}$

(C) $\dfrac{3}{10}$

(D) 3

This question is asking you to identify place value. The "3" is in the hundredths place, so its value is $\dfrac{3}{100}$. Answer choice B is the correct answer.

Some of the more challenging questions ask you to combine several operations. There is often more than one way to solve these problems, so if you get the right answer by using a different method, that is fine.

Here are some more challenging problems for you to try:

6.   Tailor spent $\dfrac{2}{3}$ of her allowance on a movie and spent the remaining $7 on candy. What was her total allowance?

(A) $3.50

(B) $7.00

(C) $14.00

(D) $21.00

Our first step is to figure out what fraction of her allowance was $7. Since the other part of her allowance was $\dfrac{2}{3}$, the fraction that she spent on candy was $\dfrac{1}{3}$ of her allowance. Now we know that $7 was $\dfrac{1}{3}$ of her total allowance. This means that the remaining $\dfrac{2}{3}$ of her allowance was $14. Now we have to add the two parts together to get the total. $7 plus $14 equals $21, so answer choice D is correct.

7. If $\frac{2}{5}$ of a cup can be filled in one minute, how many minutes would it take to fill the whole cup?

    (A) $\frac{2}{5}$

    (B) $\frac{3}{5}$

    (C) $1\frac{1}{2}$

    (D) $2\frac{1}{2}$

The first step in answering this question is to figure out how long it would take to fill $\frac{1}{5}$ of the cup. $\frac{1}{5}$ is half of $\frac{2}{5}$, so we can divide the time it takes to fill $\frac{2}{5}$ of the cup by 2 in order to figure out how long it would take to fill $\frac{1}{5}$ of the cup. Since 1 minute divided by 2 is $\frac{1}{2}$ of a minute, we know that it would take $\frac{1}{2}$ of a minute to fill $\frac{1}{5}$ of the cup. To find how long it would take to fill the entire cup, we multiply $\frac{1}{2}$ of a minute by 5, since there are 5 fifths in a whole.

$$\frac{1}{2} \times 5 = \frac{1}{2} \times \frac{5}{1} = \frac{5}{2} = 2\frac{1}{2}$$

Answer choice D is correct.

Percents

A percent is just a special kind of fraction that has 100 as the denominator. To convert between a fraction and a percent, we use the rules of equivalent fractions.

For example, let's say that we need to know what percent $\frac{1}{4}$ is equal to.

Our first step is to set up two equivalent fractions (or a proportion).

$$\frac{1}{4} = \frac{p}{100}$$

Now we can cross multiply to solve for p.

$$1 \times 100 = 4 \times p$$
$$100 = 4p$$
$$\div 4 \quad \div 4$$
$$25 = p$$

Since $\dfrac{1}{4} = \dfrac{25}{100}$, $\dfrac{1}{4}$ is equal to 25%.

Here is a basic question that tests this concept:

1.　Which is equivalent to 35%?

　　(A)　$\dfrac{1}{35}$

　　(B)　$\dfrac{7}{20}$

　　(C)　$\dfrac{7}{10}$

　　(D)　$\dfrac{100}{35}$

This question is asking us to reduce a fraction. Another way to write 35% is $\dfrac{35}{100}$. Now we have to find the answer choice that is equal to $\dfrac{35}{100}$.

$$\frac{35 \div 5}{100 \div 5} = \frac{7}{20}$$

Answer choice B is correct.

You are likely to see more challenging questions that test this concept.

Here is another example:

2. Sarah noticed that $\frac{2}{3}$ of her family members have brown hair. Of her family members that have brown hair, 60% of them also have brown eyes. What percent of her family members have both brown hair and brown eyes?

(A) 40%

(B) 45%

(C) 50%

(D) 60%

In this question, we are being asked to find $\frac{2}{3}$ of 60%. The word "of" means to multiply. To multiply, we first need to convert 60% into a fraction.

$$\frac{2}{3} \times \frac{60}{100} = \frac{120}{300}$$

Now we need to convert $\frac{120}{300}$ into a fraction that has 100 as a denominator, since we are looking for a percent.

$$\frac{120 \div 3}{300 \div 3} = \frac{40}{100}$$

Answer choice A is correct.

Converting between percents and actual numbers

On the ISEE, you may see questions that ask you to determine a certain percent of a number, or to determine what percent one number is of another number.

These questions come back to our basic definition of what a fraction and percent are:

$$\frac{\text{part}}{\text{whole}} = \frac{\text{percent}}{100}$$

To answer these questions, you need to plug in what you are given and then cross multiply to solve for the missing quantity.

For example, let's say that we need to find 15% of 60. Here is how we would set up the equation:

$$\frac{\text{part}}{\text{whole}} = \frac{\text{percent}}{100}$$

$$\frac{n}{60} = \frac{15}{100}$$

We are looking for what part of 60 is 15%, so we put in a variable for "part" in our equation. Now we can solve.

$$100 \times n = 15 \times 60$$

$$100n = 900$$

$$n = 9$$

9 is 15% of 60.

There are other methods to solve this type of question. You are not likely to see a lot of these questions though, so we are not going to go through multiple methods of solving.

Here is an example of a basic percent question for you to try:

3.   40 is 50 percent of

(A)   20

(B)   40

(C)   80

(D)   200

Let's set up our equation. We are given the part and the percent and then asked for the whole.

$$\frac{40}{n} = \frac{50}{100}$$

Now we cross multiply.

$$n \times 50 = 40 \times 100$$

$$50n = 4,000$$

$$n = 80$$

Answer choice C is correct.

Here is another example:

	Column A	Column B
4.	40% of 80	50% of 64

(A)   Quantity in Column A is greater.
(B)   Quantity in Column B is greater.
(C)   The quantities in Column A and Column B are equal.
(D)   Cannot be determined from information given.

In order to answer this question, we have to calculate the quantities in Column A and Column B.

Column A:

$$40\% \text{ of } 80 = \frac{40}{100} \times 80 = \frac{3200}{100} = 32$$

Column B:

$$50\% \text{ of } 64 = \frac{50}{100} \times 64 = \frac{1}{2} \times 64 = 32$$

Notice that the calculations are done two different ways. In the calculation for Column A, it was easy to multiply out the numbers so we used that method. For Column B, the math was more complicated, so we reduced the percent first to make it an easier calculation. Since you do not have a calculator on this test, you have to be smart about how to do calculations with the least amount of work.

We can see that the quantities in Column A and Column B are equal, so answer choice C is correct.

You may also see percent problems on the ISEE that require multiple steps. These are generally word problems. Like other multi-step problems, the trick is to follow the details carefully.

Here is an example for you to try:

5. Luke has a jar with red and green candies in it. The green candies make up 30% of the candies and the rest are red. If the jar has 12 green candies, how many red candies does the jar contain?

(A) 6

(B) 12

(C) 28

(D) 40

Let's start with the information that we have about the green candies in order to figure out how many total candies we have.

$$\frac{12}{\text{total}} = \frac{30}{100}$$

$$\text{total} \times 30 = 12 \times 100$$

$$\text{total} \times 30 = 1200$$

$$\div 30 \quad \div 30$$

$$\text{total} = 40$$

Now that we know there are 40 total candies, we can subtract the number of green candies in order to get the number of red candies. $40 - 12 = 28$, so there must be 28 red candies. Choice C is correct.

Here is an example of a quantitative comparison:

To predict the outcome of an election, a polling company polled a random selection of citizens in two different towns. The results are shown below.

	Town 1	Town 2
Percent of Voters Surveyed	50%	25%
Number of votes for Candidate A	16	22
Number of votes for Candidate B	8	25

These results were then used to predict how many people will vote for each candidate when all the voters go to the polls.

Column A	Column B

6.   The number of predicted votes for Candidate A in Town 1   The number of predicted votes for Candidate A in Town 2

(A) Quantity in Column A is greater.

(B) Quantity in Column B is greater.

(C) The quantities in Column A and Column B are equal.

(D) Cannot be determined from information given.

This question asks us to work from a part back to the whole, so we can use our percent equation. The trick is to remember to deal with each group separately. We are not trying to find the total number of voters; we are just trying to find the number of voters for Candidate A.

Column A:

$$\frac{16}{\text{votes for Candidate A}} = \frac{50}{100}$$

$$16 \times 100 = \text{votes} \times 50$$

$$1600 = \text{votes} \times 50$$

$$32 = \text{votes for Candidate A in Town 1}$$

Column B:

$$\frac{22}{\text{votes for Candidate A}} = \frac{25}{100}$$

$$22 \times 100 = \text{votes} \times 25$$

$$2200 = \text{votes} \times 25$$

$$88 = \text{votes for Candidate A in Town 2}$$

Answer choice B is correct.

Percent increase and decrease

On the Upper Level ISEE, you will probably see a question that asks you to find a percent increase or decrease.

The general equation for percent increase is:

$$\text{percent increase} = \frac{\text{final} - \text{initial}}{\text{initial}} \times 100$$

For example, let's say that we had 10 lollipops and then someone gave us 5 more lollipops.

To find the percent increase, the trick is to remember that the final number of lollipops is 15, not 5. We were given five *more,* so we now have a total of 15 lollipops. Now we can plug into the equation.

$$\text{percent increase} = \frac{\text{final} - \text{initial}}{\text{initial}} \times 100 = \frac{15 - 10}{10} \times 100 = 50\%$$

We would say that our number of lollipops has increased by 50%.

To find a percent decrease, the equation is:

$$\text{percent decrease} = \frac{\text{initial} - \text{final}}{\text{initial}} \times 100$$

Let's say that we had 10 pencils, and then we gave away 5 of them. If we want to figure out by what percent our number of pencils decreased, we can plug into the equation:

$$\text{percent decrease} = \frac{\text{initial} - \text{final}}{\text{initial}} \times 100 = \frac{10 - 5}{10} \times 100 = 50\%$$

In this case, we would say that our number of pencils decreased by 50%.

If it makes it easier to remember, the general form for percent increase/decrease is:

$$\text{percent increase/decrease} = \frac{\text{positive change}}{\text{initial}} \times 100$$

One thing to keep in mind about percent increase/decrease is that the question may not actually use the words increase or decrease – the question may use the language "percent higher" and "percent lower".

- "Percent higher" means an increase by that percent
- "Percent lower" means a decrease by that percent

Here are a couple of questions for you to try:

7. Erin had 10 pages of a report written as of yesterday. Today she wrote 4 more pages. By what percent did the number of pages she had written increase today?

    (A) 20%

    (B) 40%

    (C) 50%

    (D) 60%

    In order to answer this question, we first have to figure out the final number of pages written. She wrote 4 more pages, so she now has a total of 14 pages written.

    Now we can plug into the equation:

    $$\text{percent increase} = \frac{\text{final} - \text{initial}}{\text{initial}} \times 100 = \frac{14 - 10}{10} \times 100 = 40\%$$

    Answer choice B is correct.

8. The price of chicken increased from $4.00 a pound to $4.60 a pound. By what percent did the price of chicken increase?

(A) 15%
(B) 25%
(C) 50%
(D) 60%

To answer this question, we have to plug into our equation:

$$\text{percent increase} = \frac{\text{final} - \text{initial}}{\text{initial}} \times 100 = \frac{4.6 - 4}{4} \times 100$$

$$= \frac{0.6}{4} \times 100 = 15\%$$

Answer choice A is correct.

You may also see questions that give you the percent increase and ask for the final number.

The trick to this type of question is to remember to add back in the original number. For example, let's say that we start with 100 cats, and the number of cats then increases by 150%. Our first step is to find 150% of 100, which is 150 cats. The problem tells us that number of cats *increased* by that amount. So we do NOT now have 150 cats. We have 150 cats plus the original 100 cats. We now have 250 cats.

- If you are given a percent increase or decrease, remember to add back in the number that you started with if the question asks for the new total

Here are a couple questions for you to try:

9. The number of students in a school has increased by 150%. If the school started with 36 students, how many students does it now have?

    (A) 50
    (B) 54
    (C) 84
    (D) 90

The question tells us that the number of students increased by 150%, so our first step is to figure out how many new students were added.

> 36 students = 100% of students
>
> 18 students = 50% of students
>
> – – – – – – – – – – – – – – – –
>
> 54 students = 150% of students

We now know that 54 students were added. Now we need to add $54 + 36$ in order to include the students that were already at the school. There are now 90 students at the school, so answer choice D is correct.

10. The number of cars on the road today increased by one and a half times the number of cars on the road yesterday. By what percent did the number of cars increase?

    (A) 50%
    (B) 100%
    (C) 150%
    (D) 250%

The question tells us that the increase itself was one and half times. To increase by one time is a 100% increase. Therefore, to increase by one and half times is a 150% increase. This question does not ask us for the new total, but rather for the percent increase, so we don't have to add back in the original number of cars. Answer choice C is correct.

Multiple percent increases or discounts

You may see questions on the ISEE that ask you to take multiple discounts off of an item. The trick to these questions is that you can NOT just add the percents together. The reason that we cannot do that is that the second discount is taken off the new price and not off the original price. You need to take the first discount, find the new price, and then take the second discount off of that new price. If there is a percent increase and then a percent decrease (or vice versa), remember to take the second increase or decrease off of the new number.

- Do NOT add percents together if more than one discount is taken
- Take first discount, find new price, then take second discount off of this new price
- If there is an increase and then a decrease (or vice versa), remember to use the new number for the second increase (or decrease)

For example, let's say that a lamp costs $100. First, the price was lowered by 20%. The new price of the lamp is now $80. Then the price was lowered by another 10%. The trick is that the 10% discount is 10% of $80, not 10% of $100. 10% of 80 is $8, so we take an additional $8 off of $80 and get that the final price is $72.

Here are a few examples for you to try:

11. A hat was originally priced at $20. It was on sale for 20% off of the original price. Laura then had a coupon for an additional 10% off of the sale price. How much did Laura pay for the hat?

(A) $14

(B) $14.40

(C) $16

(D) $18

Our first step in answering this question is to take the first discount. Let's find 20% of $20:

$$\frac{x}{20} = \frac{20}{100}$$

$$100x = 400$$

$$x = 4$$

We can see that 20% of $20 is $4, so we take $4 from $20 and get that the new price is $16. Now we have to take off the additional 10% discount. We will use our trick of moving the decimal point one place to the left in order to find 10%. This tells us that 10% of $16 is $1.60. Now we subtract $1.60 from $16 and get that the final price of the hat was $14.40. Answer choice B is correct.

	Column A	Column B
12.	The amount of money saved when two separate discounts are taken of 10% and 10%	The amount of money saved when one 20% discount is taken

(A) Quantity in Column A is greater.
(B) Quantity in Column B is greater.
(C) The quantities in Column A and Column B are equal.
(D) Cannot be determined from information given.

This question is easier to answer if we make up a starting price for an item and then see how each scenario works. We are going to choose $100 as the starting price since that makes it easy to find percents. For Column A, when we take one 10% discount, the new price is $90. We then take another 10%, or $9, off of that to get a final price of $81. Now we need do the math to figure out what the final price would be after one 20% discount. Since $100 was our starting price, it is very easy to find that a 20% discount would be $20. If we take $20 from $100, we get a final price of $80. We can see that the scenario in Column A gives us a higher final price than the scenario in Column B. This means that the amount of money saved in Column B is greater, and answer choice B is correct.

In January the price of a stock was \$12.50. In February, the price of the stock was 20% higher than the price in January. In March, the price of the stock was 20% lower than the price of the stock in February.

	Column A	Column B
13.	\$12.50	The price of the stock in March

(A) Quantity in Column A is greater.
(B) Quantity in Column B is greater.
(C) The quantities in Column A and Column B are equal.
(D) Cannot be determined from information given.

Let's try to reason through this one. To find the price in March, we first add 20% of \$12.50, and then we subtract 20% of this larger number. We would subtract a greater amount than we had added, so we would be left with a final price that is less than \$12.50. Answer choice A is correct.

Exponents and square roots

Exponents tell us how many times we should multiply a number by itself.

For example:

$$3^2 = 3 \times 3 = 9$$
$$2^3 = 2 \times 2 \times 2 = 8$$

Square root radicals tell us to find the number that was multiplied by itself to get the number under the radical.

For example:

$$\sqrt{4} = 2$$
$$\sqrt{9} = 3$$

There are a couple of basic rules that you should know about exponents for the Upper Level ISEE:

1. When we multiply two terms with the same variable, we add the exponents together

    Example: $m^2 \times m^3 = m^{2+3} = m^5$

2. If a term with an exponent is raised to another exponent, we multiply the exponents together.

    Example: $(b^2)^3 = b^{2\times3} = b^6$

It is important to note that these rules work with MULTIPLICATION, but not when two terms are added.

- Do not use these rules if two terms are added (or if one term is subtracted from the other)

If two terms are added, we can only combine them if they have the same base and same exponent.

For example:

$x^2 + x^2 = 2x^2$

$x^2 + x^3 = x^2 + x^3$ (i.e., the terms cannot be combined)

There are also a few rules that you should know about taking a square root:

1. Taking a square root of a term is the same as raising that term to the $\frac{1}{2}$ exponent.

    Example: $\sqrt{w} = w^{1/2}$

2. We cannot combine two numbers just because they are both under radicals. Order of operations tells us that we must do what is under the radical first (the square root symbol is the same as raising a number or expression to the $\frac{1}{2}$ exponent).

    Example: $\sqrt{25} + \sqrt{9}$ does NOT equal $\sqrt{25 + 9}$

    $\sqrt{25} + \sqrt{9} = 5 + 3 = 8$, which is not equal to $\sqrt{34}$

Here are a few questions that test these basic rules:

1. Which is equivalent to $\sqrt{9 + 16}$?

    (A) 4
    (B) 5
    (C) 7
    (D) 9

In order to answer this question, we have to remember to combine what is under the radical first. This is true because $\sqrt{9 + 16} = (9 + 16)^{1/2}$, and according to the order of operations we must do what is in parentheses first. If we combine the 9 and the 16, we get $\sqrt{25}$, which is equal to 5, or answer choice B.

Column A	Column B
$\sqrt{16} + \sqrt{4}$	$\sqrt{20}$

2.

(A) Quantity in Column A is greater.
(B) Quantity in Column B is greater.
(C) The quantities in Column A and Column B are equal.
(D) Cannot be determined from information given.

It might be tempting to say that the two quantities are equal. However, if we remember our rules, we know that we cannot just add the two numbers in Column A together and put them under the same radical. Let's do a little math.

Column A:

$$\sqrt{16} + \sqrt{4} = 4 + 2 = 6$$

Column B:

$$\sqrt{20}$$

Since 20 is not a perfect square, we have to come up with a range.

$$\sqrt{16} = 4$$

$$\sqrt{20} = ??$$

$$\sqrt{25} = 5$$

We can see that $\sqrt{20}$ falls between 4 and 5. This means that Column B is always less than Column A, so answer choice A is correct.

3. Which operation would NOT result in an integer?

   (A) $\sqrt{16} - \sqrt{36}$
   (B) $\sqrt{16} + \sqrt{36}$
   (C) $\sqrt{36 - 16}$
   (D) $\sqrt{16} \times \sqrt{36}$

This question is essentially testing the fact that you have to combine the terms under the radical first. For answer choice C, we have to subtract 16 from 36 before taking the square root. This gives us $\sqrt{36 - 16} = \sqrt{20}$. Since $\sqrt{20}$ is NOT an integer, C is the correct answer choice.

4. If m is a positive number, which of the following could NEVER be true?

   (A) $\sqrt{121 + m} = 12$
   (B) $\sqrt{121} + \sqrt{m^2} = 12$
   (C) $\sqrt{121 + m^2} = 11 + m$
   (D) $\sqrt{121 + m^2} = 12$

For this question, let's go through each answer choice to see if we can make it work. If we can, we rule it out, because we are looking for what could never be true. Choice A would work if m was equal to 23, so we can eliminate it. Let's move on to choice B. Since $\sqrt{121}$ is equal to 11, we would need $\sqrt{m^2}$ to be equal to 1. Plugging in 1 for m makes it work, so we can rule out choice B. For choice C, it is difficult to see a number that would work for m. Instead of spending a lot of time trying different numbers, let's move on to choice D. Remember that if we can eliminate choice D, then we know that choice C must be the right answer. For choice D, if we can make m^2 equal to 23, then it would work. Since the problem does not specify that m must be a whole number, we can make $m = \sqrt{23}$ and eliminate answer choice D. We are left with choice C as the correct answer.

You may also see questions that ask you to apply these rules in order to simplify.

In order to answer these questions, you often have to apply the rule:

- If we have terms under a radical that are multiplied (NOT added), then we can break apart the terms.

$$\text{Example: } \sqrt{9x^6} = \sqrt{9} \times \sqrt{x^6}$$

Here are a couple of examples for you to try:

5. Which expression has the same value as $\sqrt{36x^{36}}$?

   (A) $6x^6$

   (B) $6x^{18}$

   (C) $18x^6$

   (D) $18x^{18}$

   To answer this question, first we break apart the terms:

   $$\sqrt{36x^{36}} = \sqrt{36} \times \sqrt{x^{36}}$$

   Now we can take the square root of 36. In order to deal with $\sqrt{x^{36}}$, we can take the radical sign and turn it into a fractional exponent.

   $$\sqrt{36} \times \sqrt{x^{36}} = 6 \times (x^{36})^{1/2}$$

   Now we apply our rule that when an exponent is raised to another exponent we multiply the exponents together:

   $$6 \times (x^{36})^{1/2} = 6 \times x^{18} = 6x^{18}$$

   Answer choice B is correct.

6. Which expression is equivalent to $4x^3\sqrt{2x}$?

(A) $\sqrt{8x^4}$

(B) $\sqrt{8x^7}$

(C) $\sqrt{32x^7}$

(D) $\sqrt{32x^{10}}$

This one is a little trickier because we have to work backwards. Let's start with figuring out what would be equivalent to $4x^3$ under a radical. If we square $4x^3$ we get $16x^6$, so $4x^3 = \sqrt{16x^6}$. Now we need to combine $\sqrt{16x^6} \times \sqrt{2x}$ (note that we can combine these because we are multiplying the terms and NOT adding them). We are left with $\sqrt{32x^7}$, or answer choice C.

Now that we have covered square roots, which are a special kind of exponent, let's move on to some other exponent questions.

How to deal with exponents in fractions

When you see a fraction that is in parentheses with an exponent, you can distribute the exponent to both the top and bottom. The key is to remember that the exponent applies to both the numerator and denominator.

- If a fraction is in parentheses, than the exponent applies to both the numerator and denominator

For example:

$$\left(\frac{1}{2}\right)^2 = \frac{1^2}{2^2} = \frac{1}{4}$$

$$\left(\frac{2x}{3y}\right)^2 = \frac{2^2 x^2}{3^2 y^2} = \frac{4x^2}{9y^2}$$

Here are a couple of questions that test this:

7.   Which is equivalent to $\left(\frac{2}{3}\right)^3$?

   (A) $\frac{2}{9}$

   (B) $\frac{8}{27}$

   (C) $\frac{2}{3}$

   (D) $\frac{8}{3}$

To answer this question correctly, we need to distribute the exponent to both the numerator and the denominator and then solve:

$$\left(\frac{2}{3}\right)^3 = \frac{2^3}{3^3} = \frac{8}{27}$$

Answer choice B is correct.

Column A	Column B

8.

$$\frac{1^2}{5} \qquad\qquad\qquad \left(\frac{1}{5}\right)^2$$

   (A)   Quantity in Column A is greater.
   (B)   Quantity in Column B is greater.
   (C)   The quantities in Column A and Column B are equal.
   (D)   Cannot be determined from information given.

If we distribute the exponent in Column B, then we can compare without having to do any calculations:

$$\left(\frac{1}{5}\right)^2 = \frac{1^2}{5^2}$$

Now we can see that Column A and Column B have the same numerator, but the denominator of Column B is larger. Since a fraction with a larger denominator has a lower value, the quantity in Column A is larger than the quantity in Column B. Answer choice A is correct.

One interesting fact to note is that raising a fraction or a decimal to a positive, whole number exponent actually decreases its value (if the original value is between 0 and 1). For example, $\left(\frac{1}{2}\right)^2 = \frac{1}{4}$. When we squared $\frac{1}{2}$, the value decreased.

- When a fraction or decimal is raised to a positive, whole number exponent, its value decreases (if the value of the fraction or decimal is between 0 and 1)

This is exactly the kind of concept that could be tested in the quantitative comparison section. Here are a couple of questions for you to try:

$$0 < x < 1$$

Column A	Column B
x^2	x^3

9.

(A) Quantity in Column A is greater.
(B) Quantity in Column B is greater.
(C) The quantities in Column A and Column B are equal.
(D) Cannot be determined from information given.

The trick to this question is to recognize that x must be a fraction since it is between 0 and 1. The question does not use the word "fraction," but it is testing whether you recognize that as a fraction is raised to a greater exponent, its value is actually reduced. This means that x^2 is greater than x^3, and answer choice A is the correct answer choice.

	Column A	Column B
10.	$(0.8)^{14}$	$(0.8)^{15}$

    (A)   Quantity in Column A is greater.

    (B)   Quantity in Column B is greater.

    (C)   The quantities in Column A and Column B are equal.

    (D)   Cannot be determined from information given.

If you were to try to do the calculations for this question, you would find that it is too much work. This is by design – the test writers want to see if you can apply a concept without doing the calculations. They also use decimals so that the concept isn't so easy to recognize. Since 0.8 is equal to $\frac{8}{10}$, we know that as we increase the exponent, we actually decrease the value of the number. This means that $(0.8)^{14}$ is greater than $(0.8)^{15}$. Answer choice A is the correct answer.

Working with negative exponents

You may see a question on the ISEE that requires you to deal with negative exponents.

The rules for negative exponents are simple:

1. If the variable with a negative exponent is in the numerator, move it to the denominator and make the exponent positive.
2. If the variable with a negative exponent is in the denominator, move it to the numerator and make the exponent positive.

Let's look at the following examples:

$$x^{-2} = \frac{1}{x^2}$$

$$\frac{1}{x^{-2}} = x^2$$

$$\frac{3x^{-2}y^3z}{2^{-3}x^4y^{-2}z^{-1}} = \frac{3 \times 2^3 \times y^3 \times y^2 \times z \times z}{x^4 \times x^2} = \frac{24y^5z^2}{x^6}$$

Here are a couple of example problems for you to try:

	Column A	Column B
11.	8^{-3}	4^2

(A)   Quantity in Column A is greater.
(B)   Quantity in Column B is greater.
(C)   The quantities in Column A and Column B are equal.
(D)   Cannot be determined from information given.

To answer this question, we do not need to do any calculations. We just need to rewrite Column A with a positive exponent:

$$8^{-3} = \frac{1}{8^3}$$

Now we can clearly see that 1 divided by a very large number is a whole lot less than 4^2. Answer choice B is correct.

12. $\dfrac{4\,b^{-3}d}{8b^2c^{-2}d} =$

(A) $\dfrac{2b^5d}{4c^2}$

(B) $\dfrac{c^2d}{2b^5}$

(C) $\dfrac{2c^2}{b^5}$

(D) $\dfrac{c^2}{2b^5}$

For our first step, we will rewrite the expression by breaking apart the like terms.

$$\frac{4\,b^{-3}d}{8b^2c^{-2}d} = \frac{4}{8} \times \frac{b^{-3}}{b^2} \times \frac{1}{c^{-2}} \times \frac{d}{d}$$

Notice that there is no "c" in the numerator, so we have to put a "1" over c^{-2}. Now we can simplify and reduce.

$$\frac{4}{8} \times \frac{b^{-3}}{b^2} \times \frac{1}{c^{-2}} \times \frac{d}{d} = \frac{1}{2} \times \frac{1}{b^5} \times \frac{c^2}{1} \times 1 = \frac{c^2}{2b^5}$$

Answer choice D is correct.

You may even see a question that combines fractions with negative exponents, like the following:

<u>Column A</u>   <u>Column B</u>

13. $\left(\dfrac{1}{15}\right)^{-2}$ $\left(\dfrac{1}{15}\right)^{-\frac{1}{2}}$

(A)   Quantity in Column A is greater.
(B)   Quantity in Column B is greater.
(C)   The quantities in Column A and Column B are equal.
(D)   Cannot be determined from information given.

Let's deal with each column individually to answer this question.

Column A:

$$\left(\frac{1}{15}\right)^{-2} = \frac{1^{-2}}{15^{-2}} = \frac{15^2}{1^2} = \frac{15^2}{1}$$

Column B:

$$\left(\frac{1}{15}\right)^{-\frac{1}{2}} = \frac{1^{-\frac{1}{2}}}{15^{-\frac{1}{2}}} = \frac{15^{\frac{1}{2}}}{1^{\frac{1}{2}}} = \frac{\sqrt{15}}{\sqrt{1}} = \frac{\sqrt{15}}{1}$$

Since 15^2 is larger than $\sqrt{15}$, the quantity in Column A is larger and answer choice A is correct.

Simplifying expressions that have negative numbers and exponents

There are three important rules that you need to know when dealing with negative numbers and exponents:

1. If the negative sign is not in parentheses, then the answer will be negative no matter what
2. If the negative sign is in parentheses and the exponent is even, then the answer will be positive
3. If the negative sign is in parentheses and the exponent is odd, then the answer will be negative

Examples:

$$-3^2 = -3 \times 3 = -9$$

$$-(3^2) = -(3 \times 3) = -9$$

$$(-3)^2 = -3 \times -3 = 9$$

$$(-3)^3 = -3 \times -3 \times -3 = -27$$

Here are some examples for you to try – remember to follow PEMDAS!

14. Evaluate the expression -2^4.

   (A) -16

   (B) -8

   (C) -4

   (D) 16

To answer this question, keep in mind that the whole thing should be negative because the negative sign is not in parentheses.

If we expand the expression, we get:

$$-2^4 = -2 \times 2 \times 2 \times 2 = -16$$

Answer choice A is correct.

15. Evaluate: $-3(-2)^3$

    (A) -24

    (B) -16

    (C) 6

    (D) 24

The important thing to remember for this question is that we have to use PEMDAS. This means that we handle what is in parentheses first. Since $(-2)^3 = -8$, then our problem becomes $-3 \times -8 = 24$. Answer choice D is correct.

Questions that require you to find a common base

There is a basic rule that is sometimes tested on the ISEE:

1. You can only combine a number that has an exponent with another number if they both have the same base

In practical terms, this means that you sometimes need to rewrite a number as a base with an exponent.

For example:

$$3^3 \times 9 = 3^3 \times 3^2 = 3^5$$

Here are a couple of questions for you to try:

16. What is the value of $\dfrac{2(2^2+2^3)}{4(2+4)}$?

    (A) -1

    (B) 0

    (C) 1

    (D) 4

In order to solve this problem, let's first rewrite all of the terms so that they have a base of 2:

$$\frac{2(2^2 + 2^3)}{4(2 + 4)} = \frac{2(2^2 + 2^3)}{2^2(2 + 2^2)}$$

Now, since we have parentheses, we will distribute:

$$\frac{2(2^2 + 2^3)}{2^2(2 + 2^2)} = \frac{(2 \times 2^2) + (2 \times 2^3)}{(2^2 \times 2) + (2^2 \times 2^2)}$$

Our next step is to use the rule that we add the exponents when we are multiplying two terms with the same base. We also have to remember that if there is no exponent written, that means the exponent is 1.

$$\frac{(2 \times 2^2) + (2 \times 2^3)}{(2^2 \times 2) + (2^2 \times 2^2)} = \frac{2^3 + 2^4}{2^3 + 2^4}$$

We can see that the numerator and the denominator are the same, so the overall value of the fraction is 1. Answer choice C is correct. You might be asking yourself why we didn't just do the calculation in the original problem. On the real test, you probably will be given much bigger numbers that would make doing the calculations without a calculator incredibly time-consuming.

	Column A	Column B
17.	$5(25 + 125)$	$25(5^3 + 5)$

(A) Quantity in Column A is greater.
(B) Quantity in Column B is greater.
(C) The quantities in Column A and Column B are equal.
(D) Cannot be determined from information given.

We need to remember that we only have to get the equations into the same form in order to compare them. We can see that all of the terms can be rewritten with a base of 5, which will allow us to compare them.

Column A:

$$5(25 + 125) = 5(5^2 + 5^3) = 5^3 + 5^4$$

Column B:

$$25(5^3 + 5) = 5^2(5^3 + 5) = 5^5 + 5^3$$

Now we can compare the two columns. They both have 5^3, but Column A has 5^4 and Column B has 5^5. This makes the value of Column B greater, so answer choice B is correct.

Scientific notation

Finally, we have a special kind of exponent problem.

Scientific notation is a way to represent numbers as the product of a decimal and 10 raised to some exponent.

For example:

$$0.000496 = 4.96 \times 10^{-4}$$

$$392{,}000 = 3.92 \times 10^5$$

You should have covered this topic more in-depth in school. If you haven't, then be sure to google "scientific notation." We aren't going into a lot of detail here because you may only see one or two questions on the ISEE that test this information and we have a lot of ground to cover!

Here is how this concept can be tested on the ISEE:

18. What is the numerical value of $\dfrac{3.6 \times 10^3}{9.0 \times 10^{-4}}$?

    (A) 4.0×10^4

    (B) 4.0×10^5

    (C) 4.0×10^6

    (D) 4.0×10^7

This problem is a little trickier than it looks. When we break apart the fraction, we get:

$$\frac{3.6 \times 10^3}{9.0 \times 10^{-4}} = \frac{3.6}{9.0} \times \frac{10^3}{10^{-4}}$$

The problem is that 3.6 divided by 9 does not give us an easy number to work with. If we rewrite 3.6×10^3 as 36×10^2, it makes it a lot easier to break apart the fraction and solve:

$$\frac{36 \times 10^2}{9.0 \times 10^{-4}} = \frac{36}{9.0} \times \frac{10^2}{10^{-4}}$$

Now we have to take care of the negative exponent:

$$\frac{36}{9.0} \times \frac{10^2}{10^{-4}} = 4 \times 10^2 \times 10^4 = 4 \times 10^6$$

Answer choice C is correct.

19. What is the value of $4.3 \times 10^{-5} + 2.6 \times 10^{-7}$

   (A) 4.326×10^{-12}
   (B) 6.9×10^{-7}
   (C) 6.9×10^{-5}
   (D) 4.326×10^{-5}

The easiest way to answer this question is to write out each number, then line up the decimals and add the numbers together.

```
0 . 0 0 0 0 4 3
0 . 0 0 0 0 0 0 2 6
-------------------------------------
0 . 0 0 0 0 4 3 2 6
```

Now we have to convert this number back into scientific notation in order to pick an answer choice. If we move the decimal place 5 places to the right, we can see that the $0.00004326 = 4.326 \times 10^{-5}$. Answer choice D is correct.

Column A	Column B
$4{,}530{,}000 \times 10^{-4}$	0.453×10^7

20.

(A) Quantity in Column A is greater.
(B) Quantity in Column B is greater.
(C) The quantities in Column A and Column B are equal.
(D) Cannot be determined from information given.

This question uses the principles of scientific notation.

Let's deal with each column individually:

Column A:

$$4{,}530{,}000 \times 10^{-4} = 453.0000$$

Since the 4,530,000 is multiplied by 10^{-4}, we move the decimal point 4 places to the left.

Column B:

$$0.453 \times 10^7 = 4{,}530{,}000$$

Since 0.453 is multiplied by 10^7, we move the decimal point 7 places to the right.

Since the quantity in Column B is greater, answer choice B is correct.

Matrices

Finally, we have the concept of a matrix. You may not have yet covered these in school, but they are pretty straightforward on the ISEE.

A matrix is an array of numbers, such as:

$$\begin{bmatrix} 1 & 2 \\ 3 & 4 \end{bmatrix}$$

On the Upper Level ISEE, you may see three basic operations with matrices:

- Adding together 2 matrices
- Subtracting one matrix from another
- Multiplying a matrix by a single number

There are other operations that can be performed with matrices that are more complicated, but you don't need to know how to perform those harder operations on the ISEE.

For addition, we simply add the numbers together for each position in the matrices:

$$\begin{bmatrix} a & b \\ c & d \end{bmatrix} + \begin{bmatrix} w & x \\ y & z \end{bmatrix} = \begin{bmatrix} (a+w) & (b+x) \\ (c+y) & (d+z) \end{bmatrix}$$

Subtraction works the same way, only we use subtraction instead of addition:

$$\begin{bmatrix} a & b \\ c & d \end{bmatrix} - \begin{bmatrix} w & x \\ y & z \end{bmatrix} = \begin{bmatrix} (a-w) & (b-x) \\ (c-y) & (d-z) \end{bmatrix}$$

Finally, if we multiply a matrix by a number, then we multiply each term by that number:

$$2 \times \begin{bmatrix} a & b \\ c & d \end{bmatrix} = \begin{bmatrix} 2a & 2b \\ 2c & 2d \end{bmatrix}$$

Here are a couple of sample problems for you to try:

1. What is the result of $\begin{bmatrix} 3 & 5 \\ 0 & 2 \end{bmatrix} - \begin{bmatrix} 2 & 3 \\ 4 & 1 \end{bmatrix}$?

   (A) $\begin{bmatrix} 5 & 8 \\ 4 & 1 \end{bmatrix}$

   (B) $\begin{bmatrix} 3 & 3 \\ 0 & 1 \end{bmatrix}$

   (C) $\begin{bmatrix} 1 & 2 \\ 0 & 1 \end{bmatrix}$

   (D) $\begin{bmatrix} 1 & 2 \\ -4 & 1 \end{bmatrix}$

To answer this question, we need to remember to subtract each term:

$$\begin{bmatrix} 3 & 5 \\ 0 & 2 \end{bmatrix} - \begin{bmatrix} 2 & 3 \\ 4 & 1 \end{bmatrix} = \begin{bmatrix} (3-2) & (5-3) \\ (0-4) & (2-1) \end{bmatrix} = \begin{bmatrix} 1 & 2 \\ -4 & 1 \end{bmatrix}$$

Answer choice D is correct.

2. What is the result of $3 \times \begin{bmatrix} 5 & 0 \\ 1 & 2 \end{bmatrix}$?

(A) $\begin{bmatrix} 15 & 3 \\ 3 & 2 \end{bmatrix}$

(B) $\begin{bmatrix} 15 & 0 \\ 3 & 6 \end{bmatrix}$

(C) $\begin{bmatrix} 15 & 0 \\ 3 & 2 \end{bmatrix}$

(D) $\begin{bmatrix} 8 & 3 \\ 4 & 5 \end{bmatrix}$

For this question, we need to multiply each term by 3.

$$3 \times \begin{bmatrix} 5 & 0 \\ 1 & 2 \end{bmatrix} = \begin{bmatrix} 15 & 0 \\ 3 & 6 \end{bmatrix}$$

Answer choice B is the correct answer.

Now you know what you need to about numbers and operations. Be sure to complete the practice set to reinforce what you have learned.

Numbers & Operations Practice Set

	Column A	Column B
1.	-3^3	$(-3)^3$

(A) Quantity in Column A is greater.
(B) Quantity in Column B is greater.
(C) The quantities in Column A and Column B are equal.
(D) Cannot be determined from information given.

2. Which is equivalent to $2 \times (3 + 4) \div (1 + 1)$?

(A) 5
(B) 7
(C) 14
(D) 28

3. What is the least common multiple of 5, 7, and 10?

(A) 5
(B) 7
(C) 35
(D) 70

4. Which of the following numbers has 1 and itself as its only factors?

(A) 4
(B) 6
(C) 13
(D) 15

	Column A	Column B

5. $\sqrt{16} + \sqrt{9}$ $\sqrt{25}$

(A) Quantity in Column A is greater.
(B) Quantity in Column B is greater.
(C) The quantities in Column A and Column B are equal.
(D) Cannot be determined from information given.

6. What is the greatest common factor of 72 and 84?

(A) 2
(B) 6
(C) 12
(D) 36

	Column A	Column B

7. $(3 \times 2) + 4 \div 2$ $3 \times (2 + 4) \div 2$

(A) Quantity in Column A is greater.
(B) Quantity in Column B is greater.
(C) The quantities in Column A and Column B are equal.
(D) Cannot be determined from information given.

$$x < 0$$

	Column A	Column B

8. x^2 x^3

(A) Quantity in Column A is greater.
(B) Quantity in Column B is greater.
(C) The quantities in Column A and Column B are equal.
(D) Cannot be determined from information given.

9. Which of the following is the solution set for $\dfrac{x^2-16}{(x+4)(x-2)} = 0$?

    (A) 4 only

    (B) 4 and −4

    (C) 4, −4, and 2

    (D) There are no real solutions

Column A	Column B
$\dfrac{2}{3}$	0.666666666666667

10.

    (A) Quantity in Column A is greater.
    (B) Quantity in Column B is greater.
    (C) The quantities in Column A and Column B are equal.
    (D) Cannot be determined from information given.

11. What is the result of $2 \times \begin{bmatrix} 3 & 0 \\ 2 & -5 \\ -2 & 1 \end{bmatrix}$?

    (A) $\begin{bmatrix} 6 & 4 & -4 \\ 0 & -10 & 2 \end{bmatrix}$

    (B) $\begin{bmatrix} 0 & -10 & 2 \\ 6 & 4 & -4 \end{bmatrix}$

    (C) $\begin{bmatrix} 6 & 0 \\ 4 & 10 \\ 4 & 2 \end{bmatrix}$

    (D) $\begin{bmatrix} 6 & 0 \\ 4 & -10 \\ -4 & 2 \end{bmatrix}$

The price of a car was increased by 20% and then for a sale this new price was decreased by 20%.

Column A	Column B

12.   The original price of the car   The sale price of the car

    (A)   Quantity in Column A is greater.

    (B)   Quantity in Column B is greater.

    (C)   The quantities in Column A and Column B are equal.

    (D)   Cannot be determined from information given.

13.   Which expression is equivalent to $3x^4\sqrt{5x}$?

    (A) $\sqrt{15x^5}$

    (B) $\sqrt{15x^5}$

    (C) $\sqrt{45x^5}$

    (D) $\sqrt{45x^9}$

14.   If $b^2 + 36 = 0$, then what is the value of b?

    (A) $6i$

    (B) $\pm 6i$

    (C) 6

    (D) ± 6

15.   The greatest minus three times the least of three consecutive integers is 4. What is the least of these consecutive integers?

    (A) -1

    (B) 1

    (C) 3

    (D) 4

	Column A	Column B
16.	3.25×10^3	$3,250,000 \times 10^{-4}$

(A) Quantity in Column A is greater.
(B) Quantity in Column B is greater.
(C) The quantities in Column A and Column B are equal.
(D) Cannot be determined from information given.

17. A bouquet has yellow and white flowers. If 40% of the flowers are yellow and there are 18 white flowers, then how many yellow flowers are there?

(A) 8
(B) 10
(C) 12
(D) 30

18. If two complex numbers are multiplied, the result

(A) will always be a complex number
(B) will never be a complex number
(C) could never be an integer
(D) could be an integer

In the expressions $2x^2y$, $3xy^2$, and $4wy^4$, the variables w, x, and y are prime integers.

	Column A	Column B
19.	The least common multiple of $2x^2y, 3xy^2$, and $4wy^4$	$12wxy^4$

(A) Quantity in Column A is greater.
(B) Quantity in Column B is greater.
(C) The quantities in Column A and Column B are equal.
(D) Cannot be determined from information given.

20. Which of the following numbers could be divided by 12 without leaving a remainder?

    (A) 1,112
    (B) 1,345
    (C) 1,448
    (D) 1,476

21. What is the value of $\frac{-3(3^3+3^2)}{9(3+3^2)}$?

    (A) -1
    (B) 0
    (C) 1
    (D) 2

22. A book collector started with 80 books in his collection. His collection was then increased by 200%. How many books are now in his collection?

    (A) 40
    (B) 80
    (C) 160
    (D) 240

Column A	Column B

23. $\left(\frac{1}{3}\right)^{-5}$ $\left(\frac{1}{4}\right)^{-5}$

    (A) Quantity in Column A is greater.
    (B) Quantity in Column B is greater.
    (C) The quantities in Column A and Column B are equal.
    (D) Cannot be determined from information given.

24. If *g* is a factor of *m*, and *h* is also a factor of *m*, then which statement is true?

(A) *h* is a factor of *gm*

(B) *g* is a multiple of *h*

(C) *h* is a multiple of *m*

(D) *m* is an odd number

Answers to Numbers & Operations Practice Set

1.	C		13.	D
2.	B		14.	B
3.	D		15.	A
4.	C		16.	A
5.	A		17.	C
6.	C		18.	D
7.	B		19.	A
8.	A		20.	D
9.	A		21.	A
10.	B		22.	D
11.	D		23.	B
12.	A		24.	A

Algebraic Concepts (Working With Variables)

On the Upper Level ISEE, there are questions that test the principles of algebra. These questions require you to set up equations, solve equations, or use the equations to find another value.

The types of algebra questions you will see include:

- Rearranging an equation to isolate a variable
- Setting up an equation (and sometimes solving)
- Patterns and sequences
- Made-up functions
- Solving inequalities
- Factoring and FOILing

The basic principle of algebra is that we must perform the same operation on both sides of an equal sign in order for the equation to remain true.

- Whatever you do to one side of an equal sign you must also do to the other

For example, let's say that we have the problem:

$$x + 5 = 7$$

We want to get the x by itself, but the problem is that right now the x has a 5 added to it. We can subtract the 5 from the left side of the equation as long as we do the same to the right side. We subtract 5 from both sides and get $x = 2$.

This is the principle that underlies all of algebra. On the Upper Level ISEE, you will not see problems as simple as $x + 5 = 7$, but you will need to remember that in order to keep the equal sign, we have to do the same thing to both sides.

Rearranging an equation to isolate a variable

Some questions on the Upper Level ISEE will ask you rearrange an equation to give one variable in terms of another. You are not likely to see many of these questions, and they are pretty straightforward, so we will just do a couple of examples as an algebra warmup. This problem type was also covered in the strategy section under Strategy #2: Plug in your own numbers.

1. If $p - q = 4$, then what is q equal to?

    (A) $4 - p$
    (B) $p - 4$
    (C) $-4 - p$
    (D) $p + 4$

    This question can be solved in two ways. First, we can solve it algebraically pretty easily. We subtract p from both sides and get $-q = -p + 4$. Now we divide both sides by -1 to get rid of the negative sign, and we are left with $q = p - 4$, or answer choice B. Another way to solve would be to choose our own numbers, since there are variables in the answer choices.

2. If $a = \frac{b}{3} + 15$, then which expression is equivalent to b?

    (A) $a - 15$
    (B) $3a - 15$
    (C) $45 - 3a$
    (D) $3a - 45$

    Again, there are variables in the answer choices, so we can either solve algebraically or by plugging in our own numbers. The trick to plugging in our own numbers for this question is that we need to pick numbers that make the equation true. We can plug in for b and then solve for a, or vice versa. Let's make $b = 3$, since that makes our lives easier. You want to choose a number for b that is divisible by 3 so that you don't have to deal with fractions. If $b = 3$, then $a = 16$. Now we plug in 16 for a in the answer choices to see which answer choice is equal to 3 (which is the value of b that we plugged in).

(A) $a - 15 = 16 - 15 = 1$

(B) $3a - 15 = 3(16) - 15 = 33$

(C) $45 - 3a = 45 - 3(16) = -3$

(D) $3a - 45 = 3(16) - 45 = 3$

Since answer choice D is equal to 3, it is the correct answer.

If we chose to solve algebraically, we would multiply the whole equation by 3 in order to get rid of the fraction. This gives us $3a = b + 45$. We would then subtract 45 from each side to find that b is equal to $3a - 45$.

Some questions may require factoring in order to isolate a variable. Factoring means that you "pull out" one factor from two or more terms and then use parentheses. Think of it as being the reverse of the distributive property. Instead of multiplying each term in the parentheses by another term, we are dividing each term by a factor and putting that factor in front of parentheses that contain the other terms. You will recognize that you need to factor when there is more than one term that contains a variable but the terms cannot be combined.

- If there is more than one term that contains a variable but the terms cannot be combined, then you probably need to factor

Since you may not see this type of question on the test, we will do just one sample problem:

3. If $pq + 1 = mq + p$ then $q =$

(A) $\dfrac{p - 1}{p - m}$

(B) $\dfrac{p - m}{p - 1}$

(C) $\dfrac{m - p}{1 - m}$

(D) $\dfrac{m - p}{1 - p}$

Our first step is to get all of the terms that contain q on the same side of the equal sign and all of the other terms on the other side:

$$pq + 1 = mq + p$$
$$\underline{-mq \quad\quad - mq}$$
$$pq - mq + 1 = p$$
$$\underline{\quad\quad -1 \quad -1}$$
$$pq - mq = p - 1$$

Now we can factor out the q so that we can then isolate it:

$$q(p - m) = p - 1$$
$$q = \frac{p - 1}{p - m}$$

Answer choice A is the correct answer.

Setting up an equation (and sometimes solving)

On the ISEE, there are several types of questions that show up frequently that require you to set up an equation and then solve. In this section we will cover those types of questions:

- Money questions
- Rate problems
- Absolute value questions

There are three basic types of money questions that we will cover: total cost questions, coin questions, and fixed cost + variable rate problems.

The first type of problem we will we go over asks you to figure out a total cost when two types of items are purchased.

The basic equation that we need to use for this type of problem is:

total cost = (# of item #1 × price of item #1) + (# of item #2 × price of item #2)

Here is an example:

1.   Jane bought five pens and five pencils at the store. The pencils cost ten cents less than the pens. Her total before tax was \$2.40. Which equation would find the cost of each pen (P)?

   (A) $5P + 5P + 0.10 = 2.40$

   (B) $5(P - 0.10) = 2.40$

   (C) $5P + 5(P - 0.10) = 2.40$

   (D) $10(P - 0.10) = 2.40$

This problem is a little involved. However, if we remember to plug into our equation, then it isn't so bad.

Here is what we know:

   $5 =$ number of item #1

   $5 =$ number of item #2

   $P =$ price of item #1 (pens)

   $P - 0.10 =$ price of item #2 (pencils)

   total cost $= 2.40$

Now we can put the pieces together:

   total cost $= $ (# of item #1 $\times$ price of item #1)
                $+ $ (# of item #2 $\times$ price of item #2)

   $2.40 = 5 \times P + 5 (P - 0.10)$

If we rearrange this equation, we get answer choice C, which is the correct answer.

You may also need to set up an equation and then solve. Here is an example:

2. Kalamazoo Playhouse wants to make a $10,000 profit from their summer production. Profit is equal to revenue minus costs. The play will cost approximately $2,200 to produce. Tickets will cost $14 in advance and $20 at the door. If they have sold 400 tickets in advance, how many tickets will they have to sell at the door in order to reach their profit goal?

    (A) 250

    (B) 300

    (C) 330

    (D) 610

For this question, we first have to find the revenue needed by using the equation that is given in words.

Profit = revenue − costs

$10,000 = revenue − $2,200

$12,200 = revenue

Now that we know the revenue that is needed, we can adapt our basic equation:

revenue = ($ presale ticket × # of tickets)
          + ($ at the door × # of tickets)

12,200 = (14 × 400) + (20 × # of tickets)

12,200 = (5,600) + (20 × # of tickets)

6,600 = (20 × # of tickets)

330 = # of tickets

Answer choice C is correct.

The next type of question involves coins. These questions are very similar to total cost questions – you can think of them as being total value questions. For these questions, we have to remember:

total value of type of coin = (# of that type of coin) × (value per coin of that type)

Here are a couple of examples of coin questions:

(The first one might look familiar. It is similar to a problem from the strategy section on plugging in answer choices. Here, we will show you how to solve algebraically since we have already covered plugging in answer choices).

3.   Janice has 12 coins in a pouch, all either dimes or quarters. If her dimes were quarters and her quarters were dimes, then her coins would be worth 60 cents more than they currently are. How many quarters does she currently have?

   (A)   4
   (B)   6
   (C)   7
   (D)   8

This problem is a doozy. First let's set up an expression for the value of the coins that she has now:

x = number of quarters

$12 - x$ = number of dimes

$0.25x + 0.10(12 - x)$ = current value of coins

Now we have to find an expression that shows the value of her coins if the number of quarters and dimes were switched. We will use the same variables, only giving the value of dimes to quarters and the value of quarters to dimes.

$0.10x + 0.25(12 - x)$ = value if coins were switched

Now we can put it all together, keeping in mind that we must add $0.60 (or 60 cents) to the existing value of the coins to get the new value of the coins.

$0.25x + 0.10(12 - x) + 0.60 = 0.10x + 0.25(12 - x)$

Now we have to work some algebra magic:

$$0.25x + 1.2 - 0.1x + 0.60 = 0.1x + 3 - 0.25x$$

$$0.15x + 1.8 = -0.15x + 3$$

$$0.3x = 1.2$$

$$x = 4$$

Since we chose x to be the number of quarters she currently has, we know that answer choice A is correct.

In a jar, there are nickels and quarters. There are twice as many nickels as quarters. The total value of the coins is $3.15.

Column A	Column B

4. The total value of the quarters. $2.50

(A) Quantity in Column A is greater.
(B) Quantity in Column B is greater.
(C) The quantities in Column A and Column B are equal.
(D) Cannot be determined from information given.

In order to answer this question, we can set up equations and then solve. As we did before, we will first define our variables.

x = number of quarters

$2x$ = number of nickels

We set x equal to the number of quarters, since Column A asks about quarters. Now we can use our equation for total value.

$$0.25x + 0.05(2x) = 3.15$$

$$0.25x + 0.1x = 3.15$$

$$0.35x = 3.15$$

$$x = 9$$

We now know that we have 9 quarters. Since the value of nine quarters is $2.25, the quantity in Column B is greater than the quantity in Column A. Answer choice B is correct.

Our final type of money problems is fixed cost + variable rate problems.

These questions give you a fixed cost for a certain first number of items and then a cost per item for additional items.

The general form of the equation for this type of questions is:

Total cost
= fixed cost + variable cost (total # of items − # of items included in fixed cost)

For example, let's say that it costs $2 for the first 20 minutes of a phone call and $0.05 for each minute after the first 20 minutes. Let's set up an equation that would tell us the total cost for a call that was w minutes long.

First, we will list what the problem gives us:

Total cost = ?

Fixed cost = $2

Variable cost = $0.05

Total # of minutes = w

# of minutes included in fixed cost = 20

Now we will put it all together:

Total cost = $2 + 0.05(w - 20)$

The reason that we subtract 20 from w is that we already paid for the first 20 minutes in the $2 part of the equation.

Here are a couple of sample problems for you to try:

5.   A taxicab charges \$4 for the first 3 miles and \$1.50 per mile for each additional mile or fraction of mile after the first 3 miles. Which equation would give the total cost (T) of a taxi ride that was m miles long?

(A) $T = 4m + 1.50m$

(B) $T = 4m + 1.50$

(C) $T = 4 + 1.50(m - 3)$

(D) $T = 4 + 3(m - 1.50)$

We will use the same method of listing out the information given in the question before setting up the equation.

Total cost $= T$

Fixed cost $= \$4$

Variable cost $= \$1.50$

Total # of miles $= m$

# of miles included in fixed cost $= 3$

Now we can plug into our equation:

$T = 4 + 1.50(m - 3)$

Answer choice C is correct.

A phone call with Company A costs $2 for the first five minutes and then $0.05 for each minute after the first five minutes. A phone call with Company B costs $0.08 a minute.

Column A	Column B

6. The cost of a 20-minute phone call with Company A. | The cost of a 20-minute phone call with Company B.

(A) Quantity in Column A is greater.
(B) Quantity in Column B is greater.
(C) The quantities in Column A and Column B are equal.
(D) Cannot be determined from information given.

Let's solve for each column separately:

Column A is a fixed cost + variable rate problem.

$$\text{Cost with Company A} = 2 + 0.05(m - 5)$$

Now we can plug in 20 for m since we are told that the call is 20 minutes long.

$$\text{Cost with Company A} = 2 + 0.05(20 - 5) = 2 + 0.05(15) = 2.75$$

Column B is a straight cost-per-minute problem.

$$\text{Cost with Company B} = 0.08m$$

Now we plug in 20 for m.

$$\text{Cost with Company B} = 0.08m = 0.08(20) = 1.60$$

We can see that the call with Company A costs more than the call with Company B, so answer choice A is correct.

The next type of problem we will work on is rate questions. The important equation to know for rate problems is:

rate × time = distance

Here is an example of a basic rate question:

7. Trevor is travelling to New Orleans, which is 30 miles away. If he travels at an average speed of 50 miles per hour, which equation will help him figure out how many minutes, m, it will it take him to get to New Orleans?

(A) $50 \times m = 30$

(B) $50 \times 30 = m$

(C) $\dfrac{60}{50} \times 30 = m$

(D) $m = 30 \times \dfrac{50}{60}$

To answer this question, we have to plug into the rate equation and then rearrange. The trick is that the speed is given in miles per hour, but the question asks for the number of minutes it would take for Trevor to get to New Orleans. This means that rather than writing the rate as $\dfrac{50 \text{ miles}}{1 \text{ hour}}$, we need to write it as $\dfrac{50 \text{ miles}}{60 \text{ minutes}}$.

$$\text{rate} \times \text{time} = \text{distance}$$

$$\dfrac{50 \text{ miles}}{60 \text{ minutes}} \times m = 30$$

This isn't one of our answer choices, so we need to keep rearranging. In order to get m by itself, we have to multiply by the inverse of $\dfrac{50}{60}$, which is $\dfrac{60}{50}$. When we do this, we are left with $\dfrac{60}{50} \times 30 = m$, or answer choice C.

You may also see a rate question that is much more involved. Here are a few examples of rate questions that are more challenging:

8. Carly and Marge started walking along a straight path at the same time and place. After 20 minutes, Marge is 500 feet ahead of Carly. If Marge's speed was twice as fast as Carly's, then which equation could be used to find Carly's speed (C) in feet per minute?

    (A) $40C - 500 = 20C$

    (B) $40C + 500 = 20C$

    (C) $40C = 20C - 500$

    (D) $40C + 20C = 500$

Our first step for this question is to write equations that represent the distance that each person has walked.

We will go back to our equation for rate:

> distance = rate × time
>
> Carly's distance = $C \times 20$
>
> Marge's distance = $2C \times 20$

Now we can use the fact that they were 500 feet apart to relate Marge's distance to Carly's distance.

> distance = rate × time
>
> Marge's distance $- 500 =$ Carly's distance

Now we can substitute in the expressions that we set up for each person's distance.

> $(2C \times 20) - 500 = C \times 20$

When we simplify, we are left with $40C - 500 = 20C$, or choice A.

9. Lawrence and Betty are driving along a straight path. After 30 minutes, Lawrence is 10 miles behind Betty. If Betty's speed is three times as fast as Lawrence's speed, then which equation could be used to find Betty's speed (B) in miles per hour?

(A) $30B - B = 10$

(B) $\dfrac{1}{2}B + \dfrac{1}{3}B = 10$

(C) $\dfrac{1}{2}\left(B + \dfrac{1}{3}\right) = 10$

(D) $\dfrac{1}{2}B = \dfrac{1}{6}B + 10$

We will begin by coming back to the rate equation:

distance = rate × time

First, we will set up an equation for Betty's speed. The trick to this is remembering that the speed is given in miles per hour. That means we have to convert 30 minutes into $\dfrac{1}{2}$ hour in order to create an equation.

$$\text{Betty's distance} = \dfrac{1}{2}B$$

Now we need to set up equations for Lawrence's rate and distance. Remember that our time has to be $\dfrac{1}{2}$ hour and NOT 30 minutes.

$$\text{Lawrence's rate} = \text{one third of Betty's rate} = \dfrac{1}{3}B$$

$$\text{Lawrence's distance} = \dfrac{1}{2}\left(\dfrac{1}{3}B\right)$$

Now we put all the pieces together, remembering that we need to add 10 to Lawrence's distance in order to get Betty's distance:

$$\dfrac{1}{2}B = \dfrac{1}{6}B + 10$$

Answer choice D is correct.

The next problem type is absolute value questions. Let's go back to the basic definition of absolute value: Absolute value tells us the distance from zero, regardless of whether the number is positive or negative. For example, the absolute value of -2, or $|-2|$, is equal to 2, since the distance from -2 to 0 is 2. Here is a basic absolute value problem for you to try:

10.   The solution for $|b| < 5$ is:

(A) $b > 5$

(B) $b < 5$

(C) $-5 < b < 5$

(D) $5 < b < -5$

For this question we have to remember that $|b| < 5$ means that the distance between 0 and b is less than 5. This means that b could be any number between -5 and 5. Answer choice C correctly represents this.

Another type of absolute value problem requires you to set up an expression using an absolute value to represent a range of possible values. The basic setup for this type of question is:

|variable − middle of range| ≤ half of range

Essentially, what this expression says is that the difference between the unknown value and the middle of the range cannot be greater than half the total range.

For example, let's say that in order to ride on a roller coaster, a rider must be between 40 and 60 inches tall. We can represent the allowable heights as $|h - 50| < 10$. This expression tells us that, in order for someone to ride on the roller coaster, the difference between his height and 50 must be less than 10. This gives us a range of 40 to 60.

Here are a couple of questions for you to try:

11. At a bottling factory, each bottle is supposed to hold 2 liters of liquid. However, each bottle is allowed to have up to $\frac{1}{8}$ of a liter more or less than 2 liters. Which expression represents the range for the number of liters of liquid (l) allowed in each bottle?

(A) $\left| l - \frac{1}{8} \right| < 2$

(B) $\left| l - \frac{1}{8} \right| > 2$

(C) $|l - 2| > \frac{1}{8}$

(D) $|l - 2| < \frac{1}{8}$

In this question, the middle of the range is 2. The difference between the actual liquid in the bottle and 2 liters must be less than $\frac{1}{8}$ liter. Answer choice D correctly represents this relationship.

12. In order to participate in a summer program, children must be between 4 and 10 years of age. Which expression correctly represents the age range (a), of children who are allowed to participate?

(A) $|a - 7| < 3$

(B) $|a - 7| > 3$

(C) $|a - 3| < 7$

(D) $|a - 6| < 7$

For this question, we first have to figure out what the middle of the range is. Since the number 7 is halfway in between 4 and 10, that is the middle of our range. Now we have to figure out how far on either side of 7 is acceptable. Since 4 is 3 less than 7 and 10 is 3 more than 7, we want an expression that shows that the difference between the child's age and 7 must be less than 3. Answer choice A correctly represents this relationship.

Patterns and sequences

A pattern or sequence is a series of numbers that has a "rule" to get from one number to the next. For example, in an arithmetic sequence, the rule might be "add 2" to find the next term. In a geometric sequence, the rule might be "multiply by 3" to find the next term.

On the Upper Level ISEE, sequence questions tend to be pretty straightforward. Typically, you are given the first few terms, and then you need to figure out the rule used to determine terms.

- Sequence and pattern questions usually test whether or not you can find the rule to determine each term
- Often you can just try out the answer choices to see which expression correctly describes each term given

One thing that can be tricky with sequences is the way that terms are named. Generally, we use n to describe the ordinal number of the term. The ordinal number tells us which position the number holds in the sequence – first, second, third, etc. To define the term itself, we generally use a_n. For example, if $a_3 = 8$, then the third term in our sequence is 8.

For example, let's say that our sequence is:

$$-4, -2, 0, 2, 4$$

There are two different ways that we can define this sequence. We can say that the rule is:

$$a_{n+1} = a_n + 2$$

This equation tells us that in order to find the next term in the sequence (a_{n+1}), we need to add 2 to the previous term (a_n).

We can also define the rule as:

$$a_n = 2n - 6$$

In this case, we are not basing our rule on the previous term. Rather, we are basing our rule on the ordinal number of that term in the sequence. For example, the third term in our sequence is 0. In order to find a_3 (or the third term), we plug in 3 for n and get:

$$a_3 = 2(3) - 6 = 0$$

- When you are evaluating whether or not a rule works, be sure to first determine whether the rule is based on the previous term or the ordinal number of the term (first, second, third, etc.)

We will try just a couple sample questions since these are pretty straightforward:

1. Shown below are the first four terms of an arithmetic sequence.

   $$-6, -1, 4, 9$$

   Which expression could be used to find the nth term of this sequence?

   (A) $n - 7$
   (B) $n + 5$
   (C) $5n - 5$
   (D) $5n - 11$

   For this question, we have to keep in mind that we are not looking for a rule that defines a term by the previous term. The question asks us to come up with the general rule for finding a term, whether or not we know the term that comes before it. Let's try the answer choices to see what works. We have to remember that n is the ordinal number of the term in the sequence (first, second, third, etc.) and not the term itself. To try out answer choice A, we plug in 1 for n and get:

   $$n - 7 = 1 - 7 = -6$$

   Since this is indeed the first term, we know that answer choice A works for that one term, but we have to keep going to make sure it works for all the terms. Let's try the next term. If we plug in 2 for n, we get:

   $$n - 7 = 2 - 7 = -5$$

   Since the second term in this sequence is not -5, we eliminate choice A. Now let's move on to choice B. We plug in 1 for n and get:

   $$n + 5 = 1 + 5 = 6$$

   Since the first term is not 6, we can rule out choice B. By the way, if you chose this answer, you most likely defined the rule by the previous term (add 5 to each term to get to the next term) instead of by a general rule that allows you to find any term. Now let's try choice C. If we plug in 1 for n, we get

$$5n - 5 = 5(1) - 5 = 0$$

Since our first term is not 0, we can eliminate choice C. Now let's try out choice D. If we plug in 1 for n, we get:

$$5(1) - 11 = -6$$

This is good news since our first term is -6. If we plug in for the other terms, we will see that they all work. Answer choice D is the correct answer.

2.   Use the table below to answer the question.

X	Y
2	4
3	7
4	10
?	?
?	?
n	m

If the pattern shown in the table above continues, then $m =$

(A) $n + 2$

(B) $2n$

(C) $3n - 2$

(D) $3n + 2$

Let's use our strategy of ruling out. If we look at choice A, it works for the first row in our table but not for the others. The same is true for answer choice B. We can eliminate both of these choices. Now let's try choice C. If we plug in 2 for n, we get $3n - 2 = 3(2) - 2 = 4$ and the first row works. Now let's try the next row. If we plug in 3 for n, we get $3n - 2 = 3(3) - 2 = 7$, so answer choice C works for the second row in our table as well. If we try the third row in our table, it also works for $m = 3n - 2$. Answer choice C is correct.

Made-up functions

A very similar problem type is made-up functions. A function is simply a fancy way of saying that one variable affects another. There is a rule that defines how one variable affects the other. For example, $y = x + 2$ tells us how y will change as x changes.

- A function tells us how one variable affects another

On the ISEE, you may see a question that defines a function for you that includes funny symbols. For example, the question may give the function $\#b\# = 3b - 7$ and ask for the value of $\#3\#$. To solve, we simply plug in 3 for b on the right side of the equation. This gives us $\#3\# = 3(3) - 7 = 2$.

- If there is an equation with a funny symbol in it, this is a made-up function
- You are not supposed to know what that funny symbol means – the function or "rule" will be defined for you

Here are a couple of questions for you to try:

1.   If $g^* = 5g + 6$, then what is the value of 4^*?

   (A) 26
   (B) 30
   (C) 36
   (D) 42

   To answer this question, we substitute in 4 for g in the equation. When we do that, we get $4^* = 5(4) + 6 = 26$. Answer choice A is correct.

   For all real numbers b and c, $b■c = b^2 - 2bc + c^2$.

	Column A	Column B
2.	1■3	3■1

   (A) Quantity in Column A is greater.
   (B) Quantity in Column B is greater.
   (C) The quantities in Column A and Column B are equal.
   (D) Cannot be determined from information given.

Since this is a quantitative comparison question, let's set up each equation and see if we have enough information to be able to compare. Using the defined function, we get $1 \blacksquare 3 = 1^2 - 2(1)(3) + 3^2$ for Column A. For Column B, we get $3 \blacksquare 1 = 3^2 - 2(3)(1) + 1^2$. Even without calculating, we can see that the two quantities are equal. Answer choice C is correct. By the way, if you didn't see that we could use the commutative property to make the two expressions equal to one another, you could have solved for each column and gotten the same answer.

Solving inequalities

An inequality is a way to define the range of numbers that a variable could be equal to. For example, $x < 5$ means that x could be any number that is less than 5.

To solve for a variable in an inequality, we use the same principles that we use to solve for a variable in an equation. The big difference is that when we multiply or divide by a negative number, we have to flip the inequality sign.

For example, let's say we have the inequality:

$$-2x < 4$$

When we divide both sides by -2, we flip the inequality sign and are left with:

$$x > -2$$

- Can use the same rules to solve for a variable in an inequality as you would with an equation
- If you multiply or divide by a negative number, you need to flip the inequality sign

On the Upper Level ISEE, inequalities are often given with a variable that needs to be solved for and an expression that includes both less than and greater than symbols. For example, a question may tell you that $5 < 2x + 7 < 15$. Here is how we would solve for the variable in this case:

$$5 < 2x + 7 < 15$$
$$-7 \quad -7 \quad -7$$
$$-2 < 2x < 8$$
$$\div 2 \quad \div 2 \quad \div 2$$
$$-1 < x < 4$$

In this case we can see that the value of x must be between -1 and 4.

Here are a couple of basic inequality questions:

1. What is the solution set for x in the inequality $4 \leq -3x - 5 \leq 13$?

    (A) $x \geq 6, x \leq 3$
    (B) $x \leq -6, x \geq -3$
    (C) $3 \leq x \leq 6$
    (D) $-6 \leq x \leq -3$

Let's go ahead and use algebra to answer this question:

$$4 \leq -3x - 5 \leq 13$$
$$+5 \qquad +5 \qquad +5$$
$$9 \leq -3x \leq 18$$
$$\div(-3) \quad \div(-3) \quad \div(-3)$$
$$-3 \geq x \geq -6$$

We can see that x should be less than or equal to -3 and greater than or equal to -6. Answer choice D correctly represents this relationship. It is important to note that in order to get the correct answer, we had to flip the inequality signs when we divided by -3.

$$x + 4 > 4x$$

Column A	Column B
-3	x

2.

(A) Quantity in Column A is greater.
(B) Quantity in Column B is greater.
(C) The quantities in Column A and Column B are equal.
(D) Cannot be determined from information given.

To answer this question, we first need to figure out what the possible values for x are. If we subtract x from both sides, we are left with $4 > 3x$. Now we divide both sides by 3 and get $\frac{4}{3} > x$. This means that x can be any value that is less than $\frac{4}{3}$. It could be 0, it could be -100, we just don't know. Since it could be a value greater than -3, equal to -3, or less than -3, we have to choose answer choice D.

You may also see questions that ask you graph the solution on a number line.

There are a couple of things to keep in mind:

1. If the inequality sign is $\leq$ or $\geq$, the circle on the number line should be filled in to show the "or equal to" part of the inequality. If the inequality sign is $<$ or $>$, then the circle on the number line should be left open to show that it cannot be equal to that number.
2. Think about whether the inequality is an "and" statement or an "or" statement. An "and" statement will be written with the variable between two numbers, and one section of the number line will be filled in. An "or" statement requires that the inequality be written in two pieces, and there will be two shaded sections of the number line.

Here is an example of an "and" inequality:

$4 \leq x < 7$

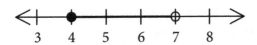

Note that the circle over the 4 is filled in because the variable is greater than or equal to 4. The circle over the 7 is not filled in because the variable is less than (but not equal to) 7.

Here is an example of an "or" inequality:

$x \geq 4, x < 2$

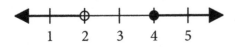

Here is an example of a very basic inequality question on the ISEE:

3.   Which is the graph that shows $x \leq 3$ or $x > 7$?

This is an "or" inequality, so we are looking for a graph that has two portions shaded. That allows us to rule out choices A and B. Now let's look for differences between C and D. We want the graph that has the circle over 3 filled in, since that inequality sign is "or equal to", and an open circle over 7. Answer choice C correctly shows this.

Sometimes you first have to isolate the variable in an inequality and then choose the correct graph. Here is an example:

4.   Which graph shows the solution set for the inequality $43 \leq 3x - 2 \leq 55$?

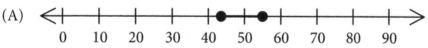

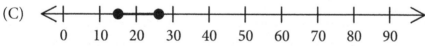

Our first step in answering this question is to isolate the variable in the inequality. Here is what the math looks like:

$$43 \leq 3x - 2 \leq 55$$

$$+2 \quad +2 \quad +2$$

$$45 \leq 3x \leq 57$$

$$\div 3 \quad \div 3 \quad \div 3$$

$$15 \leq x \leq 19$$

Now that we know the possible values for x, we need to choose the graph that represents $15 \leq x \leq 19$. Answer choice D is the only one that comes close, so we can choose it with confidence.

One of the trickier types of questions involves solving inequalities with absolute values. The key is to remember that absolute value means the distance from zero. For example, if we have $|x| \leq 4$, that means that x has to be between -4 and 4. We represent this as $-4 \leq x \leq 4$. It gets a little trickier when the absolute value is greater than a number. In this case, we have to convert the whole thing into an "or" statement. For example, if we have $|x| \geq 4$, that means that the difference between x and 0 must be greater than 4. Another way to say this is that x must be greater than or equal to 4 or less than or equal to -4. We can represent this as $x \geq 4$ or $x \leq -4$.

- If the absolute value with a variable is less than a number, then we remove the absolute value signs and make the variable greater than the negative of that number and less than the number itself

  Example: $|x| \leq 4$ becomes $-4 \leq x \leq 4$

- If the absolute value of a variable is greater than a number, we have to turn it into an "or" statement when we remove the absolute value brackets. It will be greater than the value of the number itself or less than the value of the number made negative

  Example: $|x| \geq 4$ becomes $x \geq 4$ or $x \leq -4$

Here are a couple of questions for you to try:

5.   If $|3x + 2| \geq 5$, then which of the following describes the possible values of x?

(A) $x \geq 1$

(B) $x \leq -2\dfrac{1}{3}$

(C) $x \geq 1$ or $x \leq -2\dfrac{1}{3}$

(D) $x \leq 1$ or $x \geq -2\dfrac{1}{3}$

Since this is a "greater than" statement with an absolute value, we know the answer has to be an "or" statement. We can eliminate choices A and B. If we look at choice D, it doesn't make sense to write it as an "or" statement. (If you tried to draw it out, you would see that x could be any value.) We can eliminate choice D, which leaves us with choice C as the correct answer. If you went the route of using algebra to solve, here is what the math would look like:

$$|3x + 2| \geq 5$$

$$3x + 2 \geq 5 \ \text{ or } \ 3x + 2 \leq -5$$

$$3x \geq 3 \ \text{ or } \ 3x \leq -7$$

$$x \geq 1 \ \text{ or } \ x \leq -2\dfrac{1}{3}$$

6.   The solution set of an inequality is graphed below.

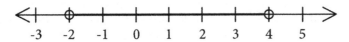

Which inequality has this solution set?

(A) $|x - 1| < 3$

(B) $|x + 1| < 3$

(C) $|x - 3| < 1$

(D) $|x + 3| < 1$

For this question, rather than solving for each individual answer choice, let's apply what we learned about absolute value in our problem types section. With absolute value, we find the middle of the range. We can see from our number line that middle of the graph is 1. We can also see that x can be up to 3 greater or less than 1. We are looking for the answer choice that tells us that the difference between x and 1 is less than 3. Answer choice A correctly represents this relationship. You also could have solved for each answer choice and seen which answer gave you $-2 < x < 4$ as an answer.

Factoring and FOILing

The next concept we are going to cover is factoring, which you may have learned as FOIL (first-outer-inner-last).

Let's say that you were presented with the expression $x^2 + 9x + 20$ and asked to factor it. In factored form, $x^2 + 9x + 20$ would be written as $(x + 4)(x + 5)$.

Factoring is a very big topic, so there isn't room in this book to cover all the basics of how factoring is done. If the above description doesn't make sense to you, please seek out other resources – factoring is incredibly important to algebra and you need to be proficient at it.

We are going to cover some of the specific aspects of factoring that commonly appear on the ISEE.

There are a couple of basic types of factoring that the ISEE favors:

1. Difference of the squares. In this type of factoring, one perfect square is subtracted from another.

    Example: $x^2 - 9 = (x + 3)(x - 3)$

2. Perfect square trinomial. In this type of factoring, both factors are the same.

    Example: $x^2 + 8x + 16 = (x + 4)(x + 4) = (x + 4)^2$

On the ISEE, the questions generally don't test factoring in a direct manner. You probably won't see a question that gives you $x^2 + 7x + 10$ and asks you for its factored form. Rather, you are more likely to see questions that require you to recognized factored forms and then apply that knowledge.

Here are some examples of how factoring is tested on the ISEE:

1. If $(x + 3)^2 = x^2 + bx + 9$, and b is a positive integer, then what is the value of b?

    (A) 3
    (B) 6
    (C) 9
    (D) 18

    This question is asking you to figure out the middle term for a perfect square trinomial. In a perfect-square trinomial, the coefficient of the middle term is twice the last term of the factored form. Since 2 times 3 is 6, answer choice B is correct. You also could have used FOIL to find the answer by multiplying $(x + 3)(x + 3)$.

2. If $x^2 - y^2 = 40$ and $x - y = 8$, then what is the value of $x + y$?

    (A) 4
    (B) 5
    (C) 32
    (D) 64

In order to answer this question, we first need to recognize that $x^2 - y^2$ is the difference of two squares. This means that $x^2 - y^2$ would factor into $(x + y)(x - y)$. Now we know that $(x + y)(x - y) = 40$. Since $x - y = 8$, then $x + y$ must be equal to 5. Answer choice B is correct.

A square has a side length of $x - 2$

	Column A	Column B
3.	The area of the square	$x^2 - 4x$

(A) Quantity in Column A is greater.
(B) Quantity in Column B is greater.
(C) The quantities in Column A and Column B are equal.
(D) Cannot be determined from information given.

This question is really testing your ability to multiply binomials. If the side length of a square is $x - 2$, then the area of the square is $(x - 2)^2$ or $x^2 - 4x + 4$. Since adding 4 to $x^2 - 4x$ will always make the value greater, answer choice A is correct.

4. If $2xy = 10$ and $x^2 + y^2 = 90$, then what is the value of $(x + y)^2$?

(A) 70
(B) 80
(C) 90
(D) 100

It is important for us to recognize that $(x + y)^2$ would multiply into $x^2 + 2xy + y^2$. We can rearrange this expression to $x^2 + y^2 + 2xy$. Now we can easily see that we can add together the value of $x^2 + y^2$, which is 90, and the value of $2xy$, which is 10, to get the value of $(x + y)^2$. Since $10 + 90 = 100$, answer choice D is correct.

You may also see a question that asks you to multiply a binomial by a trinomial. The easiest way to make sure that each term in the binomial is multiplied by each term in the trinomial is to make a box.

Here is an example:

Let's say we need to multiply $(a - b)(a^2 + ab + b^2)$:

	a^2	ab	b^2
a	a^3	a^2b	ab^2
$-b$	$-a^2b$	$-ab^2$	$-b^3$

Now we need to combine like terms, and we are left with $a^3 - b^3$. This kind of problem is called the difference of two perfect cubes. This is likely to be the only kind of trinomial you will see on the ISEE, so we will do just one sample problem.

Here is an example of a question that tests this concept:

<u>Column A</u>   <u>Column B</u>

5. $a^3 - b^3$ $(a^2 + ab + b^2)(a - b)$

     (A)   Quantity in Column A is greater.
     (B)   Quantity in Column B is greater.
     (C)   The quantities in Column A and Column B are equal.
     (D)   Cannot be determined from information given.

     From our above example, we know that the two quantities are equal. Answer choice C is correct.

Now you have covered the algebraic concepts likely to be tested on the Upper Level ISEE. Be sure to complete the practice set on the following pages.

Algebraic Concepts Practice Set

1. A concert series costs between $3,000 and $3,500 to produce. The series will consist of 12 concerts in total. Between 150 and 250 people are expected to attend each night, and tickets cost $9 each. If profit is equal to revenue minus cost, what will be the approximate profit for this concert series?

    (A) $13,000
    (B) $18,000
    (C) $24,000
    (D) $27,000

$$\frac{m}{3} + 4 = 22$$

$$2n + 5 = 113$$

Column A	Column B
2. | m | n |

    (A) Quantity in Column A is greater.
    (B) Quantity in Column B is greater.
    (C) The quantities in Column A and Column B are equal.
    (D) Cannot be determined from information given.

3.   If $b + 5 - 9 = c$, then what is the value of $b - c$?

(A) 8

(B) 4

(C) −2

(D) −4

In	Out
2	3
3	5
4	7
5	9

	Column A	Column B
4.	The output when the input is 7	The input when the output is 15

(A) Quantity in Column A is greater.

(B) Quantity in Column B is greater.

(C) The quantities in Column A and Column B are equal.

(D) Cannot be determined from information given.

5.   If $\dfrac{k+2}{k} = \dfrac{2}{6}$, then what is the value of k?

(A) −3

(B) −1

(C) 1

(D) 3

6. James and Erik ran along a straight path, starting at the same time and place. James ran twice as fast as Erik. After 5 minutes, James was 200 feet in front of Erik. Which equation could be solved to find Erik's speed (E) in feet per minute?

    (A) $2E - E = 200$
    (B) $2(E + 2E) = 200$
    (C) $200 - 5E = 10E$
    (D) $5E + 200 = 10E$

7. If $ab + 4 = cb - 3$ then $b =$

    (A) $-\dfrac{7}{a - c}$
    (B) $\dfrac{7}{a - c}$
    (C) $-\dfrac{7}{c + a}$
    (D) $\dfrac{7}{c + a}$

8. Carol has to drive 30 miles. If she drives at an average speed of 40 miles per hour, how many minutes will her trip take?

    (A) 0.5
    (B) 20
    (C) 45
    (D) 50

9. Martin has dimes and quarters in a jar. The total value of the quarters is twice the total value of the dimes. If the total value of all the coins in his jar is $5.25, how many quarters does he have?

    (A) 16
    (B) 14
    (C) 12
    (D) 9

10. A lobster fishing company requires that any lobsters it catches that are not between 1 pound and 2.4 pounds must be thrown back into the ocean. Which expression represents the weight of lobsters (p) that do NOT have to be thrown back, in pounds?

    (A) $|p - 2.4| < 1$

    (B) $|p - 1| < 2.4$

    (C) $|p - 1.7| < 0.7$

    (D) $|p - 0.7| < 1.7$

11. Which graph shows the solution set of $|2x + 5| > 3$?

    (A)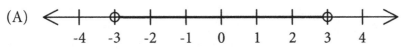

    (B)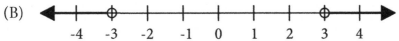

    (C)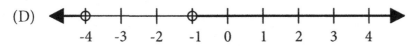

    (D)

$$a^2 + b^2 = 30 \text{ and } (a + b)^2 = 40$$

Column A	Column B
10	ab

12.

    (A) Quantity in Column A is greater.
    (B) Quantity in Column B is greater.
    (C) The quantities in Column A and Column B are equal.
    (D) Cannot be determined from information given.

13. A store is having a sale on t-shirts. The first three t-shirts purchased are $15 total, and each additional shirt after the first three is $10. Which equation represents the total cost (C) if m t-shirts are purchased?

(A) $C = 20m$

(B) $C = 15 + 10(m - 3)$

(C) $C = 15 + 10(m - 1)$

(D) $C = 15m + 10(m - 3)$

14. Shown below are the first six terms of an arithmetic sequence.

$-2, 2, 6, 10, 14, 18$

Which expression could be used to find the nth term in this sequence?

(A) $n - 4$

(B) $n + 4$

(C) $4n - 6$

(D) $4n + 6$

For all real numbers x and y, $x \uparrow y = x^2 - y^2 - 2xy$

	Column A	Column B
15.	$2 \uparrow 3$	$3 \uparrow 2$

(A) Quantity in Column A is greater.

(B) Quantity in Column B is greater.

(C) The quantities in Column A and Column B are equal.

(D) Cannot be determined from information given.

Answers to Algebraic Concepts Practice Set

1. B
2. C
3. B
4. A
5. A
6. D
7. A
8. C

9. B
10. C
11. D
12. A
13. B
14. C
15. B

Geometry & Measurement

On the Upper Level ISEE, the writers of the test classify geometry and measurement questions separately. There is so much overlap between the two categories, however, that we will review them as one.

Geometry and measurement problem types that you will see on the Upper Level ISEE include:

- Nets
- Triangles
- Polygons
- Perimeter and area
- Volume
- Coordinate geometry
- Scale
- Appropriate units
- Unit conversions

Nets

Nets are patterns that can be folded to create three-dimensional shapes, or polyhedrons. The key to this type of question is to visualize the shape that would be formed if the sides were folded up.

Here are a couple of questions that test your ability to visualize polyhedrons:

1. The pattern below is going to be folded to create a polyhedron.

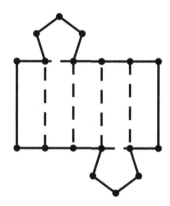

Which polyhedron could be the result if the pattern was folded along the dotted lines?

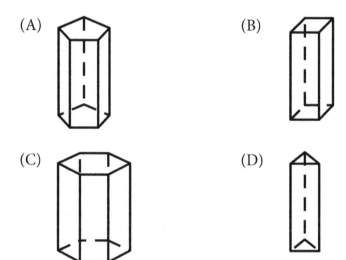

To answer this question, we can first identify the bases. We can see that there are five rectangle sides and two pentagons that would act as bases. Answer choice A is the only choice with pentagons as bases.

2.	The pattern below can be folded into a cube.

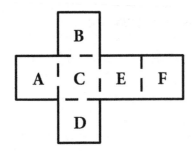

If the net is folded into a cube and side A is on the bottom, which side would be on the top?

(A)	B

(B)	C

(C)	D

(D)	E

This problem is a little tricky because you probably visualized the cube with C on the bottom. However, the question states that A is on the bottom. That means that C would be on a side and E would be on the top. Answer choice D is correct.

Triangles

On the Upper Level ISEE, there are a few facts about triangles that you may see tested. They include:

1.	Angles in a triangle add to 180 degrees
2.	If two triangles are similar, the ratios of their corresponding side lengths are the same
3.	In a right triangle, $a^2 + b^2 = c^2$
4.	Trigonometric relationships (sin, cos, tan)

Angles in a triangle add to 180 degrees

In a triangle, all angles must add to 180 degrees. You are not likely to see a question that gives you two angles and asks for the third, but you might have to apply this fact.

Here are a couple of sample questions that test this fact:

1. Use the diagram below to answer the question.

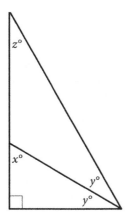

In the triangle above, $x = 2y$. What is the value of z?

(A) 30

(B) 45

(C) 50

(D) 60

In the smaller triangle, we know that one angle is 90 degrees. That means that $x + y = 90$. Now we can substitute in $2y$ for x (since $x = 2y$) and get $2y + y = 90$. We then combine like terms to get $3y = 90$, and therefore $y = 30$. Now let's look at the larger triangle. One angle is 90° and the other angle is $2y°$, or 60°. If we add these two values together, we get a total of 150°. That means that z must be equal to 30 in order for the angles in the larger triangle to add up to 180°. Answer choice A is correct.

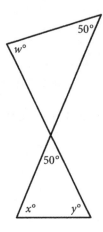

	Column A	Column B
2.	$2w$	$x + y$

(A)   Quantity in Column A is greater.

(B)   Quantity in Column B is greater.

(C)   The quantities in Column A and Column B are equal.

(D)   Cannot be determined from information given.

Let's first look at Column A. In order to figure out what w is equal to, we first have to recognize that vertical angles are congruent. This means that the bottom angle of the top triangle must be 50°. Since the two known angles in the top triangle add up to 100°, the third angle must be 80°. This means that the value of $2w$, or Column A, is 160. Now let's look at Column B. We know that one angle in the bottom triangle is 50°, so the other two angles must add to 130°. That means that $x + y = 130$. The trick here is that we can't know the value of x or y individually, but we only need to know the sum of $x + y$. Since 160 is greater than 130, answer choice A is the correct answer.

Similar triangles

On the Upper Level ISEE, you may also see questions that ask you to use similar triangles to solve for a side length. If you have two similar triangles, the ratio of the corresponding side lengths for each triangle is the same.

For example:

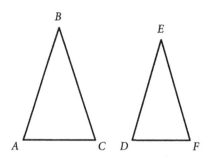

If triangle ABC is similar to triangle DEF, then

$$\frac{AB}{DE} = \frac{BC}{EF} = \frac{AC}{DF}$$

Here are a couple of examples of questions that test this concept:

3.   Triangles PQR and STU are similar. The length of $\overline{PQ}$ is 2 cm, and the length of $\overline{ST}$ is 3 cm. If the length of $\overline{QR}$ is 6 cm, what is the length of $\overline{TU}$?

   (A)   3 cm

   (B)   5 cm

   (C)   6 cm

   (D)   9 cm

   For this question, we can set up a proportion that uses the segments that we are given and what we want to solve for:

   $$\frac{PQ}{ST} = \frac{QR}{TU}$$

   Now we can substitute the values that we have:

   $$\frac{2}{3} = \frac{6}{TU}$$

Our next step is to cross-multiply and solve:

$$2 \times TU = 6 \times 3$$

$$2 \times TU = 18$$

$$TU = 9$$

Answer choice D is the correct answer.

4.   In the figure below, triangle ABC is similar to triangle DEF.

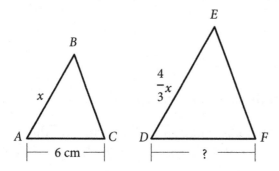

What is the length of $\overline{DF}$?

(A)   6 cm

(B)   8 cm

(C) $6x$ cm

(D) $8x$ cm

For this question, let's set up a proportion again:

$$\frac{AB}{DE} = \frac{AC}{DF}$$

Now we will plug in what we have:

$$\frac{x}{\frac{4}{3}x} = \frac{6}{DF}$$

Let's cross-multiply:

$$x \times DF = 6 \times \frac{4}{3}x$$

Now we are going to divide both sides by x in order to eliminate the variable. We are left with:

$$DF = 6 \times \frac{4}{3} = 8$$

Answer choice B is correct. If you chose answer choice D, your error was that you didn't divide *both* sides by x in order to get rid of the variable.

Another classic problem type is the "shadow" question. These questions do not use the words "similar triangle" at all, but rather are expecting you to recognize that the principles of similar triangles must be applied. In these questions, there are two objects with shadows. The height of one object and the length of its shadow is given, and you must use that to solve for either the height of the other object or the length of its shadow.

- If a question has two objects with shadows, odds are good that it is a similar triangle problem

Here is an example for you to try:

5.   A fence post that is 3 feet high casts a shadow that is 5 feet long. At the same time, a nearby flagpole casts a shadow that is 35 feet long. How tall is the flagpole?

  (A) 7 ft
  (B) 21 ft
  (C) 30 ft
  (D) 35 ft

This question is all about recognizing that we are dealing with similar triangles. Let's go ahead and do a rough sketch so that we can keep everything straight:

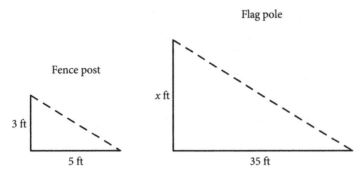

Note - This figure is not to scale.

Now we set up a proportion to solve:

$$\frac{3}{x} = \frac{5}{35}$$

$$3 \times 35 = 5x$$

$$105 = 5x$$

$$x = 21$$

Answer choice B is correct.

The Pythagorean Theorem

In a right triangle, the sum of the squares of the two legs is equal to the square of the hypotenuse, or the side opposite the right angle. This relationship is called the Pythagorean Theorem.

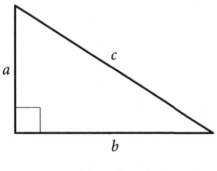

$$a^2 + b^2 = c^2$$

On the Upper Level ISEE, you are not likely to see a question that simply asks you to solve for a side. Rather, you may see a question that asks you to apply the principles of Pythagorean Theorem without directly stating that.

The best way to practice this is through examples:

6.   *ABCD* and *WXYZ* are both squares, and *WXYZ* is inscribed inside *ABCD*.

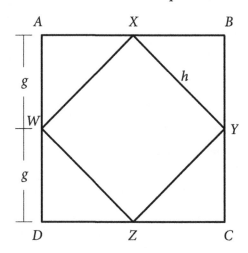

What is the length of line segment *h*?

(A) $2g$

(B) $2g^2$

(C) $g\sqrt{2}$

(D) $2g\sqrt{2}$

Since *WXYZ* is inscribed inside *ABCD*, and both $\overline{AW}$ and $\overline{WD}$ are equal to g, we know that $\overline{XB}$ and $\overline{BY}$ must also be equal to g. Since *ABCD* is a square, we know that $\angle B$ must be a right angle and triangle *XBY* must be a right triangle. If we then use the Pythagorean theorem, we know that $g^2 + g^2 = h^2$.

Now we have to solve for *h*:

$$g^2 + g^2 = h^2$$

$$2g^2 = h^2$$

$$\sqrt{2g^2} = \sqrt{h^2}$$

$$g\sqrt{2} = h$$

Answer choice C is the correct answer.

Car A left the library and drove north for 5 miles. Car B left the library and drove east for 6 miles.

	Column A	Column B
7.	The shortest distance between Car A and Car B.	8 miles

(A) Quantity in Column A is greater.
(B) Quantity in Column B is greater.
(C) The quantities in Column A and Column B are equal.
(D) Cannot be determined from information given.

Let's go ahead and draw this one out:

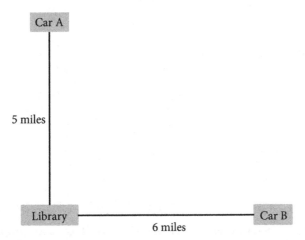

The shortest distance between two points is a straight line. If we draw in that line, we can see that we have a right triangle and can therefore use the Pythagorean Theorem:

$$5^2 + 6^2 = c^2$$

$$25 + 36 = c^2$$

$$61 = c^2$$

$$\sqrt{61} = c$$

Now we have to determine which is longer: $\sqrt{61}$ miles or 8 miles. We can rewrite 8 as $\sqrt{64}$. Now we can see that $\sqrt{64}$ is larger than $\sqrt{61}$, so answer choice B is the correct answer.

Trigonometric relationships (sin, cos, tan)

On the Upper Level ISEE, you may see a question that asks you to use trigonometry. If you have never worked on trigonometry before, it may not be worth your time to learn a whole new concept when there may only be one question on this test. However, if you have done this in school before but it may be just a little rusty for you, please work through this section.

Trigonometry gives us the relationships between angles and sides in a right triangle.

The first step in determining the relationships is to determine which angle is the reference point. For example, the side that is "opposite" will depend on what angle we are talking about.

In the drawing below, θ represents the angle that is being used in each relationship.

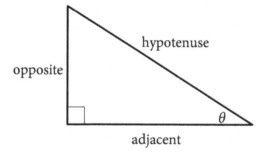

If we are given two sides and asked to find an angle, or if we are given the angle measure and one side and asked to find another, we can use the following relationships:

$$\sin \theta = \frac{\text{opposite}}{\text{hypotenuse}}$$

$$\cos \theta = \frac{\text{adjacent}}{\text{hypotenuse}}$$

$$\tan \theta = \frac{\text{opposite}}{\text{adjacent}}$$

You may have learned the acronym SOHCAHTOA to remember these relationships. This is a way to remember:

$$s = \frac{o}{h}, c = \frac{a}{h}, t = \frac{o}{a}$$

You won't need to know the values of sin, cos, or tan or be given tables for these values. Rather, the test will want you to apply these concepts in a very basic way.

Here are a couple of examples of questions that test trigonometry:

8.   Below is Triangle ABC. The length of $\overline{AB}$ is 4 cm and the length of $\overline{BC}$ is 3 cm.

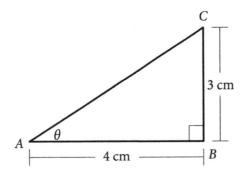

Which equation could be used to determine the angle measure of θ?

(A) $\sin \theta = \dfrac{3}{4}$

(B) $\cos \theta = \dfrac{3}{4}$

(C) $\tan \theta = \dfrac{3}{4}$

(D) $\tan \theta = \dfrac{4}{3}$

If we look at angle θ, we can see that we are given values for the opposite and adjacent sides. This means that we will be using *tan*, and we can eliminate choices A and B. Answer choice C correctly shows the opposite side length over the adjacent side length, so it is the correct answer.

9.   Shown below is Triangle *DEF*. The measure of angle *DEF* is 30°, as shown. The length of $\overline{DF}$ is 5 cm.

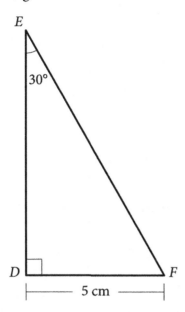

Which expression is equal in value to the length of $\overline{EF}$?

(A) $\dfrac{\sin 30°}{5}$

(B) $\dfrac{5}{\sin 30°}$

(C) $\dfrac{\cos 30°}{5}$

(D) $\dfrac{5}{\cos 30°}$

Let's start out by setting up an equation using trigonometry. We are given the side opposite the angle given and then asked for the length of the hypotenuse, so we are going to use *sin*:

$$\sin 30° = \frac{5}{\overline{EF}}$$

Now we need to rearrange the equation to get $\overline{EF}$ by itself. We will multiply both sides by $\overline{EF}$:

$$\overline{EF} \times \sin 30° = 5$$

Now we will divide by sin 30° to get $\overline{EF}$ by itself:

$$\overline{EF} = \frac{5}{\sin 30°}$$

Answer choice B is correct.

Polygons

On the Upper Level ISEE, there aren't many questions about polygons. You may need to know some basic terminology, though:

1. Interior angles are the angles that are inside a polygon. In a quadrilateral, the angles add up to 360°.

   Example:

   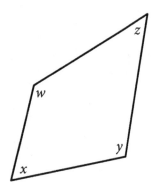

   Angles $w, x, y,$ and z are all interior angles. The degree measures of $w, x, y,$ and z add up to 360°.

2. Exterior angles are the angles that are created when a side is extended, as shown on the next page. In a regular polygon (all sides are the same length and all interior angles have the same measure), any exterior angle and any interior angle add to 180°.

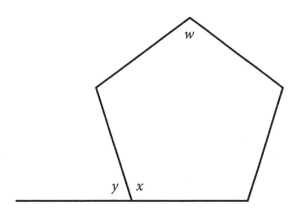

The pentagon shown is a regular polygon, meaning that all the sides are the same length and all interior angles have the same measure. In this figure, angles w and x are interior angles. Angle y is an exterior angle. This means that $m\angle x + m\angle y = 180°$ and $m\angle w + m\angle y = 180°$. (Note: The notation $m\angle x$ means the degree measure of angle x.)

3. The number of sides for a few polygons:

   - Quadrilateral – 4 sides
   - Pentagon – 5 sides
   - Hexagon – 6 sides
   - Octagon – 8 sides
   - Decagon – 10 sides

Here are a few sample questions for you to try:

1. Use the figure below to answer the question.

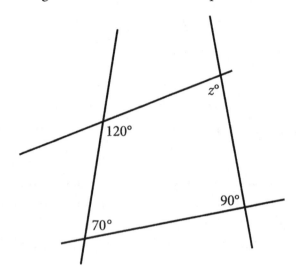

What is the value of z in the figure above?

(A) 70
(B) 75
(C) 80
(D) 90

In order to answer this question, we need to recognize that the area bounded by the lines is a quadrilateral. Once we recognize that, we know that $120 + 70 + 90 + z$ must be equal to 360, or $280 + z = 360$. In order to make this equation true, z must be equal to 80. Answer choice C is the correct answer.

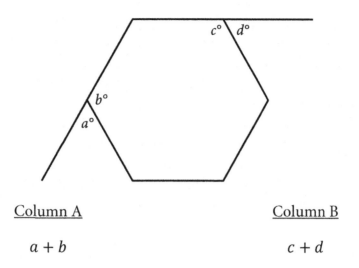

	Column A	Column B
2.	$a + b$	$c + d$

(A) Quantity in Column A is greater.

(B) Quantity in Column B is greater.

(C) Quantities in Columns A and B are equal.

(D) Not enough information to determine relationship.

In this case, angles a and b are adjacent interior and exterior angles, so they add to 180°. Angles c and d are also adjacent interior and exterior angles, so they also add to 180°. Answer choice C is correct.

The measure of an interior angle in a regular polygon is given by $\frac{180\,(n-2)}{n}$, where n is the number of sides in the polygon.

	Column A	Column B
3.	The sum of the measures of the interior angles in a regular pentagon	The sum of the measures of the interior angles in a regular hexagon

(A) Quantity in Column A is greater.

(B) Quantity in Column B is greater.

(C) The quantities in Column A and Column B are equal.

(D) Cannot be determined from information given.

Remember that this is a quantitative comparison question, so we should first evaluate whether or not we can answer this question without doing any actual math. We need to be able to compare, but we don't always need to find exact values. Let's picture a pentagon (with 5 sides) and a hexagon (with 6 sides). Can you see that each interior angle of a regular hexagon is larger than each interior angle of a regular pentagon? Each angle of a hexagon has a larger measure, and there are more interior angles in a hexagon. So even without doing the math, we know that the sum of the interior angles in a regular hexagon must be greater than the sum of the measures of the interior angles in a regular pentagon. Answer choice B is correct.

Perimeter and area

The perimeter is the distance around a figure. To find the perimeter of a polygon, simply add the side lengths together. When we are dealing with circles, we call the distance around the edge the circumference. The equation for circumference of a circle is:

circumference $= 2\pi r$, where r is the radius

Note: You may have also seen the formula written as circumference $= \pi d$, where d is the diameter. This is equivalent to the formula above since $d = 2r$.

On the Upper Level ISEE, you are unlikely to see a question that simply asks you to find the perimeter of a rectangle or the circumference of a circle. Rather, you will likely be given a shape that is a combination of the two and then asked for the distance around.

- If the question asks for the "distance around", you often have to break the figure into pieces and use the formulas for perimeter and/or circumference

Here are a couple of examples:

1. A garden is created by taking a rectangle and then adding on semi-circles to each end, as shown below. The dimensions of the center rectangle are 20 yards wide by 40 yards long.

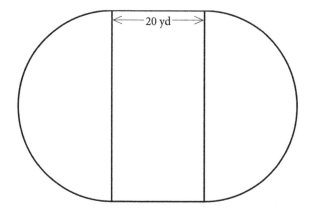

If fencing is to be placed around the outside border of this garden, how many yards of fencing will be needed?

(A) $20\pi + 40$

(B) $40\pi + 40$

(C) $40\pi + 120$

(D) $80\pi + 120$

In this question, you have to recognize that the distance around the garden will be the circumference of a full circle plus two sides of a rectangle. The diameter of the circle is equal to the length of the rectangle, or 40 yards. This means that the circumference of the circle is 40π. We can rule out choices A and D since they do not have 40π in them. Now let's add in the two sides of the rectangle, which are each 20 yards. This gives us $40\pi + 40$. Answer choice B is correct. If you chose answer choice C, you added in the sides of the rectangle that would not be part of the border of the garden.

2. In the figure below, arc *GHI* is a semi-circle.

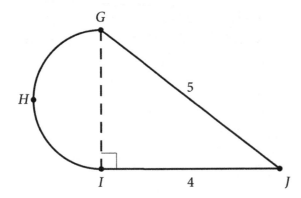

What is the perimeter of *GHIJ*?

(A) $9 + \dfrac{3\pi}{2}$

(B) $9 + 3\pi$

(C) $12 + \dfrac{3\pi}{2}$

(D) $12 + 3\pi$

The tricky part about this question is that we have to solve for the diameter of the circle. We have a right triangle, though. If we recognize that the triangle is a 3-4-5 triangle, then we know that the missing side length is 3. If you didn't see that, you can always use $a^2 + b^2 = c^2$. Just remember that the unknown length has to be a or b, because c is always the hypotenuse. Since the missing side of the triangle is also the diameter of the semi-circle, we know if it was a full circle the circumference would be 3π. We don't have a full circle, however, we only have half a circle. That means that the length of arc *GHI* is $\dfrac{3\pi}{2}$. Now we add in the two sides of the triangle that lie along the perimeter and get $\dfrac{3\pi}{2} + 4 + 5$, or $\dfrac{3\pi}{2} + 9$. Answer choice A is correct.

On the Upper Level ISEE, you will also need to know how to find the areas of rectangles, triangles, and circles. The important formulas are:

area of rectangle = length × width

area of triangle = $\dfrac{b \times h}{2}$, where b is the base and h is the height

area of circle = πr^2, where r is the length of the radius

On the Upper Level ISEE you probably won't see a question that just asks you for the area of a figure. Rather, these concepts are generally tested through "shaded region" questions. In these questions, you are asked for the area of a shaded region. The shaded region is often the result of inscribing one figure in another. The trick to these questions is that you generally have to find the area of a larger shape and then subtract off the area of a smaller shape in order to find the area of the shaded region.

- If you are asked to find the area of a shaded region, you usually have to find the area of a larger shape and then subtract the area of a smaller shape to find the area of what is left (or the shaded region)

Here are some examples of questions that test these concepts:

3. A picture frame measures 10 inches by 8 inches on the outside. Within that frame is a wood border that is $1\frac{1}{2}$ inches wide and goes all the way around the frame, as shown below.

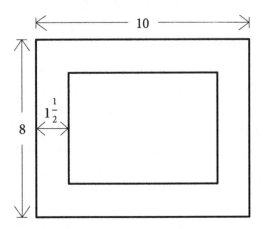

What is the area of the wood frame?

(A) $2\frac{1}{4}$ in²

(B) 24 in²

(C) 35 in²

(D) 45 in²

To answer this question, we could divide the frame into rectangular pieces and then add the areas together. We don't need to make life that hard, though. To find the area of the border, we can just find the area of the larger rectangle and then subtract off the area of the smaller rectangle within the frame. The area of the larger rectangle is 8 in × 10 in = 80 in². Now we have to figure out the dimensions of the smaller rectangle. Since there is a border that reduces each side by $1\frac{1}{2}$ inches, each dimension is actually reduced by 3 inches. This means that the dimensions of the inner rectangle are 5 inches by 7 inches, for an area of 35 in². Now we subtract the smaller rectangle from the larger rectangle (80 − 35) to get that the area of the border is 45 in². Answer choice D is correct.

A circle is inscribed in a square as shown below. The square has a side length of x and the circle has a radius of length y as shown.

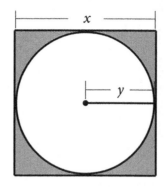

	Column A	Column B

Column A   Column B

4.   The area of the shaded $x^2 - y^2$
            region

(A)   Quantity in Column A is greater.
(B)   Quantity in Column B is greater.
(C)   Quantities in Columns A and B are equal.
(D)   Not enough information to determine relationship.

This is a shaded region problem, so our first step is to find the area of the larger shape. The only thing that is a little tricky is that we aren't given real numbers. Let's go back to the basic concept. The area of a square is s^2 where s is the side length, so the area of the square in our question is x^2. Now we need to subtract off the area of the circle that is inscribed in the square. Since the radius of the circle is y, its area is $y^2\pi$. The area of the shaded region is therefore $x^2 - y^2\pi$. Answer choice B is correct since $y^2\pi$ will always be greater than y^2, and subtracting a larger value makes the final answer smaller.

5.   In the figure below, the two semi-circles shown have a radius of 3 cm.

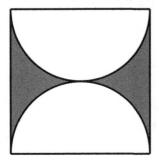

What is the area of the shaded region?

(A) $(9 - 3\pi)$ cm²

(B) $\left(18 - \dfrac{9}{2}\pi\right)$ cm²

(C) $\left(36 - \dfrac{9}{2}\pi\right)$ cm²

(D) $(36 - 9\pi)$ cm²

For this question, we have to first recognize that the side length of the square is equal to two radii, or 6. This means that the area of the square is 36 cm². Now we have to subtract off the area of the semi-circles. Since we have two semi-circles, both with a radius of 3 cm, their combined area would be same as that of a complete circle with a radius of 3 cm. The area of a circle with a radius of 3 cm is 9π cm², so the area of the shaded region is $(36 - 9\pi)$ cm². Answer choice D is correct.

Another common question type asks you to convert between perimeter or side length and area.

Here is an example of a basic problem that requires you to do this:

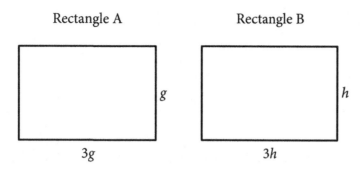

Rectangle A   Rectangle B

Note: Figures not drawn to scale.

The area of Rectangle A is 27 cm². The perimeter of Rectangle B is 24 cm.

Column A	Column B

6. g h

(A)   Quantity in Column A is greater.
(B)   Quantity in Column B is greater.
(C)   The quantities in Column A and Column B are equal.
(D)   Cannot be determined from information given.

For this question, the easy answer would be that g is larger since the area of Rectangle A is greater than the perimeter of Rectangle B. However, we know that the easy answer is often the wrong one on quantitative comparisons. We can't compare a perimeter to an area, so we need to do the actual math.

Column A:

$$\text{area of Rectangle A} = 3g \times g = 27$$
$$3g^2 = 27$$
$$g^2 = 9$$
$$g = 3$$

Column B:

$$\text{perimeter of Rectangle B} = 2(3h + h) = 24$$
$$2(4h) = 24$$
$$8h = 24$$
$$h = 3$$

We can see that the value of Column B is the same as the value of Column A, so answer choice C is correct.

You may see a question that asks you to transition between area and perimeter while also requiring you to recognize that several side length combinations can produce rectangles with the same area. For example, let's say we have a rectangle with an area of 20 cm^2, and the side lengths are measured in whole centimeters. Our dimensions could be 1 cm × 20 cm, 2 cm × 10 cm, or 4 cm × 5 cm.

- If you have to convert from area to perimeter, remember to consider all factor pairs of the area given

Here are a couple of questions for you to try:

7. Rectangle X has an area of 130 cm^2. What is the greatest possible perimeter of Rectangle X if the side lengths are whole centimeters and each side is longer than 1 cm?

   (A) 23 cm
   (B) 31 cm
   (C) 62 cm
   (D) 134 cm

Our first step is to figure out the factor pairs for 130. Let's go ahead and use a factor tree:

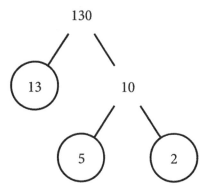

This tells us that the prime factorization of 130 is $13 \times 5 \times 2$. To find our factor pairs, we have to use every combination of these numbers. For example, one factor pair is 13 and 5×2 (or 10). Now let's try a different combination. If one member of the factor pair is 5, then the other factor is 13×2, or 26. If we continue, then the final factor pair is 65 and 2. (Note that 1 and 130 would be another factor pair, but the question states that each side is longer than 1 cm.) Now we know that if the area is 130 cm^2, then the possible combinations for dimensions are:

13 cm $\times$ 10 cm

5 cm $\times$ 26 cm

65 cm $\times$ 2 cm

We want the dimensions that give us the greatest perimeter, so we will choose 65 cm $\times$ 2 cm since those two dimensions have the greatest sum. Since the perimeter is equal to $2 \times$ (length + width), or $2 \times (65 + 2)$, the greatest perimeter is 134 cm, or answer choice D.

A garden has an area of 120 ft². A fence is to be built around the garden.

Column A	Column B

8. Number of feet of fencing needed to go around garden   64 ft

(A) Quantity in Column A is greater.
(B) Quantity in Column B is greater.
(C) The quantities in Column A and Column B are equal.
(D) Cannot be determined from information given.

Since this is a quantitative comparison, let's try out different scenarios and see what works. If the garden was 12 ft × 10 ft, then 44 ft of fencing would be needed, so the quantity in Column B would be greater. If the dimensions were 2 ft × 60 ft, however, then 124 ft of fencing would be needed, so the quantity in Column A would be greater. Since we can get either column to be greater, we have to choose answer choice D as the correct answer.

Another type of question asks you how the area of a figure is changed when its side lengths are changed. The key to this type of question is that we have to remember that area is in two dimensions, and we have to multiply these two dimensions together to figure out how the area of a figure is changed.

- We have to multiply the changes made to each side length by each other in order to figure out the change to the area

Let's take a look at the two squares below:

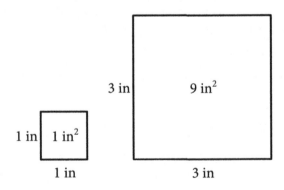

From the first square to the second square above, we tripled the side length. However, the area was not tripled. The area was multiplied by 3^2, or 9. Each side length was multiplied by three, so we had to multiply 3×3 in order to figure out how the area was changed.

Here are a couple of questions that test this concept:

9. A rectangle was enlarged by making the length $\frac{3}{2}$ as long and tripling the width. If the area of the original rectangle was R square inches, then how many square inches is the new rectangle?

   (A) $2R$

   (B) $3R$

   (C) $\frac{9}{2}R$

   (D) $9R$

   In this case, the length was multiplied by $\frac{3}{2}$ and the width was multiplied by 3. When we multiply these two together, we find that we have to multiply the old area by $\frac{9}{2}$ in order to find the new area. Answer choice C is correct.

10. The base length of a triangle was increased by 20% and the height was decreased by 30%. By what percent was the area of the triangle decreased?

    (A) 10%

    (B) 16%

    (C) 20%

    (D) 24%

    This question is a little trickier since one dimension is being increased and the other is being decreased. Since this is a percent question, however, we can just make up our own numbers. We will make each of the dimensions 10 to start with in order to make the percentages easier. If we increase the base by 20%, then the new base length would be 12. If we decrease the height by 30% the new height would be 7. Now let's compare the areas of these figures:

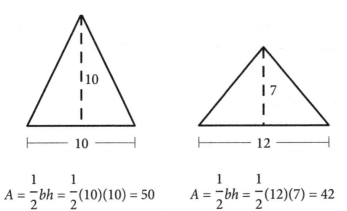

$$A = \frac{1}{2}bh = \frac{1}{2}(10)(10) = 50 \qquad A = \frac{1}{2}bh = \frac{1}{2}(12)(7) = 42$$

Now we can see that the area was originally 50 but was reduced by 8 when the dimensions were changed. Now we just need to convert that into a percent:

$$\text{percent decreased} = \frac{\text{change}}{\text{original}} = \frac{8}{50} = \frac{16}{100}$$

We can see that the area was reduced by 16%, or answer choice B.

Volume

On the Upper Level ISEE, if you are asked for the volume of a three-dimensional figure other than a prism, you will be given the equation for volume of that shape. Generally, there will be some figuring that needs to be done other than just plugging numbers into the volume formula. Just like with any other word problem, follow each step carefully.

- The questions will give you the formulas for volumes of cones, cylinders, spheres, and pyramids if you need them
- Follow the wording carefully – you will probably have to solve for at least one variable

You may also see questions that ask you how volume will be affected if the dimensions of a three-dimensional figure are changed. These are similar to the area questions that we saw before, except we have to remember that there are three dimensions and not two.

- If you have to figure out the effect on volume when side lengths are changed, then remember that you will have multiply the change in three dimensions, not two

Here are a couple of examples:

1. The cone shown below has a diameter of 6 cm. Its height is $\frac{3}{2}$ times its diameter.

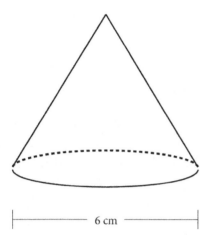

6 cm

If the volume of a cone can be found using the formula $V = \frac{1}{3}r^2h\pi$, then what is the volume of the cone shown above?

(A) 27π cm^3

(B) 81π cm^3

(C) 108π cm^3

(D) 324π cm^3

In order to use the formula given, we first have to do a couple of calculations. First, the question tells us that the height is $\frac{3}{2}$ times the diameter. Since the diameter is 6 cm, this means that the height is 9 cm. Now if we look at the formula, we can see that it uses radius, but we are given diameter. The radius is equal to half of the diameter, so the radius of the cone is 3 cm. Now we can plug into the formula:

$$V = \frac{1}{3}r^2h\pi = \frac{1}{3}(3^2)(9)\pi = 27\pi$$

Choice A is correct.

2.   A cube has a volume of V cubic inches. Each of the side lengths is doubled. Which expression correctly represents the volume, in cubic inches, of this new cube?

(A) $2V$

(B) $3V$

(C) $4V$

(D) $8V$

Perhaps the easiest way to answer this question is to come up with our own example. Let's start out with a cube that is 1 inch × 1 inch × 1 inch. The volume of this cube is 1 in³. Now let's double the lengths of all of the sides. The dimensions of our new cube are 2 inches × 2 inches × 2 inches, so the volume of this new cube is 8 in³. We can see that doubling the side lengths led to a volume that was 8 times larger. Answer choice D is the correct answer.

Coordinate geometry

Coordinate geometry uses a grid. The important thing to remember about points on a coordinate grid is that the x-coordinate is given first and then the y-coordinate. Ordered pairs are written (x, y). If you have trouble remembering what comes first, just think "first you run, then you jump".

Here is an example:

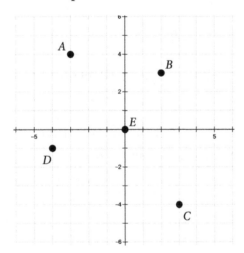

In the coordinate grid above, there are several points plotted.

On this grid, we would call point E the origin. The coordinates of point E are $(0, 0)$.

The coordinates of point B are $(2, 3)$ because we go over 2 and up 3 to get to point B from the origin.

If we have to go to the left of the origin, then the x-coordinate is a negative number. If we have to go down (instead of up), then the y-coordinate is negative.

Therefore, the coordinates of point A are $(-3, 4)$.

What are the coordinates of point D?

We have to go the left 4 spots to get from the origin to point D, so the x-coordinate is -4. We then have to go down 1 place, so the y-coordinate of point D is -1. We write the coordinates of point D as $(-4, -1)$.

What about point C?

Let's remember to run then jump. To get from the origin to point C, we have to go 3 places to the right in the positive direction and then go down 4 places in the negative direction. The coordinates of point C are $(3, -4)$.

You may see a question on the Upper Level ISEE that combines coordinate geometry with polygon definitions.

Here are a few examples for you to try:

1. Jackie plots the points $(1, 2), (2, 3), (4, 3)$, and $(5, 2)$. She then connects these points to make a quadrilateral. Which term could describe that quadrilateral?

    (A) square
    (B) diamond
    (C) hexagon
    (D) trapezoid

    The best way to answer this question is to draw our own grid. It does not have to be exact since we are just looking for a rough idea of where the points are in relation to one another.

Your grid should look something like this:

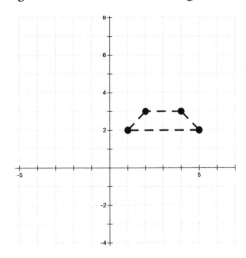

We can see that the shape is clearly not a square or a diamond, so we can rule out choices A and B. Choice C, a hexagon, is not even a quadrilateral, so it can be eliminated. Answer choice D is the correct answer.

2. Harriet is drawing a rhombus on the grid below. She has plotted three of the vertices.

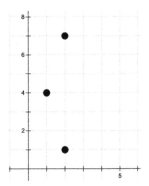

What are the coordinates of the fourth vertex of her rhombus?

(A) $(3, 4)$

(B) $(4, 3)$

(C) $(5, 4)$

(D) $(5, 7)$

Let's think about the definition of a rhombus. In a rhombus, all four sides are the same length, and opposite sides are parallel. We can see that to get from the vertex $(1, 4)$ to the vertex $(2, 7)$ we have to go over 1 and up 3. That means that to find our fourth vertex, we need to start at the vertex $(2, 1)$ and go over 1 and up 3. This gets us to the point $(3, 4)$ as shown:

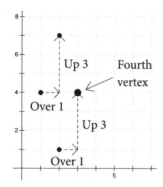

Answer choice A is the correct answer.

3.   In the figure below, point O is the center of a circle. Point A is on that circle.

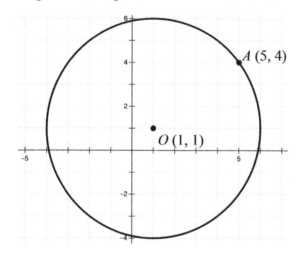

What is the radius of this circle?

(A)   2 grid units
(B)   3 grid units
(C)   4 grid units
(D)   5 grid units

If we connect points O and A, we can see that the distance between these two points is also a radius of the circle. The easiest way to figure out the distance between two points on a grid is to create a right triangle and then use the Pythagorean Theorem:

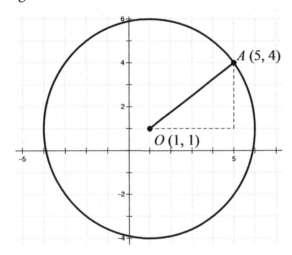

We can count the grid spaces and see that the base of the triangle is 4 grid units and the height of the triangle is 3 grid units. Since we are trying to solve for the hypotenuse $(\overline{AO})$, we can use $a^2 + b^2 = c^2$:

$$3^2 + 4^2 = c^2$$

$$25 = c^2$$

$$5 = c$$

We now know that the length of $\overline{AO}$ is 5, so the radius of the circle must also be 5. Answer choice D is correct.

Note: You may have also used the distance formula to answer this question. The distance formula is derived from the Pythagorean Theorem, however, so as long as you create a right triangle, you don't need to memorize the distance formula. Also, you may have recognized that the triangle is a 3-4-5 triangle. If the two legs of a right triangle are 3 and 4, then the hypotenuse will be 5. It saves a little work if you recognize this, but you will never get the wrong answer by completing the calculation using the Pythagorean Theorem.

Slope and equations of lines

On the ISEE, you will need to know the following about equations of lines:

- $y = mx + b$
- What slope is and what it really means
- How to rearrange an equation to find slope
- How to use two points to find slope
- How the slopes of perpendicular and parallel lines are related
- How to come up with an equation when you are given point(s) and/or slope
- What the y-intercept is and what it really means

The basic equation of a line

There are different ways that you can write the equation of a line. The most useful way to write the equation of a line on the ISEE is to use slope-intercept form. The basic form for slope-intercept is:

$y = mx + b$, where m is equal to the slope and b is equal to the y-intercept

The y-intercept is the point on the y-axis that the line crosses, or where the line intercepts the y-axis.

What slope is and what it really means

Slope tells us how y-values change as x-values change. You can think of slope as telling us how "steep" a line is. You can also say that slope describes the rate of change. Another description of slope is rise over run.

For example:

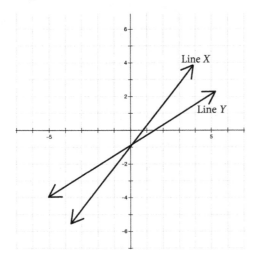

In the above diagram, Line X has a greater slope than Line Y. This means that the rate of change is greater for Line X than for Line Y.

Slope can be positive or negative. If slope is positive, that means that as x-values increase, y-values also increase. If slope is negative, that means that as x-values increase, y-values decrease.

For example:

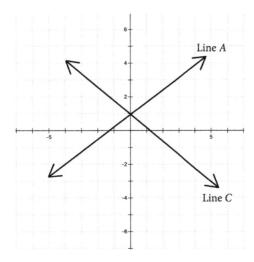

On the above coordinate graph, Line A has a positive slope and Line C has a negative slope.

Here is an example of how slope could be tested on the ISEE:

4.   For which of the following functions do the y-values decrease at the greatest rate as x-values increase?

(A)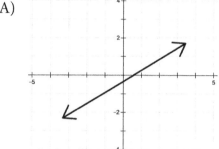

(B)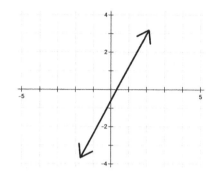

(C)

(D)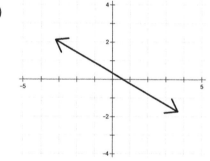

First we need to decide whether the slope we are looking for is positive or negative. Since the question says that the y-values decrease as the x-values increase, we know that the slope must be negative. That means that choices A and B cannot be the correct answer, because they both show functions with positive slope. We are down to choices C and D. Now we are looking for the function that changes at the greatest rate. Another way to say that is we are looking for the line that is steepest. Answer choice C is correct.

Here is another one for you to try:

5. For which of the following functions do the y-values increase at the lowest rate as x-values increase?

(A)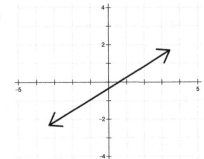

(B)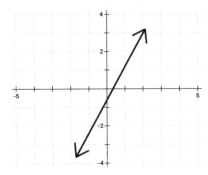

(C)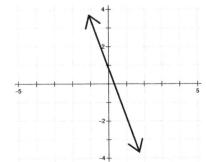

(D)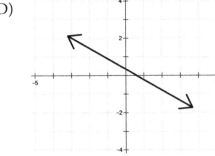

The question says that as the y-values increase, the x-values also increase, which means that we are looking for a positive slope. That means we can rule out C and D.

Now we are looking at choices A and B and need to choose the one that increases at the lowest rate, or has the smaller slope. Answer choice A is the correct answer.

How to rearrange an equation to find slope

Some questions on the ISEE will ask you rearrange an equation in order to find the slope.

The easiest way to do this is to use the rules of isolating a variable in order to get the equation into the form:

$$y = mx + b$$

Think of it like any other equation where you are trying to get y by itself.

Here are a couple of examples of questions that ask you to find slope:

6. What is the slope of the line with the equation $2x + 7y = 1$?

(A) $\dfrac{2}{7}$

(B) 2

(C) $-\dfrac{2}{7}$

(D) -2

To find the slope, we have to get the equation into the form $y = mx + b$, where m is the slope. This basically means that we need to get y by itself.

$$2x + 7y = 1$$
$$-2x \qquad\quad - 2x$$
$$7y = -2x + 1$$
$$\div 7 \quad\ \div 7$$
$$y = -\dfrac{2}{7}x + \dfrac{1}{7}$$

Now that we have the equation in the form $y = mx + b$, we can easily see that the slope is $-\dfrac{2}{7}$ and answer choice C is correct.

Here is another one for you to try:

7. What is the slope of the line with the equation $5x - 2y = 15$?

(A) $\dfrac{2}{5}$

(B) $-\dfrac{5}{2}$

(C) 2

(D) $\dfrac{5}{2}$

Again, we have to get the equation in the form $y = mx + b$.

$$5x - 2y = 15$$
$$-5x \qquad\quad -5x$$
$$-2y = -5x + 15$$
$$\div(-2) \quad \div(-2)$$
$$y = \frac{5}{2}x - \frac{15}{2}$$

Since our equation is now in $y = mx + b$ form, we can clearly see that the slope is $\frac{5}{2}$. Choice D is correct.

How to use two points to find slope

Another way to find slope is to use two points. Slope can be described as:

$$\frac{\text{rise}}{\text{run}}$$

This means that slope is equal to how far the line goes up over how far it moves to the side.

Here is an example:

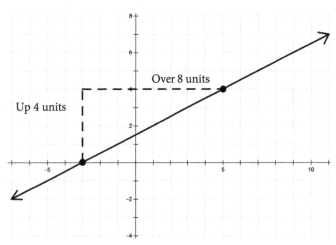

If you look at the line above, you can see that to go from one chosen point to the other chosen point, we have to go up 4 units and over 8 units.

Remember that slope is equal to:

$$\frac{\text{rise}}{\text{run}} = \frac{4}{8} = \frac{1}{2}$$

From this, we can see that the slope is $\frac{1}{2}$.

If we are given two points not on a graph, we can turn rise over run into a usable equation:

$$\frac{\text{rise}}{\text{run}} = \frac{\text{difference in } y\text{-coordinates}}{\text{difference in } x\text{-coordinates}} = \frac{y_1 - y_2}{x_1 - x_2}$$

Here is an example of how you may have to apply this on the ISEE:

8.   What is the slope between the points $(5, 4)$ and $(3, 7)$?

(A) $-\dfrac{3}{2}$

(B) $\dfrac{3}{2}$

(C) $-\dfrac{2}{3}$

(D) $\dfrac{2}{3}$

To find the answer, we need to plug into our equation:

$$\frac{y_1 - y_2}{x_1 - x_2} = \frac{4 - 7}{5 - 3} = \frac{-3}{2}$$

Answer choice A is correct.

Now here is an example of a question that combines what you have learned about finding slope:

	Column A	Column B
9.	The slope of $3x - 5y = 7$	The slope between $(6, 2)$ and $(1, 5)$

(A) Quantity in Column A is greater.
(B) Quantity in Column B is greater.
(C) The quantities in Column A and Column B are equal.
(D) Cannot be determined from information given.

Our first step is to find the slope of the line in Column A. In order to do that, we need to get it into the form $y = mx + b$. Here is what the math looks like:

$$3x - 5y = 7$$
$$-3x \qquad -3x$$
$$-5y = -3x + 7$$
$$\div (-5) \quad \div (-5)$$
$$y = \frac{3}{5}x - \frac{7}{5}$$

From this, we can see that the slope of the line in Column A is $\frac{3}{5}$.

Now we have to use the two points in Column B to find the slope between them. Here is what the math looks like:

$$\frac{y_1 - y_2}{x_1 - x_2} = \frac{2 - 5}{6 - 1} = -\frac{3}{5}$$

We can now see that the slope in Column A is $\frac{3}{5}$ and the slope in Column B is $-\frac{3}{5}$. The correct answer is A.

How the slopes of perpendicular and parallel lines are related

If two lines are parallel, then they have the same slope.

Here is how this could be tested on the ISEE:

10.   The graph below shows line l.

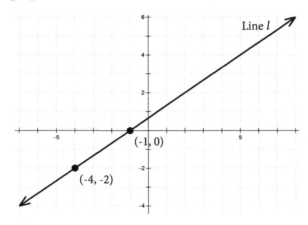

Which of the following lines is parallel to line l?

(A) $y = -\dfrac{2}{3}x + 4$

(B) $y = -\dfrac{2}{5}x - 5$

(C) $y = \dfrac{2}{3}x + 2$

(D) $y = \dfrac{2}{5}x + 3$

Our first step is to figure out the slope of line l. We are given two points that are on that line.

Since we have a picture, we can count rise over run:

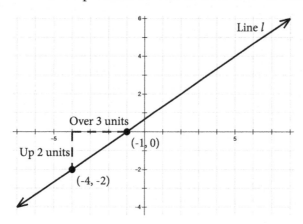

From this, we can see that the slope of line l is $\frac{2}{3}$. Now we have to look at the answer choices to see which one has a slope of $\frac{2}{3}$. Answer choice C is correct.

If two lines are perpendicular, then their slopes are negative reciprocals. This means that if you flip the numerator and denominator of the slope of a line and add a negative sign, you will then have the slope of a line that is perpendicular to the first line.

Here are some examples:

If $m = \frac{2}{3}$, then a perpendicular line would have $m = -\frac{3}{2}$

If $m = 2$, then a perpendicular line would have $m = -\frac{1}{2}$

If $m = -\frac{1}{3}$, then a perpendicular line would have $m = 3$

Here is an example of a question that tests the concept of the slopes of perpendicular lines:

11. The graph below shows line m.

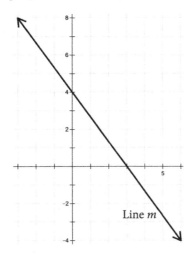

Which of the following could be the equation of a line that is perpendicular to m?

(A) $y = -\dfrac{4}{3}x + 3$

(B) $y = -\dfrac{3}{4}x + 7$

(C) $y = \dfrac{4}{3}x + 6$

(D) $y = \dfrac{3}{4}x + 5$

Line m goes through the points $(0, 4)$ and $(3, 0)$. If we count $\dfrac{\text{rise}}{\text{run}}$, we see that the slope of m is $-\dfrac{4}{3}$. A perpendicular line would have a slope of $\dfrac{3}{4}$, which is the slope of answer choice D. D is the correct answer.

How to come up with an equation when you are given point(s) and/or slope

You may be given two points and then asked to find the equation of a line. You may also be given a point and the slope and then asked to find the equation of a line.

Here are the basic steps:

1. Solve for slope (if it is not given)
2. Set up the equation $y = mx + b$
3. Plug the x and y values from one point into the equation for x and y, and also plug in the slope for m
4. Use this equation to solve for b
5. Rewrite $y = mx + b$ by plugging in the values you found for m (slope) and b (y-intercept) – your final equation should have x and y in it

Here is an example of how this question could be asked on the ISEE:

12. Line s has a slope of $\frac{3}{2}$ and goes through the point $(4, 6)$. What is the equation of line s?

   (A) $y = \frac{3}{2}x$

   (B) $y = \frac{3}{2}x + 6$

   (C) $y = 4x + \frac{3}{2}$

   (D) $y = 3x + \frac{3}{2}$

   We are given slope, so we can jump right to setting up our equation.

   $$y = mx + b$$

   Now we substitute in the values that were given for slope, x, and y.

   $$6 = \frac{3}{2} \times 4 + b$$

   Now we solve for b.

   $$6 = 6 + b$$

   $$0 = b$$

Since $b = 0$, we now know that the equation of the line is $y = \frac{3}{2}x$, and answer choice A is correct.

Here is an example of a problem where you first have to solve for slope.

13. Line g runs through the points $(-2, 3)$ and $(2, 7)$. What is the equation of line g?

(A) $y = 4x + 5$

(B) $y = x + 5$

(C) $y = \frac{1}{4}x + 5$

(D) $y = \frac{2}{3}x + 4$

In this question, we are not given slope, so we must first solve for it.

$$\text{slope} = \frac{y_1 - y_2}{x_1 - x_2} = \frac{3 - 7}{-2 - 2} = \frac{-4}{-4} = 1$$

Now that we have found that the slope is 1, we can plug into $y = mx + b$ and then solve for b. When we are given two points, we can pick either one of them to plug into the equation. It does not matter which one we pick.

$y = mx + b$

$7 = 1 \times 2 + b$

$7 = 2 + b$

$5 = b$

When we plug back into $y = mx + b$, we can see that the equation of our line is $y = x + 5$, so answer choice B is correct.

Now here is a problem that combines a lot of what you have learned about slope:

14. The graph below shows $\overline{XY}$.

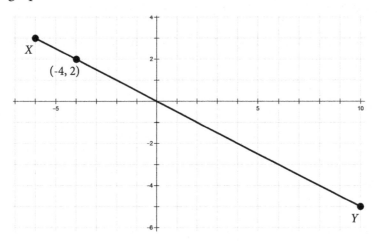

Line d is perpendicular to $\overline{XY}$ at the point $(8, -4)$. What is the equation of d?

(A) $y = -\dfrac{1}{2}x + 12$

(B) $y = -\dfrac{1}{2}x - 20$

(C) $y = 2x + 12$

(D) $y = 2x - 20$

First, we have to find the slope of $\overline{XY}$ from the picture. We can see that the segment goes through the point $(-4, 2)$ and the origin $(0,0)$. If we count down and then over, we get that the slope of $\overline{XY}$ is $-\dfrac{1}{2}$. This means that the slope of d is 2, and either answer choice C or D must be correct. Now we have to determine if the y-intercept is positive or negative. If we sketch in a line that is perpendicular to $\overline{XY}$ at the point $(8, -4)$, we can clearly see that the y-intercept has to be negative. Answer choice D is correct.

What the y-intercept is and what it really means

In literal terms, the y-intercept is where a line crosses the y-axis. What it represents, however, is the non-variable part of an equation. It can also represent the starting point if the graph is showing how something changes as time progresses.

Here are some examples:

- The cost of printing books is a $500 set up fee plus $2 per book. If we were to graph this, the y-intercept would be 500 since that is the fixed cost. The slope would then be 2 since that is the variable cost.
- If we were plotting the temperature throughout the day, starting at 12 AM, then the y-intercept would represent the temperature at 12 AM.

Here is an example of how this could be tested on the ISEE:

15. The cost (in dollars) for renting a truck, c, depends upon how miles, m, the renter drives the truck. To figure out the total cost, the formula $c = 2.5m + 100$ can be used. What is the meaning of the 100 in this formula?

    (A) for every 100 miles driven, it costs one dollar

    (B) for every 1 mile driven, it costs $100

    (C) when the truck is driven 0 miles, the cost is $100

    (D) when 100 miles are driven the cost is $2.50

    Since the y-intercept represents the fixed cost, choices A, B, and D can be eliminated. Choice C is correct.

Scale

You may see a question on the Upper Level ISEE that asks you to apply the concept of scale. These questions are easy to answer – just use a proportion. The key is to label the top and bottom of each fraction so that you can be sure that you are plugging numbers into the right places.

- Use a proportion to answer scale questions
- Label each part of the proportion to keep it all straight

Here are a couple of examples:

1. Eric is building a boat model to scale. The length of the actual boat is 32 meters, and the length of Eric's model is 25 centimeters. If the width of the actual boat is 20 meters, what is the width of Eric's model?

    (A) 14 cm

    (B) $15\dfrac{5}{8}$ cm

    (C) 17 cm

    (D) $20\dfrac{1}{2}$ cm

    In order to answer this question, we need to set up a proportion, being sure to include units:

    $$\frac{25 \text{ cm}}{32 \text{ m}} = \frac{x \text{ cm}}{20 \text{ m}}$$

    Now we can cross-multiply to solve:

    $$25 \times 20 = 32 \times x$$

    $$500 = 32x$$

    $$15\frac{5}{8} = x$$

    Answer choice B is correct.

2. The diagram below shows a scaled map of the library, school, and park.

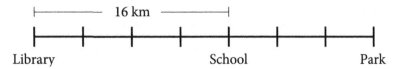

How many kilometers is it from the school to the park?

(A) 9 km

(B) 10 km

(C) 12 km

(D) 28 km

For this question, we can first determine the scale and then use that, or we can set up a direct proportion. There are 4 segments between the library and the school, and there are 3 segments between the school and the park.

$$\frac{4 \text{ segments}}{16 \text{ km}} = \frac{3 \text{ segments}}{x \text{ km}}$$

Now we can cross-multiply:

$$4 \times x = 16 \times 3$$

$$4x = 48$$

$$x = 12$$

Answer choice C is correct.

Appropriate units

You may see a question that asks you which unit should be used for a particular measurement. These questions are pretty straightforward and not very common, so we will just do a couple of sample questions:

1. What would be the most appropriate unit for measuring the mass of an apple?

    (A) liters
    (B) meters
    (C) grams
    (D) kilograms

    Our first step is to rule out choices A and B since liters and meters are not even units of mass. Now we have to think about which is more appropriate, grams or kilograms. An apple is relatively light, so grams is more appropriate. Answer choice C is correct.

2. What is the most appropriate unit for measuring the length of a field?

    (A) inches
    (B) pounds
    (C) quarts
    (D) yards

    We can rule out choices B and C because they are not units of length. It would take us a long time to try to measure a field in inches. A yard is a larger unit of length, so it is the more appropriate unit. Answer choice D is correct.

Unit conversions

You may also see questions that require you to convert between different units. These questions will generally give you the conversions, but you will need to know what to do with them.

*   You will generally be given the conversions

There are two things you should know to answer this type of question:

1. We want units to cancel

    For example, let's say we want to convert 50 miles per hour into miles per minute:

    $$\frac{50 \text{ miles}}{1 \text{ hour}} \times \frac{1 \text{ hour}}{60 \text{ minutes}} = \frac{5}{6} \text{ miles per minute}$$

2. We can write a unit conversion in whatever way we need to make units cancel

    For example, let's say we wanted to convert 9 yards into feet. The conversion factor given is 1 yard = 3 feet.

    $$9 \text{ yards } \times \frac{3 \text{ feet}}{1 \text{ yard}} = 27 \text{ feet}$$

    In this case we wrote the conversion factor as $\frac{3 \text{ feet}}{1 \text{ yard}}$ so that the yards would cancel and leave us with feet.

On the Upper Level ISEE, conversions are likely to be tested in multi-step problems. Here are a couple of questions for you to try:

1. A car is traveling at a speed of 30 miles per hour. If there are 1,760 yards in a mile, which expression could be used to figure out how fast the car is travelling in yards per second?

    (A) $\dfrac{30 \times 1,760}{60 \times 60}$

    (B) $\dfrac{30 \times 60}{1,760 \times 60}$

    (C) $\dfrac{60 \times 1,760}{30 \times 60}$

    (D) $\dfrac{30 \times 1,760}{60}$

We are going to use our two principles (making sure that the units cancel and writing the conversion factors to make that happen):

$$\frac{30 \text{ miles}}{1 \text{ hour}} \times \frac{1,760 \text{ yards}}{1 \text{ mile}} \times \frac{1 \text{ hour}}{60 \text{ minutes}} \times \frac{1 \text{ minute}}{60 \text{ seconds}}$$
$$= \frac{30 \times 1,760 \text{ yards}}{60 \times 60 \text{ seconds}}$$

We set up our expression so that miles, hours, and minutes would cancel and leave us with yards per second, which is what the question asks for. Keep in mind that we also had to go through an intermediary step. We had to go from hours to minutes to seconds. Answer choice A is the correct answer.

2. A rocket is travelling at a speed of 300 meters per second. There are 0.305 meters in one foot and 5,280 feet in one mile. Which expression could be used to find the rocket's speed in miles per hour?

(A) $\dfrac{300 \times 60}{0.305 \times 5,280 \times 60}$

(B) $\dfrac{0.305 \times 60 \times 60}{300 \times 5,280}$

(C) $\dfrac{300 \times 0.305}{60 \times 5,280}$

(D) $\dfrac{300 \times 60 \times 60}{0.305 \times 5,280}$

Let's use the same method here. We will start with what we have and then set up conversion factors so that the units cancel to leave us with miles per hour:

$$\frac{300 \text{ m}}{1 \text{ sec}} \times \frac{60 \text{ sec}}{1 \text{ min}} \times \frac{60 \text{ min}}{1 \text{ hr}} \times \frac{1 \text{ ft}}{0.305 \text{ m}} \times \frac{1 \text{ mile}}{5,280 \text{ ft}}$$

If we then cancel units, we are left with:

$$\frac{300 \times 60 \times 60 \text{ miles}}{0.305 \times 5,280 \text{ hours}}$$

Answer choice D is correct.

Unit conversions with area

Earlier, we discussed how if we do something like doubling the side lengths in rectangle, the area will not be doubled. It will be multiplied by 2^2.

A related concept is that we have to square unit conversion factors when we are dealing with area.

For example, let's say we have a square that is 1 foot on each side:

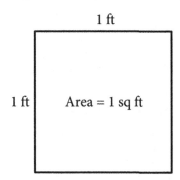

The area of this square is 1 square foot. There are 12 inches in a foot. Let's see what happens when we determine how many square inches are in this square:

1 ft = 12 in

1 ft = 12 in   Area = 144 sq in

The area of the square is not 12 square inches, rather it is 144 square inches.

Here are a couple of questions that test this concept:

3.   A rectangular room is 10 feet by 15 feet. About how many square yards of carpet would be needed to cover the floor of this room? (3 feet = 1 yard)

(A)   15

(B)   17

(C)   50

(D)   150

If we multiply the dimensions of the room, we find that the area of the floor is 150 sq ft. Now we have to remember that while 1 yard equals 3 feet, 1 square yard actually equals 9 square feet. We can then use a proportion to solve:

$$\frac{1 \text{ sq yd}}{9 \text{ sq ft}} = \frac{x \text{ sq yd}}{150 \text{ sq ft}}$$

Now we can cross-multiply:

$$1 \times 150 = 9 \times x$$

$$150 = 9x$$

From here, if we do the calculation, we find that x is equal to a little more than 16, but not quite 17. Since the question asks for "about" how many square yards of carpet are needed, answer choice B is the correct answer.

4.   The cost of a certain fabric is $3 per square foot. If a piece of this fabric is 18 inches by 36 inches, how much would it cost?

(A) $4.50

(B) $13.50

(C) $16.20

(D) $162.00

In this case, the cost is given by the square foot, so we need to figure out how many square feet of fabric we have. By converting the inches into feet, we get that the piece of fabric is 1.5 ft × 3ft. When we multiply these dimensions, we get that area of the fabric is 4.5 sq ft. Now we multiply 4.5 × $3 to get a total cost of $13.50. Answer choice B is correct.

Geometry & Measurement Practice Set

Column A	Column B

1. The slope of $4y - 3x = 10$ The slope between $(1, 2)$ and $(5, 5)$

    (A) Quantity in Column A is greater.

    (B) Quantity in Column B is greater.

    (C) The quantities in Column A and Column B are equal.

    (D) Cannot be determined from information given.

2. The cost (in dollars), c, of getting groceries delivered is given by the formula $c = 0.2p + 10$, where p is pounds of food. Which of the following statements correctly describes how much it costs to get groceries delivered?

    (A) For every 10 pounds of food delivered, it costs $0.20

    (B) The fixed cost for a delivery is $10 plus $0.20 per pound of food

    (C) It costs $10 to have any amount of food delivered

    (D) It costs $10.20 to have 20 pounds of food delivered

3.   What is the slope of a line that is parallel to the line $7x + 2y = 8$?

(A) $-\dfrac{7}{2}$

(B) $\dfrac{7}{2}$

(C) $-\dfrac{2}{7}$

(D) $\dfrac{2}{7}$

4.   The pattern below can be folded to create a prism.

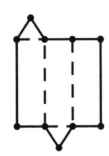

Which prism could result from the above figure being folded?

(A)      (B)

(C)   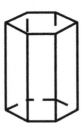   (D)

5. The coordinate points $(2, 6)$, $(3, 8)$, $(4, 6)$, and $(3, 1)$ are connected to form a quadrilateral. What term would best describe this quadrilateral?

    (A) square
    (B) kite
    (C) trapezoid
    (D) rhombus

6. The graph below shows line n.

    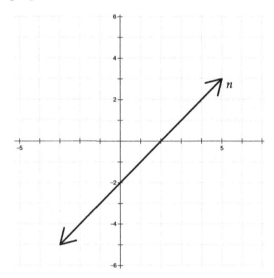

    What is the equation of the line that is perpendicular to n at $(4, 2)$?

    (A) $y = x - 6$
    (B) $y = x + 6$
    (C) $y = -x - 6$
    (D) $y = -x + 6$

7. Which equation shows the greatest increase in y-values as x-values increase?

(A) $y = 2x + 5$

(B) $y = \dfrac{1}{2}x + 5$

(C) $y = -\dfrac{1}{2}x + 5$

(D) $y = -2x + 5$

Column A	Column B

8. $a + b$ $q + r$

(A) Quantity in Column A is greater.
(B) Quantity in Column B is greater.
(C) The quantities in Column A and Column B are equal.
(D) Cannot be determined from information given.

9.   The figure below shows a regular hexagon.

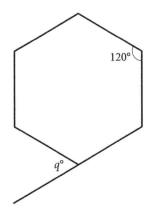

What is the value of *q*?

(A) 60

(B) 70

(C) 85

(D) 90

The area of a rectangle is 90 cm²

Column A	Column B
10. The perimeter of the rectangle	180 cm

(A) Quantity in Column A is greater.

(B) Quantity in Column B is greater.

(C) The quantities in Column A and Column B are equal.

(D) Cannot be determined from information given.

11. Triangle *GHI* is similar to triangle *XYZ*, as shown below.

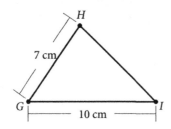 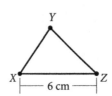

What is the length of $\overline{XY}$?

(A) 3 cm

(B) $3\frac{1}{2}$ cm

(C) $4\frac{1}{5}$ cm

(D) 5 cm

12. The cylinder shown below has a diameter equal to half of its height.

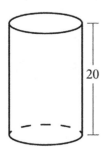

If the volume of a cylinder can be found using the formula $V = \pi r^2 h$, then what is the volume of the cylinder shown above?

(A) 25π

(B) 100π

(C) 250π

(D) 500π

13. The figure below was created by combining a right triangle with a semi-circle. The length of $\overline{AB}$ is 6 cm and the length of $\overline{AD}$ is 8 cm, as shown.

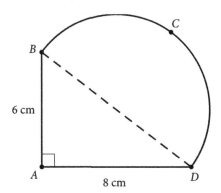

What is the perimeter of this figure?

(A) $14 + 5\pi$

(B) $14 + 10\pi$

(C) $24 + 10\pi$

(D) $24 + 25\pi$

14. The scale on a map shows that 3 cm is equal to 50 miles. If two towns are 5 cm apart on the map, about how far apart are they in reality?

(A) 83 miles

(B) 96 miles

(C) 110 miles

(D) 150 miles

15. A rectangular room has the dimensions 12 feet by 16 feet. If carpet costs $3 per square yard installed, about how much would it cost to install carpet in this room? (3 feet = 1 yard)

(A) $22

(B) $64

(C) $192

(D) $576

16. The figure below shows a square with side length of 4 inscribed in a circle.

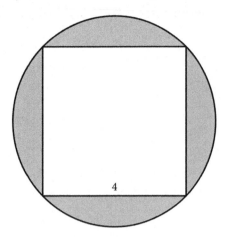

What is the area of the shaded region?

(A) $8\pi - 16$

(B) $16\pi - 16$

(C) $32\pi - 16$

(D) $32\pi - 32$

17. What is the equation of a line that is perpendicular to $4x + 2y = 8$ at the point $(3, -2)$?

(A) $y = -\dfrac{1}{2}x - 3\dfrac{1}{2}$

(B) $y = \dfrac{1}{2}x - 3\dfrac{1}{2}$

(C) $y = -\dfrac{1}{2}x + 3\dfrac{1}{2}$

(D) $y = \dfrac{1}{2}x + 3\dfrac{1}{2}$

18. The length of a rectangle was increased by 10% and the width of the rectangle was decreased by 20%. By what percent was the area of the rectangle decreased?

(A) 8%

(B) 10%

(C) 12%

(D) 15%

19. Which would be the most appropriate unit for measuring the height of a large tree?

(A) millimeters

(B) gallons

(C) kilometers

(D) meters

20. A car is traveling at the speed of 40 miles per hour. If there are 5,280 feet in one mile, which expression could be used to find the car's speed in feet per second?

(A) $\dfrac{40 \times 60 \times 5,280}{60 \times 60}$

(B) $\dfrac{40 \times 60}{5,280 \times 60}$

(C) $\dfrac{40 \times 5,280}{60 \times 60}$

(D) $\dfrac{40 \times 5,280}{60}$

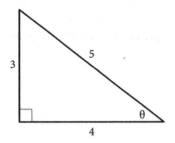

Column A	Column B

21. $\sin \theta$ $\cos \theta$

(A)   Quantity in Column A is greater.

(B)   Quantity in Column B is greater.

(C)   The quantities in Column A and Column B are equal.

(D)   Cannot be determined from information given.

Answers to Geometry & Measurement Practice Set

1. C
2. B
3. A
4. B
5. B
6. D
7. A
8. C
9. A
10. D
11. C

12. D
13. A
14. A
15. B
16. A
17. B
18. C
19. D
20. C
21. B

Data Analysis & Probability

Some of the most challenging math problems on the Upper Level ISEE are the questions involving the interpretation of data and figuring out probabilities. The good news is that the concepts themselves are relatively straightforward.

The question types we will cover include:

- Different types of graphs
- Central tendencies in data
- Basic probability
- Probability with multiple events
- Complementary events

Different types of graphs

We will start by going over the different types of graphs that you are likely to see on the Upper Level ISEE. You won't be asked to identify the type of a graph, but you will be asked to interpret data in various formats.

Types of graphs you need to know:

- Bar graph
- Histogram
- Stem and leaf plot
- Line graph
- Scatter plot
- Circle graph
- Box-and-whisker plot (we will cover this type in the central tendencies section)

Bar graph

A bar graph is great way to compare data. It allows you to easily see data recorded at different times.

One important detail that you always want to look for is the scale on the left side. You may need to figure out a data value that doesn't fall exactly on a line, so you will need to know the scale in order to figure out the data value.

- Always check the scale on a bar graph before answering any questions about it

Sometimes it is also hard to tell exactly where a bar falls if it is far away from the numbers on the y-axis. If you are finding this difficult, use the side of your answer sheet to trace across a straight line to the axis.

- If you are having trouble figuring out how a bar corresponds to the numbers on the y-axis, use the side of your answer sheet to trace across

Here is an example of how you might see bar graphs on the ISEE:

1. The graph below shows how many cars a dealership sold in each month.

Number of sales

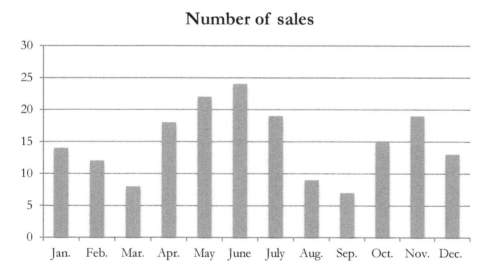

According to the graph, how many more cars were sold in June than in January?

- (A) 2
- (B) 5
- (C) 10
- (D) 14

The important thing to keep in mind here is the scale. The scale shows us that each line delineates 5 cars sold. The graph shows that in January, just under 15 cars were sold. In June, just under 25 cars were sold. That makes the difference around 10 cars, so answer choice C is correct.

Histogram

A histogram looks a lot like a bar graph. The difference is that while a bar graph generally gives you data points arranged in some sort of chronological order, a histogram shows you how data is clustered, or distributed, instead. It groups numbers into ranges.

- Bar graphs tend to be chronological, histograms show how data is distributed
- Histograms group data into ranges

Here is an example of how you could see histograms on the ISEE:

2. A student took a survey of the ages of the residents on her street. The range of ages of the residents on her street are shown in the histogram below.

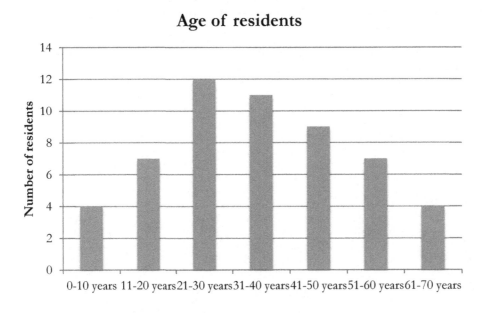

Which of the following age groups has the greatest number of residents?

(A) 0-20 years old
(B) 21-30 years old
(C) 31-50 years old
(D) 51-70 years old

In order to answer this question, we have to be careful to not jump on the obvious answer. Since the biggest bar on the histogram is for the age range of 21-30 years old, it is tempting to choose B. However, the other answer choices require you to combine more than one range from the histogram. For answer choice A, you have to add the 4 residents in the 0-10 years range to the 7 residents in the 11-20 years range, for a total of 11 residents in the range of 0-20 years old. For answer choice B, there are 12 residents in the range of 21-30 years old. For answer choice C, you have to add 11 and 9 to get 20 residents in the range of 31-50 years old. For answer choice D, you have to add 7 and 4 to get that there are 11 residents in the range of 51-70 years old. Therefore, answer choice C is correct.

Stem and leaf plot

Stem and leaf plots are also used to illustrate frequency, or how often a number shows up. The advantage of a stem and leaf plot is that it is super easy to show where numbers cluster without a lot of work. They function a lot like histograms, but are easier to create. On this test, however, you don't need to create any graphs, you just need to able to read them!

A stem and leaf plot is created by grouping numbers by their first digits.

For example, let's say that we want to create a stem and leaf plot for the following numbers:

2, 2, 3, 5, 7, 9, 10, 10, 13, 14, 14, 14, 16, 16, 17, 19, 20, 21, 22, 22, 24, 25

Here is what the stem and leaf plot would look like:

0	2	2	3	5	7	9			
1	0	0	3	4	4	4	6	6	7	9
2	0	1	2	2	4	5			

From this stem and leaf plot, we can see that there are six numbers that fall between 0 and 9, there are ten numbers that fall between 10 and 19, and there are six numbers that are between 20 and 29. We can also see that the number that shows up most often is 14.

With a stem and leaf plot, each data point gets its own input, even if it repeats another input. For example, 14 shows up three times in the original data set, so it shows up three times in the stem and leaf plot.

Here is an example of a question that tests stem and leaf plots:

3.   A local farmer surveyed his neighbors and asked them how many animals they had on their farms. The stem and leaf plot below reflects the results of the farmer's survey.

0	3	3	5	5	6	6	7	7	8				
1	0	0	0	2	2	3	3	3	4	4	5	7	7	8
2	0	1	1	2	5	7							

How many neighbors did the farmer survey?

(A)   3

(B)   15

(C)   29

(D)   32

In order to solve this question, we need to count up how many numbers there are on the right side of the bar. The trick here is to not count the numbers on the left side of the bar, because these are not separate numbers, but rather they are the first digits of the numbers on the right side of the bar. Answer choice C is correct.

Line graph

The next type of graph is a line graph. A line graph is best used for data where one variable affects the other.

- With a line graph, one variable usually affects the other variable

For example, as time increases, the height of a plant often increases, so a line graph would be appropriate.

With a line graph, the slope tells you how one variable affects the other.

For example, here is a graph that shows a positive relationship, such as with hours worked and wages earned.

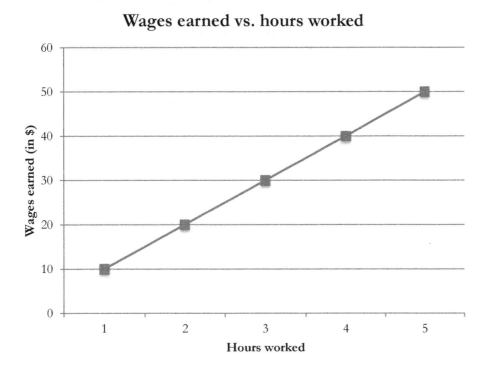

Sometimes there is a negative relationship, such as how the value of a car declines the longer that it is owned, as shown below.

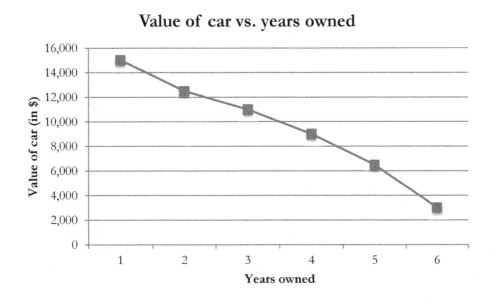

Keep in mind that the relationship can change from positive to negative, or even flatten out. For example, a child may grow continually up until age 18, so the graph would have a positive relationship for that period. Then height might remain constant (or flat) for decades.

The trick is to take a close look at the axes and what they really mean.

- Take a close look at the axes and think about what the relationship between the axes is

Here is an example of how a line graph could be tested on the ISEE:

4. The following graph shows the distance of four different cars from the repair shop.

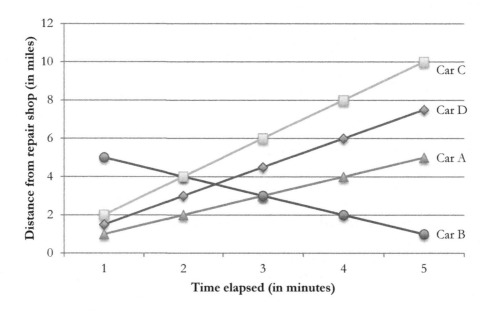

Which car is driving toward the repair shop at the greatest speed?

(A) Car A
(B) Car B
(C) Car C
(D) Car D

This is a bit of a trick question. Only one car is actually driving toward the repair shop. The distance from the repair shop is decreasing for Car B, so that means that Car B is getting closer to the shop. Choice B is correct.

Here is another one for you to try:

5.   The graph below shows Mike's distance from his school as a function of the number of minutes after dismissal time.

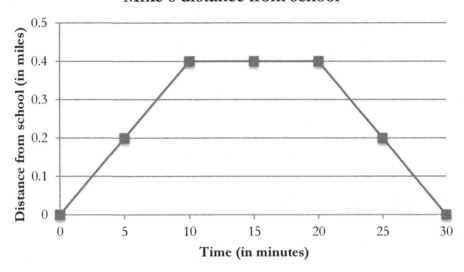

At one point Mike stopped to look for a book in his bag, realized he didn't have it, and then returned to school. How many minutes did Mike spend looking for his book and not walking?

(A)   5

(B)   10

(C)   15

(D)   20

The graph shows the distance that Mike is from school. We can see that he steadily walked away from school for 10 minutes. Then his distance from school did not increase or decrease for the next 10 minutes. He therefore spent ten minutes not walking, and answer choice B is correct.

Scatter plot

The next type of graph that we are going to cover is a scatter plot. A scatter plot simply gives you data points, and you have to look for the trends.

For example, the following scatter plot gives the ages of the cars sold at one dealership in a day and the amount of money that they sold for.

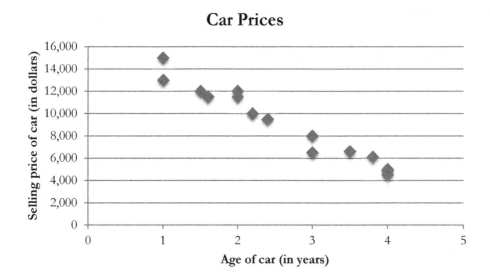

Many scatter plot questions on the ISEE ask you to use the line of best fit.

The *line of best fit* is a line that you draw through your data points to help you figure out a trend. A line of best fit is far from an exact science. You want to draw the line so that you have about the same number of points above the line as below the line.

An *outlier* is a point that is pretty far separated from the other points. Generally, we don't worry about taking outliers into consideration when we are drawing a line of best fit.

If we were to add a line of best fit to the previous scatter plot, it would look something like this:

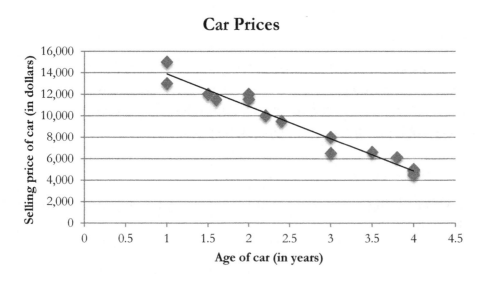

Notice that the line does not go through every single point, but rather it captures a kind of average of all the points.

Here is an example of a question on the ISEE that uses a line of best fit:

6. The graph below shows the relationship between the cost of a book and the number of books ordered.

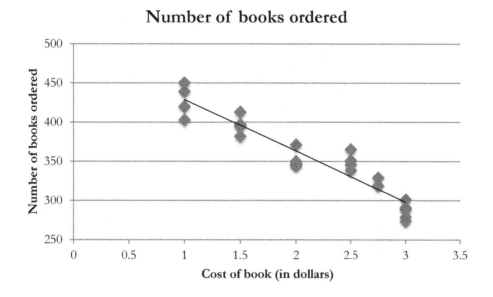

Number of books ordered

Using the line of best fit, what would be the total cost of an order if 400 books were ordered?

(A) $1.50
(B) $450
(C) $550
(D) $600

The graph provides a line of best fit for us, so we use that line to figure out how much each book would cost if 400 books were ordered. If we trace across from 400 on the y-axis, we can see that the cost of each book would be about $1.50. Now we have to multiply 400 by $1.50 to get the total cost of the order. Since $1.50 × 400 = $600, answer choice D is correct.

Some problems require you to draw in your own line of best fit. You can use the side of your answer sheet to get a roughly straight line. Aim to have as many points above the line as below the line, and try to run halfway in between two points if possible. Remember, this is not an exact science!

- If you have to draw in your own line of best fit, do your best and use the side of your answer sheet to approximate a straight line

Here is an example of a question that requires you to come up with your own line of best fit:

7. According to the scatter plot, what would it cost to buy a lot that is 1.1 acres?

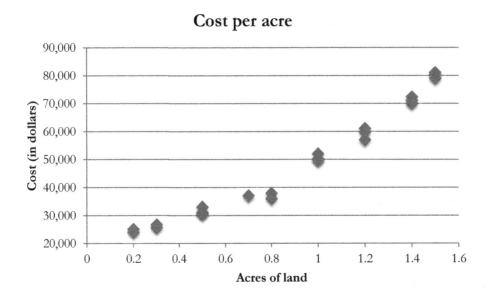

(A) $45,000

(B) $50,000

(C) $55,000

(D) $70,000

We can see from the scatter plot that 1.0 acres costs about $50,000 and that 1.2 acres costs about $60,000. Since 1.1 is halfway in between 1.0 and 1.2, we would expect the cost of 1.1 acres to be halfway in between $50,000 and $60,000, so choice C, or $55,000, is correct.

Circle graphs

The next type of graph that we will go over is a circle graph. Circle graphs give us a visual representation of how different categories of data compare to each other in terms of the entire set of data. Another way to say that is that circle graphs give us a representation of the fractional breakdown of data (a percent is really just a particular type of fraction).

- Circle graphs show us what percent (or fraction) of the total data that different categories represent

An important concept with circle graphs is the central angle. The central angle is the angle that is created at the center of a circle for a portion representing one data point. We can use the following proportion to solve for a central angle:

$$\frac{\text{value of one data point}}{\text{total value of data points}} = \frac{\text{central angle}}{360°}$$

For example, let's say a total of 50 students were asked what their favorite food is, and 15 of them replied pizza:

$$\frac{15}{50} = \frac{\text{central angle}}{360°}$$

$$15 \times 360° = 50 \times \text{central angle}$$

$$108° = \text{central angle}$$

We now know that the central angle of the portion of the circle graph representing students who chose pizza as their favorite food is 108°.

Here are a couple of examples of how circle graphs are tested on the ISEE:

8.   Clark conducted a survey of his classmates to find out how many of his classmates preferred chocolate ice cream, how many preferred vanilla ice cream, and how many preferred strawberry ice cream. The results are shown in the circle graph below.

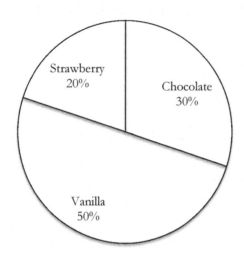

Which data could correspond to this circle graph?

(A)   15 chocolate lovers, 10 strawberry lovers, and 25 vanilla lovers
(B)   15 chocolate lovers, 15 strawberry lovers, and 30 vanilla lovers
(C)   15 chocolate lovers, 10 vanilla lovers, and 5 strawberry lovers
(D)   15 chocolate lovers, 30 vanilla lovers, and 10 strawberry lovers

The first thing that we should note is that all the answer choices begin with 15 chocolate lovers. If we look at the graph, we can see that 30% is equal to 15.

We can then set up proportions to solve for the other numbers:

$$\frac{15 \text{ chocolate lovers}}{30 \%} = \frac{v \text{ vanilla lovers}}{50\%}$$

Now we can cross-multiply to solve:

$$15 \times 50 = 30 \times v$$

$$750 = 30v$$

$$\div 30 \quad \div 30$$

$$25 = v$$

This tells us that if there were 15 chocolate lovers, then there must have been 25 vanilla lovers. Only answer choice A has this combination, so it is correct.

9. Tracy took a survey of 45 of her classmates. She asked each classmate what his or her favorite weekend activity was.

FAVORITE WEEKEND ACTIVITY

Activity	Number of classmates
Video games	14
Movies	10
Sports games	13
Trips	8

Tracy then made a circle graph from this data. What was the central angle of the section of her graph that represented video games?

(A) 8°

(B) 14°

(C) 80°

(D) 112°

Let's go ahead and set up our proportion:

$$\frac{14 \text{ students who chose video games}}{45 \text{ total students}} = \frac{x°}{360°}$$

Now we can cross-multiply:

$$14 \times 360° = 45 \times x°$$

$$5,040 = 45x$$

$$x = 112°$$

Answer choice D is correct.

Box-and-whisker plot

We are going to cover box-and-whisker plots in the central tendencies section. In order to construct or interpret a box-and-whisker plot, you need to first know the concept of median, which we will cover in the next section.

Central tendencies in data

Central tendencies are different ways for us to interpret data and take meaning from it.

The central tendencies that you need to know are:

- Mean
- Median
- Mode
- Range

Mean

Mean tells us the average of data. To find the mean, we add up all of the data points and then divide by the number of data points.

- To find the mean, add up all of the data points and then divide by the number of data points (i.e., find the average)

Here is an example of a question that asks you to apply the concept of mean on the ISEE:

1.   The graph below shows the number of flights delayed at Airport X over a six-month period last year.

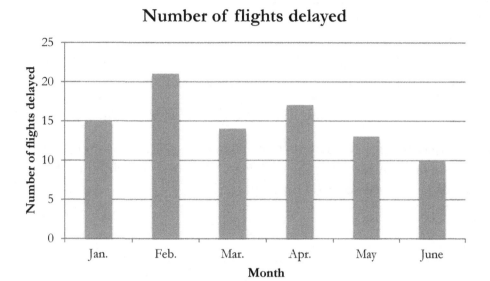

Number of flights delayed

According the graph, what was the mean number of flights delayed monthly?

(A)   14

(B)   15

(C)   16

(D)   17

If we add up all the delayed flights over the six-month period, we find that 90 flights were delayed. We then divide this by the number of months to get the mean monthly number of flights delayed. Since 90 divided by 6 is 15, answer choice B is correct.

Another important concept on the Upper Level ISEE is weighted average. A weighted average is used when we want to be sure that each data point contributes equally to the average (or mean) of a data set.

$$\text{weighted average} = \frac{\text{sum of group 1} + \text{sum of group 2} ...}{\text{total number of numbers}}$$

For example, let's say that a student's average for four test scores is a 90. The student then scores a 95 on a fifth test. If we simply add together 90 and 95 and divide by two, we would be giving way too much weight to the fifth test score. Instead, we do a weighted average:

$$\text{weighted average} = \frac{4(90) + 95}{5} = 91$$

The average (or mean) of all five test scores is 91. Note that in order to find the sum of group 1, we can multiply the average of the four scores by the number of scores.

Here are a couple of examples of questions that test the concept of weighted average:

2. Jody knew that the mean of six tests that she took was 82. The sum of the scores on the first five tests that she took was 415, but she couldn't find the sixth test. What did she score on the sixth test?

(A) 77
(B) 80
(C) 82
(D) 83

In order to answer this question, we have to work backwards from the weighted average that we are given. If the mean of the six tests is 82, then the sum of those scores is $82 \times 6 = 492$. Now we can subtract off the sum of the first five tests. Since $492 - 415 = 77$, answer choice A is correct.

3. Lucia has taken 4 tests in her math class, and the mean of her scores is 92. Her final test will be counted twice for her final mean. What is the lowest score that she could get on the final test and still have a mean score of at least 90?

(A) 84
(B) 86
(C) 88
(D) 90

This question is very similar to the previous question, only we have to remember that the final test counts twice. We will have the equivalent of six scores, not five, if the final test counts twice. The sum of the first four tests is $4 \times 92 = 368$. If she wants her final average to be at least 90, then the sum of all her scores must be $6 \times 90 = 540$. When we subtract $540 - 368$, we get that her final test must contribute 172 points to the sum. Because it counts twice, we divide 172 by 2 to get that she must score at least 86 on her final test. Answer choice B is correct.

Median

Median is the number that is right in the middle when you line up the data from least to greatest.

- To find the median, put the data in order from least to greatest and then find the middle number
- If there is an even number of numbers, take the average of the two middle numbers in order to find the median

Here is an example of a question that tests median:

4. The students in Mr. Zim's class made a graph of the snowfall reported by local ski areas in the month of January.

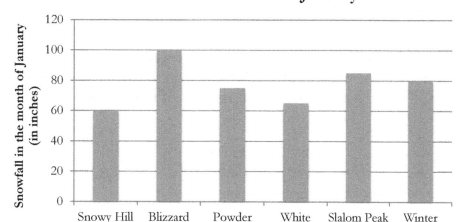

Snowfall in the month of January

What was the median snowfall in the month of January at these six ski areas?

(A) 77.5

(B) 80

(C) 82.5

(D) 85

First, we have to list out the snowfall at each area: $60, 100, 75, 65, 85,$ and 80. Remember to use the edge of a piece of paper as a straightedge if there are not lines provided. You may have to estimate a little, but remember that this is a multiple-choice test. Now we have to list those numbers in order from least to greatest: $60, 65, 75, 80, 85, 100$. Since we have an even number of numbers, the median will not be one of our data points. Rather, we have to average our two middle data points. Since $\frac{75+80}{2} = 77.5$, our median is 77.5 and answer choice A is correct.

You may see a question that tests box-and-whisker plots. A box-and-whisker plot is created using the median as well as quartiles, which are the medians of the first half of the numbers and the second half of the numbers.

The basic form of a box-and-whisker plot is:

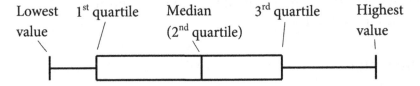

Box-and-whisker plot questions tend to be very basic, so we won't go into the particulars of how to find quartiles. Just know that the end of the "whisker" on the left is the minimum value, the line in the middle of the box is the median, and the end of the "whisker" on the right is the maximum value.

- End of left "whisker" gives us the minimum value
- End of right "whisker" gives us maximum value
- Line in the middle of box gives us the median

Here is an example of a question that tests box-and-whisker plots:

5. The snow on the ground in a certain spot in Town A was recorded on the same day in January for the last 40 years. It was measured in inches, and the box-and-whisker plot below was created using this recorded data.

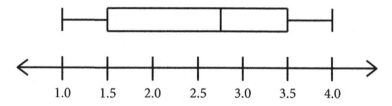

What is the median of this data?

(A) 1.25 inches
(B) 1.5 inches
(C) 2.75 inches
(D) 3 inches

The line in the middle of the box represents the median of the data. In this case, the line falls in between the 2.5 and 3.0 measurements on the number line, so 2.75 is the median. Answer choice C is correct.

Mode

The mode of a data set is the number that shows up most often. This number tells us which data point is most likely to show. Not every set of data has a mode. Data can have more than one mode if multiple numbers show up more than one time.

- Mode is the number that shows up most often in a data set
- Not every set of data has a mode
- Data can have more than one mode

Here is an example of how mode could be tested on the ISEE:

6. Mrs. Taylor made a stem and leaf plot of the grades that the students in her class received on the last test.

6	2	5	6					
7	5	6						
8	3	3	3	5	6	6	7	9
9	0	0	2	4	5	6	6	8	9

What is the mode of the test scores in her class?

(A) 6

(B) 83

(C) 90

(D) 96

To answer this question, we have to remember to combine the first digit (on the left of the bar) with the numbers on the right to form complete data points. Remember that the number on the left is the tens digit and the number on the right is the units digit. This means that our data points are really: $62, 65, 66, 75, 76, 83, 83, 83, 85, 86, 86, 87, 89, 90, 90, 92, 94, 95, 96, 96, 98,$ and 99. From this, we can see that 83 shows up more often than any other number, so this is our mode. Answer choice B is correct.

Range

Range tells us the difference between the highest and the lowest points on the graph. Sometimes the questions will use the word "range," and sometimes they will just ask for the difference between the highest and lowest points on the graph.

- To find range, subtract the lowest number from the highest number

Here is an example of a question that tests range, even though it doesn't use the word "range" at all:

7. Mr. McGarry's class recorded the average rainfall for every month in the school year. Their results are shown in the graph below.

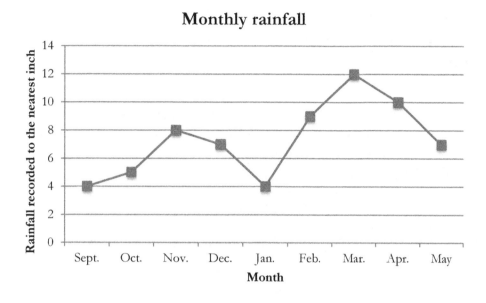

What was the difference between the highest and lowest amounts of rainfall recorded in a month?

(A) 4 inches
(B) 6 inches
(C) 8 inches
(D) 10 inches

To answer this question, we first have to figure out what the highest and lowest amounts of rain recorded were. From the graph, we can see that the lowest amount recorded was 4 inches. The highest recorded rainfall in a month was 12 inches. To find the difference, we simply subtract 4 from 12 and get a difference of 8. Answer choice C is correct.

Here is another example for you to try:

8.   Mr. Moss decides to add 5 points to each student's score on a test. What would happen to the range?

    (A)   It would increase by 5 points
    (B)   It would decrease by 5 points
    (C)   It would increase by 15 points
    (D)   It would remain unchanged

Let's think about what range is. It is the difference between the least and greatest data points. If the least number was increased by 5 and the greatest number was also increased by 5, then the difference between the two would remain constant. Answer choice D is correct.

Here is a question that puts together a couple of different concepts:

The box-and-whisker plot below was created using the final exam test scores for 100 students.

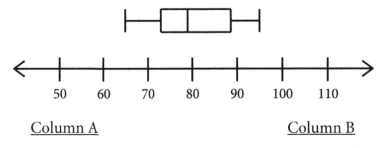

Column A	Column B

9.   The range of the scores   The mean of the scores

    (A)   Quantity in Column A is greater.
    (B)   Quantity in Column B is greater.
    (C)   The quantities in Column A and Column B are equal.
    (D)   Cannot be determined from information given.

If we look at the box-and-whisker plot, we can see that the scores range roughly from 65 to 95. This means that the range of our scores is around 30, which is far below any of the individual scores. Since the mean must be somewhere between the least and the greatest data points, the mean must always be greater than the range in this case. Answer choice B is correct.

Basic probability

Probability tells us the likelihood of a certain event occurring.

$$\text{Probability} = \frac{\text{desired outcome}}{\text{total number of outcomes}}$$

For example, let's say that we have a bowl with three red candies and four blue candies. Let's say we want to know the probability of choosing a red candy.

$$\text{Probability of choosing red candy} = \frac{\text{desired outcome}}{\text{total number of outcomes}} = \frac{3}{7}$$

Our desired candy is red and there are 3 red candies in the bowl, so that is the top number in our probability. There are a total of 7 candies in the bowl, so that is our bottom number. The key is that you have to add together all the outcomes to get the total number of outcomes.

Here is what basic probability problems look like on the ISEE:

1. There are 6 red cards, 5 green cards, and 8 blue cards in a pile. If a card is drawn at random, what is the probability that the card will be red?

    (A) $\dfrac{6}{13}$

    (B) $\dfrac{6}{19}$

    (C) $\dfrac{5}{13}$

    (D) $\dfrac{8}{19}$

    If we add up the total number of cards, we get that there are a total of 19 cards. Of those cards, 6 are the desired outcome (or red). That means that the probability of drawing a red card is $\dfrac{6}{19}$, so answer choice B is correct.

Here is what a basic probability question could look like in the quantitative comparison section:

There are four red marbles, four green marbles, and eight black marbles in a bag. A marble is to be chosen at random.

	Column A	Column B

2. The probability that the marble drawn will be black

The probability that the marble drawn will not be black

(A) Quantity in Column A is greater.
(B) Quantity in Column B is greater.
(C) The quantities in Column A and Column B are equal.
(D) Cannot be determined from information given.

In this case, there are an equal number of black marbles and marbles that are not black. This means that the two probabilities are the same, and answer choice C is correct.

On the ISEE, the test writers love to use a spinner to illustrate probability.

3. Bernadette is playing a game with a spinner labeled #1-7 (as shown below). She spins twice and then adds together the two numbers that the spinner lands on. If the sum of these two numbers is either 4 or 6, she gives herself a point. What is the probability that she will earn a point?

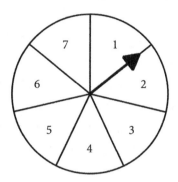

(A) $\dfrac{4}{7}$

(B) $\dfrac{3}{7}$

(C) $\dfrac{14}{49}$

(D) $\dfrac{8}{49}$

Since this is a probability question, we first have to figure out how many total possibilities there are. There are 7 possible numbers to land on with the first spin and 7 possible numbers to land on with the second spin. If we multiply these together, we get that there are 49 possibilities for how the spinner could land. Of those possibilities, let's make a systematic list of the combinations that would add to 4 or 6.

1 + 3	3 + 1
1 + 5	3 + 3
2 + 2	4 + 2
2 + 4	5 + 1

We can see that out of the 49 possibilities, there are 8 combinations that would add to 4 or 6. This means that the probability is $\frac{8}{49}$ and answer choice D is correct.

Probability with multiple events

You are also likely to see questions where first one event occurs and then a second event must occur. The two events can be independent of one another, or the probability of the second event can depend upon the outcome of the first event. For example, if we roll a cube and then flip a coin, these are independent events. The number we roll doesn't affect the outcome of the coin flip. An example of dependent events is to draw marbles from a bag and not replace the first marble drawn. For example, let's say we have a bag with 10 white marbles and 10 black marbles. The probability of drawing a white marble first is $\frac{1}{2}$, but if that marble is not replaced then the probability of drawing a white marble the second time is $\frac{9}{19}$ since there are now 9 white marbles in a bag of 19 marbles.

- Make sure that you figure out whether events are dependent or independent
- With independent events, the outcome of the first event does not affect the outcome of the second event
- With dependent events, the outcome of the first event does affect the outcome of the second event

Here is an example of a question that tests these principles:

A die is rolled that is numbered 1 through 6. Then a marble is drawn from a bag that has 3 red marbles and 4 blue marbles.

Column A	Column B
1. If a number less than 4 is rolled, the probability that a red marble will be drawn	If a number greater than 4 is rolled, the probability that a blue marble will be drawn

(A) Quantity in Column A is greater.
(B) Quantity in Column B is greater.
(C) The quantities in Column A and Column B are equal.
(D) Cannot be determined from information given.

In this question, the first part of each statement in Column A and Column B is completely irrelevant. The number rolled on the die will not affect the color of the marble drawn, because the two events are independent. There is a greater probability of drawing a blue marble than drawing a red marble, so Column B is greater and choice B is correct.

The formula for figuring out the probability of two events occurring is:

probability of event 1 occurring × probability of event 2 occurring
= probabilty of both events occurring

Whether the events are independent or dependent doesn't change this formula, rather it affects the probability of the second event occurring.

Here is an example of a question that uses this equation:

2. Sharon is using a random number generator. She has set her computer to randomly pick a number between 1 and 9. If she uses the random number generator twice to pick a number, what is the probability that both numbers will be odd?

(A) $\dfrac{1}{9}$

(B) $\dfrac{25}{81}$

(C) $\dfrac{4}{9}$

(D) $\dfrac{5}{9}$

We have two independent events occurring in this problem. First, the computer must choose an odd number. Since there are nine numbers, and five of them are odd, the probability of the first event occurring is $\dfrac{5}{9}$. Since the second event is the same as the first, the probability of the second event occurring is also $\dfrac{5}{9}$. Now, to get the probability of BOTH events occurring, we must multiply the two together.

$$\frac{5}{9} \times \frac{5}{9} = \frac{25}{81}$$

Answer choice B is correct.

Here is another problem that uses the same concept of multiplying together probabilities, only in this case there are three events occurring:

3. Kara has one red, one blue, one green, one yellow, and one brown shirt in her suitcase. She has one pair of red pants, one pair of blue pants, and one pair of tan pants in her suitcase as well. She also has one pair of red shoes and one pair of white shoes. If she randomly selects a shirt, a pair of pants, and a pair of shoes from her suitcase, what is the probability that they will all be red?

(A) $\frac{1}{30}$

(B) $\frac{3}{30}$

(C) $\frac{1}{6}$

(D) $\frac{1}{3}$

In order to answer this question, we have to first figure out the probability of each individual event occurring. Since she has 5 shirts in her suitcase, the probability of choosing a red shirt is $\frac{1}{5}$. Since she has three pairs of pants in her suitcase, the probability of choosing a red pair of pants is $\frac{1}{3}$. Since she has only two pairs of shoes, the probability of choosing red shoes is $\frac{1}{2}$. To find the probability of all three events occurring, we simply multiply them together:

$$\frac{1}{5} \times \frac{1}{3} \times \frac{1}{2} = \frac{1}{30}$$

Answer choice A is correct.

Here is an example of how this could be tested in a quantitative comparison question:

A jar has 10 paperclips in it. There are three green paperclips, four red paperclips, and three blue paperclips. A paperclip is randomly selected and replaced. A second paperclip is then selected.

	Column A	Column B
4.	The probability that the first paperclip will be red	The probability that both of the paperclips will be red

(A) Quantity in Column A is greater.
(B) Quantity in Column B is greater.
(C) The quantities in Column A and Column B are equal.
(D) Cannot be determined from information given.

Let's look first at Column A. The probability that the first paperclip will be red is $\frac{4}{10}$. Now let's look at Column B. The probability that both paperclips will be red is $\frac{4}{10} \times \frac{4}{10}$, or $\left(\frac{4}{10}\right)^2$. Since this is a quantitative comparison question, we want to see if we can avoid doing the actual calculation. In this case, we are squaring a fraction, so the value decreases. We know that Column A has to be larger than Column B, so answer choice A is correct.

Now let's take a look at some questions that use dependent events. Here is a basic question:

5. A jar contains 5 red candies, 7 blue candies, 10 green candies, and 4 orange candies. Lela removes one blue candy from the jar and eats it. Robert then randomly picks a candy. What is the probability that he picks a green candy?

(A) $\frac{5}{13}$

(B) $\frac{2}{5}$

(C) $\frac{7}{26} \times \frac{5}{13}$

(D) $\frac{7}{26} \times \frac{2}{5}$

The first step in this question is to recognize that these are dependent events, since the blue candy is not replaced before Robert picks a candy. There were originally 26 candies, but after Lela ate a blue candy, there were only 25 left. Of those 25, 10 were green, so the probability of choosing a green candy is $\frac{10}{25}$. This reduces to $\frac{2}{5}$, so answer choice B is correct. Don't be fooled by answer choice D. The question only asked for the probability of the second event occurring, not the probability of both events occurring.

Here is another one to try:

A jar has 6 red marbles, 10 blue marbles, 4 green marbles, and 2 black marbles. Three marbles are going to be randomly chosen from the jar.

	Column A	Column B
6.	The probability that all three marbles will be blue	The probability that at least one marble will be blue

(A) Quantity in Column A is greater.
(B) Quantity in Column B is greater.
(C) The quantities in Column A and Column B are equal.
(D) Cannot be determined from information given.

It is particularly important to keep in mind that we don't need to find exact numbers; we just need to compare the two probabilities. To figure out the probability that "at least one" marble will be blue requires using a complicated equation. But that is why this question is a quantitative comparison and not a multiple-choice question. If we think about it logically, the probability that all three marbles are blue has to be less than the probability that one, two, or three marbles are blue. Answer choice B is correct.

Complementary events

Complementary events are events that occur if and only if the other event does not. The probabilities of each event occurring also add to 1.

Here are some examples of complementary events:

- If you have a spinner labeled 1 through 6, landing on a number greater than or equal to 4 is complementary to landing on a number less than 4 because they can't happen at the same time and their probabilities add to 1.
- If you roll a die, rolling an even number is complementary to rolling an odd number because they can't both happen at once and the probabilities of these two events add to 1.
- If you have a bag of pink, brown, and violet marbles, choosing a pink marble and then choosing either a brown or a violet marble are complementary events because their probabilities add to 1 (assuming that the pink marble is replaced after it is drawn).

Here are some events that are NOT complementary:

- If you have a spinner labeled 1 through 6, spinning a factor of 6 and then spinning a factor of 2 are not complementary. The probabilities of these two events do add to 1, but there is overlap (1 and 2 are factors of both 6 and 2), so they aren't complementary.
- If you roll a die, rolling a 4 is not a complementary event to rolling a 2. The probabilities of these two events don't add to 1.
- If you have a bag of pink, brown, and violet marbles, choosing a pink marble and then a brown marble are not complementary events because the probabilities of these two events do not add to 1.

Following is a question that demonstrates how complementary events could be tested on the ISEE:

1. Cheryl has two spinners, both with equally-sized sections labeled 1-3. She is going to spin both of them. Which of the following describes complementary events?

   (A) The first spinner lands on 1 and the second spinner lands on 2.
   (B) The first spinner lands on 2 and the second spinner lands on 2.
   (C) The first spinner lands on 3 and the second spinner lands on 2 or 3.
   (D) The first spinner lands on 2 and the second spinner lands on 1 or 3.

   Only answer choice D gives two events that do not overlap with probabilities that add to 1. It is the correct answer choice.

You now know the concepts of data analysis and probability that are likely to be tested on the Upper Level ISEE. Be sure to complete the following practice set.

Data Analysis & Probability Practice Set

1. There are 5 green shirts, 7 blue shirts, and 4 white shirts in a drawer. If a shirt is selected at random, what is the probability that it will be green?

   (A) $\dfrac{5}{11}$

   (B) $\dfrac{5}{16}$

   (C) $\dfrac{5}{7}$

   (D) $\dfrac{7}{16}$

   A die is rolled that is numbered 1 through 6.

Column A	Column B

2. The probability that the die will land with a factor of 4 on the side facing up | The probability that the die will land with a factor of 3 on the side facing up

   (A) Quantity in Column A is greater.
   (B) Quantity in Column B is greater.
   (C) The quantities in Column A and Column B are equal.
   (D) Cannot be determined from information given.

3. The graph below shows the number of cars recorded passing through an intersection in one eight-hour time period.

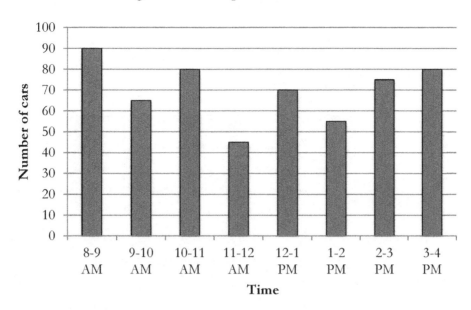

What is the median of this data?

(A) 70

(B) 72.5

(C) 75

(D) 80

A student counted up how many cars were in the school parking at lot at 9 AM each day for 30 days. The data collected is displayed in the histogram below.

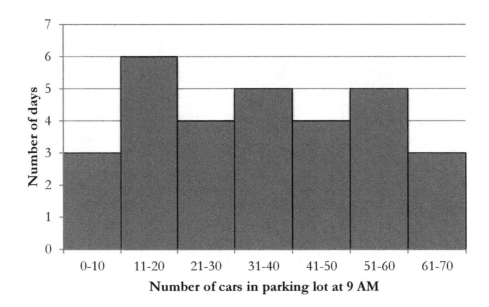

Number of cars in parking lot at 9 AM

	Column A	Column B
4.	The range of the data	The mode of the data

(A) Quantity in Column A is greater.
(B) Quantity in Column B is greater.
(C) The quantities in Column A and Column B are equal.
(D) Cannot be determined from information given.

Cameron spins Spinner 1 and Spinner 2 (both of which have equally-sized sections). He then adds the results together.

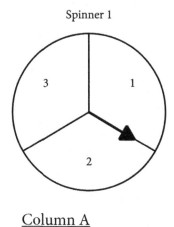

Spinner 1   Spinner 2

| Column A | Column B |

5.   The probability that the sum will be greater than 4 | The probability that the sum will be less than or equal to 4

(A)   Quantity in Column A is greater.
(B)   Quantity in Column B is greater.
(C)   The quantities in Column A and Column B are equal.
(D)   Cannot be determined from information given.

6.   Charles scored 84, 88, 64 and 90 on his first four tests. He has two tests left to take. If he wants the mean score for all 6 tests to be 86, then what must the mean be for the two tests that he still has to take?

(A)   86
(B)   90
(C)   95
(D)   98

7. Lindsey took a survey of 60 of her classmates. She asked them whether they prefer cheese pizza, pepperoni pizza, mushroom pizza, or sausage pizza. Her results are shown in the table below.

PREFERRED TYPE OF PIZZA

Type of Pizza	Number of Students
Cheese	14
Pepperoni	16
Mushroom	20
Sausage	10

Lindsay wants to turn this data into a circle graph. What would be the measure of the central angle for the section that represents the students who prefer cheese pizza?

(A) 84°

(B) 90°

(C) 108°

(D) 120°

8. In a bag there are 5 red marbles, 3 green marbles, and 4 blue marbles. One marble is drawn and then not replaced. Then a second marble is drawn. What is the probability that both of these marbles are red?

(A) $\dfrac{5}{33}$

(B) $\dfrac{25}{144}$

(C) $\dfrac{5}{12}$

(D) $\dfrac{10}{12}$

A spinner is divided into six equal parts.

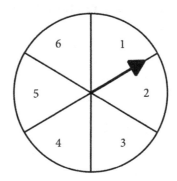

	Column A	Column B
9.	The probability that the spinner will land on an even number	The probability that the spinner will land on a number less than 4

(A) Quantity in Column A is greater.

(B) Quantity in Column B is greater.

(C) The quantities in Column A and Column B are equal.

(D) Cannot be determined from information given.

10. A library display has four novels, five non-fiction books, and six poetry books. The display contains the novel that is checked out most often, the non-fiction book that is checked out most often, and the poetry book that is checked out most often. If a student is to randomly choose a novel, a non-fiction book, and a poetry book, what is the probability that each of the three books chosen will be the book that is checked out most often in that genre?

(A) $\dfrac{1}{120}$

(B) $\dfrac{1}{15}$

(C) $\dfrac{3}{120}$

(D) $\dfrac{3}{15}$

11. A certain store uses a reward system based on how much money a customer spends. The graph below shows the relationship between dollars spent and reward points received.

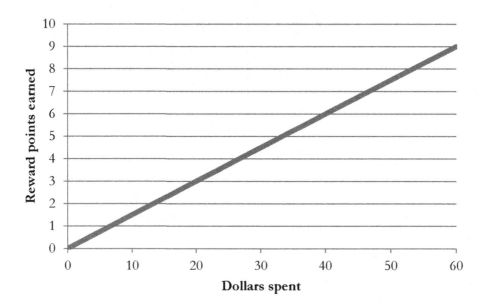

If a customer spent $100 in this store, how many rewards points would he receive?

(A) 9

(B) 10

(C) 14

(D) 15

12. A bag contains four marbles. One is red, one is green, and two are blue. A marble is randomly chosen, then replaced in the bag, and then another marble is randomly chosen. Which of the following scenarios best describes complementary events?

(A) The first marble is red and the second marble is green.
(B) Both of the marbles drawn are blue.
(C) The first marble is blue and the second marble is green or blue.
(D) The first marble is green and the second marble is blue or red.

13. The graph below shows how far four students were from school as a function of time.

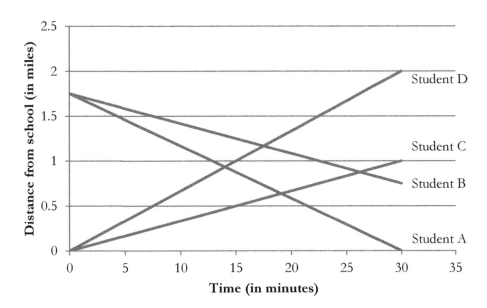

Which student is walking away from the school at the greatest rate?

(A)   Student A
(B)   Student B
(C)   Student C
(D)   Student D

14. Mrs. Mullins made a stem and leaf plot of the ages of the residents in her apartment building.

0	2 2 7
1	3 3 3 4 6 8 9
2	1 2 2 5 7
3	0 0 1 2 4 6
4	1 1 2 9
5	2 3 4
6	0 5 6 7
7	2 3

What is the median of this data?

(A) 0

(B) 3

(C) 27

(D) 30.5

15. A class recorded the average temperature each day for 60 days. The box-and-whisker plot below shows the data.

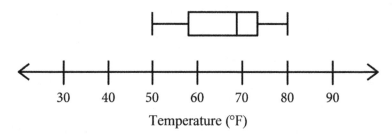

Which of the following two central tendencies could not have the same value for this data?

(A) mean and mode

(B) mean and range

(C) mean and median

(D) mode and median

Answers to Data Analysis & Probability Practice Set

1. B
2. A
3. B
4. D
5. C
6. C
7. A
8. A

9. C
10. A
11. D
12. D
13. D
14. D
15. B

Tips for the Essay

When you take the ISEE, you will be asked to complete an essay at the very end of the test. You will be given 30 minutes and two pages to write your response. You will also be given a piece of paper to take notes on.

- Essay is at the end of the test
- 30 minutes to complete
- Two pages to write on, plus one piece of paper for notes

Your writing sample will NOT be scored. Rather, a copy of it will be sent to the schools that you apply to. This essay is a great way for the admissions committee to get to know you better.

- Let your personality shine through so that admissions officers can get to know you better

You will be given a question to write from. The questions are topics that you can relate to your own life.

Here are some examples that are like the questions that you will see on the ISEE:

1. If you could change one thing about your community, what would it be? Describe what you would change and how it would improve your community.
2. Who is your favorite teacher? Describe how this person has influenced your thoughts and actions.
3. We live in a world that is rapidly changing. Describe one change that you have seen recently and whether or not you think it is an improvement.

(There are more sample questions in ERB's official guide, *What to Expect on the ISEE*.)

To approach the essay, follow this three-step plan:

Step 1: Plan

- Take a couple of minutes to plan – it will be time well spent
- Be sure to know what your main idea is and how each paragraph will be different
- Use the piece of paper provided

Step 2: Write

- Break your writing into paragraphs – don't do a two-page blob
- Write legibly – it does not have to be perfect and schools know that you are writing with a time limit, but if the admissions officers can't read what you wrote, they can't judge it
- Remember that each paragraph should have its own idea

Step 3: Edit / proofread

- Save a couple of minutes at the end to look over your work
- You won't be able to do a major editing job where you move around sentences and rewrite portions
- Look for where you may have left out a word or misspelled something
- Make your marks simple and clear – if you need to take something out, put a single line through, it and use a carat (^) to insert words that you forgot

The essay is not graded, but the schools that you apply to do receive a copy.

What are schools looking for?

Organization

There should be structure to your essay. You need to have an introduction, good details to back up your main point, and a conclusion. Each paragraph should have its own idea.

Word choice

Use descriptive language. Don't describe anything as "nice" or "good". Describe specifically why something is nice or good. Good writing shows us and DOESN'T tell us.

Creativity and development of ideas

It is not enough just to be able to fit your writing into the form that you were taught in school. These prompts are designed to show how you think. This is your chance to shine!

The writing sample is a place for you to showcase your writing skills. It is one more piece of information that the admissions committee will use in making their decisions.

The best way to get better at writing an essay is to practice. Try writing about one or more of the questions above. Use the prompts from *What to Expect on the ISEE*. Have a trusted adult help you analyze your writing sample and figure out how you can improve.

- Practice writing an essay before the actual test
- Have a teacher or parent help you analyze your practice essays

Practice Test

Answer Sheets

The following pages contain answer sheets for the practice test. Additional copies can be downloaded at:

www.testprepworks.com/student/download

Student Name: _____   Grade Applying For: _____

Use pencil to fill in your answers below.

Section 1: Verbal Reasoning

1	(A) (B) (C) (D)	15	(A) (B) (C) (D)	29	(A) (B) (C) (D)
2	(A) (B) (C) (D)	16	(A) (B) (C) (D)	30	(A) (B) (C) (D)
3	(A) (B) (C) (D)	17	(A) (B) (C) (D)	31	(A) (B) (C) (D)
4	(A) (B) (C) (D)	18	(A) (B) (C) (D)	32	(A) (B) (C) (D)
5	(A) (B) (C) (D)	19	(A) (B) (C) (D)	33	(A) (B) (C) (D)
6	(A) (B) (C) (D)	20	(A) (B) (C) (D)	34	(A) (B) (C) (D)
7	(A) (B) (C) (D)	21	(A) (B) (C) (D)	35	(A) (B) (C) (D)
8	(A) (B) (C) (D)	22	(A) (B) (C) (D)	36	(A) (B) (C) (D)
9	(A) (B) (C) (D)	23	(A) (B) (C) (D)	37	(A) (B) (C) (D)
10	(A) (B) (C) (D)	24	(A) (B) (C) (D)	38	(A) (B) (C) (D)
11	(A) (B) (C) (D)	25	(A) (B) (C) (D)	39	(A) (B) (C) (D)
12	(A) (B) (C) (D)	26	(A) (B) (C) (D)	40	(A) (B) (C) (D)
13	(A) (B) (C) (D)	27	(A) (B) (C) (D)		
14	(A) (B) (C) (D)	28	(A) (B) (C) (D)		

Section 2: Quantitative Reasoning

1	(A) (B) (C) (D)	14	(A) (B) (C) (D)	27	(A) (B) (C) (D)
2	(A) (B) (C) (D)	15	(A) (B) (C) (D)	28	(A) (B) (C) (D)
3	(A) (B) (C) (D)	16	(A) (B) (C) (D)	29	(A) (B) (C) (D)
4	(A) (B) (C) (D)	17	(A) (B) (C) (D)	30	(A) (B) (C) (D)
5	(A) (B) (C) (D)	18	(A) (B) (C) (D)	31	(A) (B) (C) (D)
6	(A) (B) (C) (D)	19	(A) (B) (C) (D)	32	(A) (B) (C) (D)
7	(A) (B) (C) (D)	20	(A) (B) (C) (D)	33	(A) (B) (C) (D)
8	(A) (B) (C) (D)	21	(A) (B) (C) (D)	34	(A) (B) (C) (D)
9	(A) (B) (C) (D)	22	(A) (B) (C) (D)	35	(A) (B) (C) (D)
10	(A) (B) (C) (D)	23	(A) (B) (C) (D)	36	(A) (B) (C) (D)
11	(A) (B) (C) (D)	24	(A) (B) (C) (D)	37	(A) (B) (C) (D)
12	(A) (B) (C) (D)	25	(A) (B) (C) (D)		
13	(A) (B) (C) (D)	26	(A) (B) (C) (D)		

Section 3: Reading Comprehension

1	(A) (B) (C) (D)	13	(A) (B) (C) (D)	25	(A) (B) (C) (D)
2	(A) (B) (C) (D)	14	(A) (B) (C) (D)	26	(A) (B) (C) (D)
3	(A) (B) (C) (D)	15	(A) (B) (C) (D)	27	(A) (B) (C) (D)
4	(A) (B) (C) (D)	16	(A) (B) (C) (D)	28	(A) (B) (C) (D)
5	(A) (B) (C) (D)	17	(A) (B) (C) (D)	29	(A) (B) (C) (D)
6	(A) (B) (C) (D)	18	(A) (B) (C) (D)	30	(A) (B) (C) (D)
7	(A) (B) (C) (D)	19	(A) (B) (C) (D)	31	(A) (B) (C) (D)
8	(A) (B) (C) (D)	20	(A) (B) (C) (D)	32	(A) (B) (C) (D)
9	(A) (B) (C) (D)	21	(A) (B) (C) (D)	33	(A) (B) (C) (D)
10	(A) (B) (C) (D)	22	(A) (B) (C) (D)	34	(A) (B) (C) (D)
11	(A) (B) (C) (D)	23	(A) (B) (C) (D)	35	(A) (B) (C) (D)
12	(A) (B) (C) (D)	24	(A) (B) (C) (D)	36	(A) (B) (C) (D)

Section 4: Mathematics Achievement

1	(A) (B) (C) (D)	17	(A) (B) (C) (D)	33	(A) (B) (C) (D)
2	(A) (B) (C) (D)	18	(A) (B) (C) (D)	34	(A) (B) (C) (D)
3	(A) (B) (C) (D)	19	(A) (B) (C) (D)	35	(A) (B) (C) (D)
4	(A) (B) (C) (D)	20	(A) (B) (C) (D)	36	(A) (B) (C) (D)
5	(A) (B) (C) (D)	21	(A) (B) (C) (D)	37	(A) (B) (C) (D)
6	(A) (B) (C) (D)	22	(A) (B) (C) (D)	38	(A) (B) (C) (D)
7	(A) (B) (C) (D)	23	(A) (B) (C) (D)	39	(A) (B) (C) (D)
8	(A) (B) (C) (D)	24	(A) (B) (C) (D)	40	(A) (B) (C) (D)
9	(A) (B) (C) (D)	25	(A) (B) (C) (D)	41	(A) (B) (C) (D)
10	(A) (B) (C) (D)	26	(A) (B) (C) (D)	42	(A) (B) (C) (D)
11	(A) (B) (C) (D)	27	(A) (B) (C) (D)	43	(A) (B) (C) (D)
12	(A) (B) (C) (D)	28	(A) (B) (C) (D)	44	(A) (B) (C) (D)
13	(A) (B) (C) (D)	29	(A) (B) (C) (D)	45	(A) (B) (C) (D)
14	(A) (B) (C) (D)	30	(A) (B) (C) (D)	46	(A) (B) (C) (D)
15	(A) (B) (C) (D)	31	(A) (B) (C) (D)	47	(A) (B) (C) (D)
16	(A) (B) (C) (D)	32	(A) (B) (C) (D)		

Student Name: _____

Grade Applying For: _____

Write in blue or black pen for this essay

Write your essay topic below

_____

_____

_____

Write your essay below and on the next page

_____

_____

_____

_____

_____

_____

_____

_____

_____

_____

_____

_____

_____

_____

_____

_____

_____

_____

_____

_____

_____

_____

_____

Verbal Reasoning

40 questions
20 minutes

The Verbal Reasoning section has two parts. When you finish Part One, be sure to keep working on Part Two. For each answer that you choose, make sure to fill in the corresponding circle on the answer sheet.

Part One – Synonyms

Each question in Part One has a word in all capital letters with four answer choices after it. Choose the answer choice with the word that comes closest in meaning to the word in all capital letters.

SAMPLE QUESTION:

1. SPEEDY:

    (A) loud
    (B) messy
    ● quick
    (D) small

Part Two – Sentence Completions

The questions in Part Two each have a sentence with one or two blanks. Each blank takes the place of a word that is missing. The sentence has four answer choices after it. Choose the answer choice with the word or word pair that best completes the sentence.

SAMPLE QUESTION:

1. Since the weather is getting warmer every day, it is particularly important to -------- more water.

    (A) create
    ● drink
    (C) leave
    (D) waste

STOP

DO NOT MOVE ON TO THE SECTION UNTIL TOLD TO

Part One – Synonyms

Directions: Choose the word that is closest in meaning to the word that is in all capital letters.

1. ADVANTAGEOUS:

    (A) devout
    (B) overdue
    (C) positive
    (D) willowy

2. TREACHEROUS:

    (A) deceitful
    (B) earnest
    (C) obedient
    (D) simple

3. MEEK:

    (A) controversial
    (B) familiar
    (C) literal
    (D) shy

4. PIOUS:

    (A) beneficial
    (B) domestic
    (C) occasional
    (D) religious

5. PROSAIC:

    (A) absent
    (B) dull
    (C) lanky
    (D) sturdy

6. TRANSLUCENT:

    (A) clear
    (B) exaggerated
    (C) humorous
    (D) rugged

7. INGENIOUS:

    (A) brilliant
    (B) disagreeable
    (C) nervous
    (D) relieved

8. RENOWN:

    (A) absence
    (B) damage
    (C) fame
    (D) jubilance

CONTINUE TO THE NEXT PAGE

9. ONEROUS:

(A) able
(B) burdensome
(C) gruesome
(D) monotonous

10. CAPER:

(A) disgrace
(B) prank
(C) reminder
(D) tablet

11. PREPOSTEROUS:

(A) flourishing
(B) hospitable
(C) mournful
(D) ridiculous

12. HOODWINK:

(A) deceive
(B) employ
(C) observe
(D) smear

13. DILIGENT:

(A) dreary
(B) necessary
(C) responsible
(D) typical

14. INANE:

(A) definite
(B) meager
(C) silly
(D) tawny

15. PEDESTRIAN:

(A) boring
(B) flawless
(C) objective
(D) remorseful

16. FANATIC:

(A) adviser
(B) emigrant
(C) phantom
(D) zealot

17. DEBACLE:

(A) amusement
(B) catastrophe
(C) innovation
(D) leader

18. BOISTEROUS:

(A) fearless
(B) graceful
(C) loud
(D) ordinary

CONTINUE TO THE NEXT PAGE

19. RIGHTEOUS:

   (A) important
   (B) moral
   (C) possessive
   (D) trespassing

Part Two – Sentence Completions

Directions: Choose the word or word pair to best complete the sentence.

20. Fertilizer runoff from farms has led to algae bloom in waterways, which means that the abundant growth of algae has -------- the growth of other plants and reduced food available to aquatic life that does not consume algae.

   (A) curbed
   (B) immersed
   (C) misguided
   (D) tolerated

21. Jackson Pollock revolutionized the art world when he started producing abstract paintings instead of the -------- pictures that more conventional artists had been creating.

   (A) borrowed
   (B) larger
   (C) majestic
   (D) realistic

CONTINUE TO THE NEXT PAGE

22. When Richard Drew visited an automobile painting shop in 1925 and witnessed the difficulty the painters were having painting two differently colored sections without an adhesive strip, he came up with the -------- of masking tape.

    (A) calamity
    (B) examination
    (C) innovation
    (D) sequence

23. Styrofoam is often used in surfboards and boats because it is a lightweight material with a high level of ---------.

    (A) agreement
    (B) buoyancy
    (C) harmony
    (D) mythology

24. When animals are released into the wild after being in captivity for an extended period of time, it can be difficult for them to adapt because they are --------- to having food provided for them.

    (A) accustomed
    (B) employed
    (C) perplexed
    (D) treated

25. Because the Galapagos Islands are highly secluded, species survive there that have long ago ------- in other locations.

    (A) assisted
    (B) declined
    (C) maximized
    (D) thrived

CONTINUE TO THE NEXT PAGE

26. Martha Graham considered dancing to be a(n) --------- part of her life that could not be avoided.

   (A) aggressive
   (B) dignified
   (C) inevitable
   (D) unusual

27. Clearly the conditions for growing corn on the plains were --------- given the tremendous harvest that was produced.

   (A) delicate
   (B) favorable
   (C) static
   (D) tapering

28. During World II, the supply of natural rubber from Southeast Asia was cut off and American scientists had to quickly develop a -------- replacement.

   (A) backward
   (B) fragrant
   (C) lagging
   (D) synthetic

29. It can be difficult to treat diseases that are -------- because symptoms often go away and then reappear later.

   (A) chronic
   (B) humbling
   (C) lazy
   (D) questionable

CONTINUE TO THE NEXT PAGE

30. Opponents of the bridge project had to be -------- before construction could begin on the massive span crossing the Ohio River.

    (A) explained
    (B) fortified
    (C) pacified
    (D) replaced

31. Although it is possible to --------- a quick fix during a race, it is better for a sailing team to plan ahead for potential problems they might encounter during a long race.

    (A) appreciate
    (B) improvise
    (C) pronounce
    (D) shelter

32. Although many people consider air conditioning to be essential, it is often ------- if a house is built to capture surrounding winds and be -------- from the sun by tall trees.

    (A) complimented... protected
    (B) fraudulent... faded
    (C) protective.... hidden
    (D) superfluous... sheltered

33. When pure olive oil has been ------- by other oils it must be -------- so that consumers do not pay more for a product that has been mixed with other ingredients.

    (A) adulterated... relabeled
    (B) eclipsed... poured
    (C) hosted.... limited
    (D) thawed.... simulated

CONTINUE TO THE NEXT PAGE

34. Although many people believe that voter turnout was reduced by the -------- weather, the effect of the rain on the number of voters was actually ---------.

    (A) sunny… flattering
    (B) inconsistent…massive
    (C) inclement…negligible
    (D) blustery… requested

35. Before the Great Depression in America, there was great ------ in income with some Americans experiencing tremendous wealth and others confined to a life of -------.

    (A) compatibility… affluence
    (B) disparity… penury
    (C) equality… poverty
    (D) performance… mediocrity

36. Before the Pilgrims came to North America, they fled from the ------- political situation in England to the relatively ------- environment in Holland.

    (A) conscientious… responsible
    (B) experimental… unstable
    (C) misguided… chaotic
    (D) volatile… calm

37. When too much ------ builds up in a river bed, the river must be ------- in order to keep water flowing in the same path.

    (A) algae… waded
    (B) garbage… neglected
    (C) sediment…dredged
    (D) water…. flooded

CONTINUE TO THE NEXT PAGE

38. Bonnie and Clyde were famous for their ------- bank robberies, often entering a bank in broad daylight without wearing -------.

   (A) brazen… disguises
   (B) honest…shoes
   (C) mystical… hats
   (D) vivid… masks

39. Despite the words of -------- that the director received from movie critics, she still felt ------ every time she released a new film.

   (A) astonishment… placid
   (B) encouragement… apprehensive
   (C) praise… confident
   (D) wistfulness… timid

40. The downtown area became a far more attractive place to spend time when ------ buildings were ------ and replaced by small parks.

   (A) derelict… razed
   (B) historic… restored
   (C) new … constructed
   (D) residential… painted

STOP

IF YOU HAVE TIME LEFT YOU MAY CHECK YOUR ANSWERS IN THIS SECTION ONLY

Quantitative Reasoning

37 questions
35 minutes

Each math question has four answer choices after it. Choose the answer choice that best answers the question.

Make sure that you fill in the correct answer on your answer sheet. You may write in the test booklet.

SAMPLE QUESTION:

1.   What is the perimeter of a rectangle that has a length of 3 cm and a width of 5 cm?
     ($P = 2l + 2w$)

     (A)   6 cm

     (B)   10 cm

     (C)   8 cm

     ●   16 cm

The correct answer is 16 cm and circle D is filled in.

STOP
DO NOT MOVE ON TO THE SECTION UNTIL TOLD TO

Part One – Word Problems

1. If $\#m = 5m - 3$, then what is the value of $\#6$?

   (A) 27
   (B) 30
   (C) 33
   (D) 39

2. If $b - c = 6$, then c is equal to which expression?

   (A) $b + 6$
   (B) $6 - b$
   (C) $b - 6$
   (D) $-b - 6$

3. If x represents the number of even numbers between 1 and 20 inclusive, which expression represents the number of even numbers between 1 and 10 inclusive?

   (A) $x - 10$
   (B) $x - 5$
   (C) $x + 5$
   (D) $x + 10$

4. If the height of a triangle is increased by 10 percent and the base length is increased by 10 percent, then what is the percent increase in the area of the triangle?

   (A) 20%
   (B) 21%
   (C) 25%
   (D) 30%

CONTINUE TO THE NEXT PAGE

5. If $(x + n)^2 = x^2 + 10x + 25$, then what is the value of n?

    (A) 5
    (B) 10
    (C) 15
    (D) 25

6. Differently colored buckets were filled with water and then placed in a sunny spot. The temperature in each bucket was measured when the buckets were filled and again one hour later. Recorded below is the temperature rise measured in each bucket, in degrees.

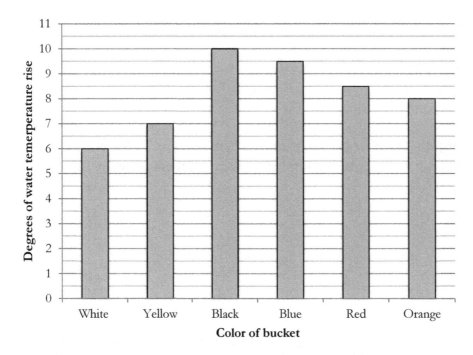

    According to the above graph, which is closest to the mean number of degrees that the temperature rose?

    (A) 6.5 degrees
    (B) 7.0 degrees
    (C) 7.5 degrees
    (D) 8.0 degrees

CONTINUE TO THE NEXT PAGE

7.   A set of 6 numbers had a mean of 8. One number was removed and the mean of the remaining numbers was 7. What number was removed?

   (A) 7
   (B) 13
   (C) 35
   (D) 48

8.   If $xy = 70$ and x and y are both integers, then what is the greatest possible value of $x + y$?

   (A) 17
   (B) 19
   (C) 35
   (D) 71

9.   The volume of a sphere can be found using the formula $V = \frac{4}{3}\pi r^3$. If the length of the radius of Sphere A is 2 times the length of the radius of Sphere B, then which statement is true?

   (A)   The volume of Sphere A is 2 times the volume of Sphere B.
   (B)   The volume of Sphere B is 2 times the volume of Sphere A.
   (C)   The volume of Sphere A is 8 times the volume of Sphere B.
   (D)   The volume of Sphere B is 8 times the volume of Sphere A.

CONTINUE TO THE NEXT PAGE

10. The two triangles shown below are similar.

Triangle 1   Triangle 2

A = 40 cm^2 A = 10 cm^2

What is the ratio of a side length in Triangle 1 to the length of the corresponding side in Triangle 2?

(A) 2 to 1
(B) 4 to 1
(C) 8 to 1
(D) 16 to 1

11. Brian and Meredith start at the same place and time walking along a straight path. If Brian walks twice as fast as Meredith and after 20 minutes they are 600 feet apart, which equation would give Meredith's speed (M) in feet per minute?

(A) $2M - M = 600$
(B) $40M - 600 = 20M$
(C) $40M = 600 - 20M$
(D) $20(M + 2M) = 600$

CONTINUE TO THE NEXT PAGE

12. Justin took his boat out on the bay, pausing along the way to admire the sunset. The following graph shows how far Justin was from shore as a function of time.

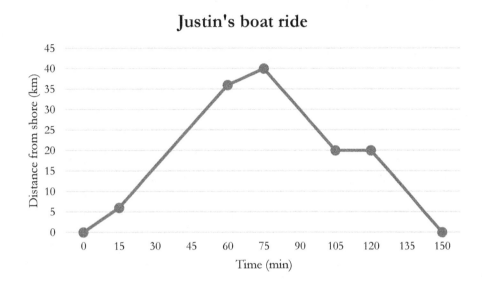

Justin's boat ride

How far was Justin from shore when he paused to admire the sunset (assume the boat did not move while he paused)?

(A) 20 km
(B) 36 km
(C) 40 km
(D) 150 km

13. Perry is using a random number generator. He sets the computer to choose a whole number between 1 and 10 inclusive for each trial. What is the probability that both numbers chosen will both be less than 5?

(A) $\dfrac{4}{25}$

(B) $\dfrac{2}{5}$

(C) $\dfrac{7}{10}$

(D) $\dfrac{4}{5}$

CONTINUE TO THE NEXT PAGE

14. Glenda compiled the number of hits for each player on the team. She summarized the results in the following table of statistical measures.

Statistical Measures	
Measure	Value
Mean	75
Median	65
Mode	67
Range	104

If a player with 65 hits had gotten 105 hits instead, which of the measures could possibly remain the same?

(A) mean and median
(B) median and mode
(C) median, mode and range
(D) range

15. A baseball team played 20 games during the summer. The range of attendance for each game is shown in the histogram.

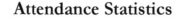

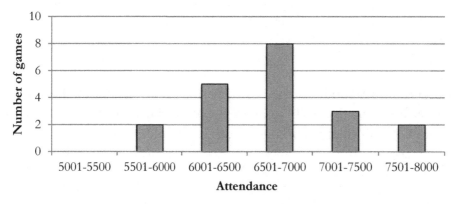

Which measure of central tendency could never equal one of the 20 individual attendance figures?

(A) median
(B) mode
(C) range
(D) mean

CONTINUE TO THE NEXT PAGE

16. Albert conducts an experiment by tossing 10 quarters, recording the number of quarters that landed on heads, and then repeating. After 40 tosses, he collects his results and determines that the mean and median number of heads is 5 and that the data is symmetric about that value.

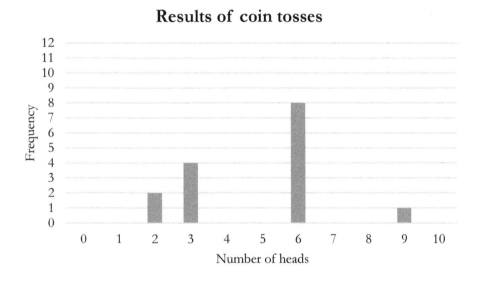

Results of coin tosses

Albert starts to create the graph above but does not finish. If the range of the data is 8 and the maximum value is 9, then how many times did exactly 5 quarters land on heads?

(A) 0

(B) 6

(C) 9

(D) 10

CONTINUE TO THE NEXT PAGE

17. The net below is going to be folded into a cube.

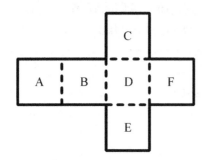

If side D is going to be on the bottom of the cube, which side will be on the top?

(A) side A
(B) side B
(C) side C
(D) side F

18. An elementary school has set up a phone tree. At noon, the first person calls four people. At one o'clock, those four people each call four more people. At two PM, those sixteen people each call another four people. If this pattern continues, which expression would represent the total number of people called by 4:30 PM?

(A) $1 + 4^5$
(B) $1 + 4^6$
(C) $1 + 4 + 4^2 + 4^3 + 4^4 + 4^5$
(D) $4 + 4^2 + 4^3 + 4^4 + 4^5$

19. If $y = 3x^2 + 2$ and $-3 \leq x \leq 2$, then what is the greatest possible value for y?

(A) 14
(B) 29
(C) 32
(D) 40

CONTINUE TO THE NEXT PAGE

20. If 8 is a multiple of x and 12 is a multiple of y, then which value must xy be a factor of?

    (A) 4
    (B) 20
    (C) 24
    (D) 96

Part Two – Quantitative Comparisons

Directions: Use the information in the question to compare the quantities in Columns A and B. After comparing the two quantities, choose the correct answer choice:

    (A) Quantity in Column A is greater.
    (B) Quantity in Column B is greater.
    (C) The quantities in Column A and Column B are equal.
    (D) Cannot be determined from information given.

	Column A	Column B
21.	$6 \times (2 + 3) - 5$	25

Caleb has $1.32 in quarters, dimes, nickels, and pennies. (Note: 1 quarter = $0.25, 1 dime = $0.10, 1 nickel = $0.05, and 1 penny = $0.01.)

	Column A	Column B
22.	10	The smallest number of coins that Caleb could have

CONTINUE TO THE NEXT PAGE

Area of triangle = 18 in²   Area of square = 25 in²

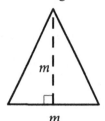 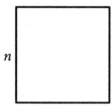

Note: Figures are not drawn to scale

	Column A	Column B
23.	m	n

	Column A	Column B
24.	M	$\dfrac{1}{M}$

x and y are positive integers

	Column A	Column B
25.	$(x-y)(x+y)^2$	$x^3 - x^2y - xy^2 - y^3$

Line q has the equation $y = 2x + 6$. Line m is perpendicular to line q.

	Column A	Column B
26.	The slope of line m	$\dfrac{1}{2}$

CONTINUE TO THE NEXT PAGE

Carol has $1.65 in quarters and nickels. She has twice as many quarters as nickels.

(Note: 1 quarter = $0.25, 1 nickel = $0.05)

	Column A	Column B
27.	$1.50	The value of Carol's quarters

The area of a rectangle is 30 inches^2

	Column A	Column B
28.	The perimeter of the rectangle	26 inches

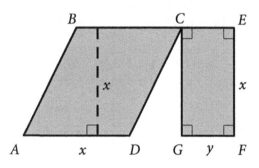

The parallelogram $ABCD$ and the rectangle $CEFG$ are shown in the figure above. The distance between points D and G is equal to y.

	Column A	Column B
29.	The area of the shaded region	$x(x + y)$

	Column A	Column B
30.	The price of a shirt after a 20% discount.	The price of the same shirt after two separate 10% discounts

CONTINUE TO THE NEXT PAGE

	Column A	Column B
31.	The slope of a line between $(2, 4)$ and $(4, 5)$	The slope of a line that is perpendicular to the line $y = \dfrac{1}{2}x + 7$

The product of 3 consecutive even integers is 480.

	Column A	Column B
32.	The smallest of the 3 consecutive even integers	6

Before an election, a survey was done in two separate towns to see which of two candidates voters were planning to vote for. This data was then used to predict who would win the election.

	Town 1	Town 2
Percent of town surveyed	50%	25%
Number of votes for Candidate A	200	101
Number of votes for Candidate B	150	225

	Column A	Column B
33.	The number of predicted votes for Candidate A in Town 1	The number of predicted votes for Candidate A in Town 2

CONTINUE TO THE NEXT PAGE

Rhombus *CDEF*   Triangle *GHJ*

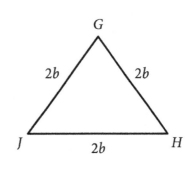

Column A	Column B
34. The perimeter of Rhombus *CDEF*	The perimeter of Triangle *GHJ*

The spinner below is divided into six equally-sized pieces. It was spun twice.

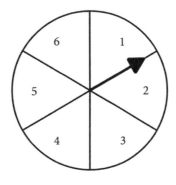

Column A	Column B
35. If the spinner lands on 3 the first time, the probability that the spinner will land on 3 with the second spin	If the spinner lands on 3 the first time, the probability that the spinner will land on a number other than 3 with the second spin

CONTINUE TO THE NEXT PAGE

Column A | Column B

36. The number of multiples of 8 between 4 and 58 | The number of multiples of 8 between 2 and 63

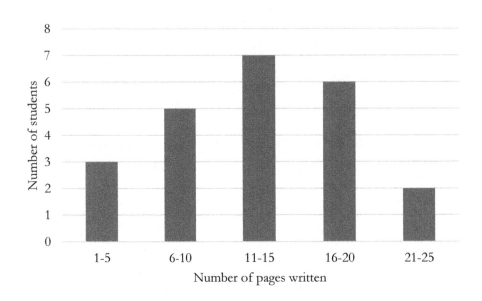

The histogram above shows the number of pages written by each student in the class.

Column A | Column B

37. The median number of pages written | The range of the number of pages written

STOP

IF YOU HAVE TIME LEFT YOU MAY CHECK YOUR ANSWERS IN THIS SECTION ONLY

Reading Comprehension

36 questions
35 minutes

The Reading Comprehension section has six short passages. Each passage has six questions after it. Choose the answer choice that comes closest to what is stated or implied in the passage. You may write in the test booklet.

STOP

DO NOT MOVE ON TO THE SECTION UNTIL TOLD TO

Questions #1-6

1　　Stretching approximately 2,200 miles over 14 states, the Appalachian Trail is a
2　popular hiking route that many hiking enthusiasts dream of one day completing. Some
3　hikers, called "section hikers," choose to cover the trail in smaller sections over the
4　course of multiple trips, or sometimes even several years. Others, who have the luxury
5　of time and seek a more difficult challenge, attempt to hike the entire length within one
6　hiking season. These adventurers are called "thru-hikers." Whether a section hiker or
7　a thru-hiker, anyone who successfully completes the trail in its entirety is designated a
8　"2,000 Miler" by the Appalachian Trail Conservancy. To date, there are more than
9　10,000 people who have been bestowed with that title.
10　　Beginning in March or April, most thru-hikers set off from Georgia and travel
11　north along the trail toward Maine. Of the more than 1,000 people who begin the
12　journey each year, only a few hundred actually complete it, usually within five to seven
13　months. Along the way, the main path is marked by white paint and any side trails that
14　extend to shelters are marked with blue paint. Hikers can stop at any of the more than
15　200 shelters to rest, go to the privy (bathroom) if there is one, and possibly meet up with
16　other hikers who are at the same location.
17　　Many hikers would likely say that one of the best parts of the experience is the
18　camaraderie among the hikers. As with many specific interests, there is a particular
19　culture that surrounds the activity of thru-hiking. Many hikers give themselves a special
20　trail nickname or have one assigned to them by other hikers. Another custom is for
21　hikers to leave items, such as food, candy, or some other type of gift behind for a fellow
22　hiker to find. These gifts, called "Trail Magic," can make for a pleasant surprise after a
23　long day of intense hiking.
24　　Because the majority of the trail passes through wilderness, many dangers lurk
25　along the path and threaten to interfere with hikers' mission of reaching their final post.
26　Each year only a small percentage of people who have intentions of thru-hiking
27　accomplish the feat. Right from the beginning of the northbound journey, steep hills in
28　Georgia pose a difficult, often painful, challenge that defeats some hikers who are less-
29　seasoned mountain climbers. Similarly, overwhelming fatigue after months on the road,
30　and minor injuries, such as sprained and broken bones, are also common reasons hikers
31　depart from the trail early. And although animal attacks and animal-borne illnesses are
32　rare, they do occur on occasion.
33　　For an adventurous thru-hiker who thrives on adrenaline, though, all of these
34　dangers are merely just part of the excitement of joining the exclusive club of 2,000
35　Milers.

CONTINUE TO THE NEXT PAGE

1. Which best expresses the main idea of the passage?

    (A) The Appalachian Trail is approximately 2,000 miles long.
    (B) It is a great accomplishment to hike the entire Appalachian Trail.
    (C) There is a risk of injury with any hiking experience.
    (D) If hikers make it past Georgia, they are likely to complete the hike to Maine.

2. The first paragraph implies all of the following about the Appalachian trail EXCEPT

    (A) many hikers choose to hike different portions of the trail over several years.
    (B) it is easy to hike the entire trail in a season.
    (C) it is considered an honor to be named a "2,000 Miler".
    (D) it requires a large time commitment to hike the entire trail at one time.

3. The author describes Trail Magic as

    (A) nicknames given to thru-hikers.
    (B) dangerous animal-borne diseases.
    (C) treats that hikers leave for one another.
    (D) thru-hikers.

4. Which of the following can be inferred from the second paragraph?

    (A) Bathroom facilities are not always available along the trail.
    (B) Most hikers who don't complete the journey are stopped by the steep trails that they encounter in Georgia.
    (C) The trail is regularly maintained and well-kept.
    (D) Hikers are not allowed to begin in Maine and hike south towards Georgia.

5. According to the last paragraph, hikers who manage to complete the roughly 2,200-mile journey are generally

    (A) injured by the time they finish hiking.
    (B) worried about animal attacks.
    (C) already planning when they will be able to come back and complete the Appalachian Trail again.
    (D) motivated by the exhilaration they feel from completing an adventure.

6. The main purpose of the fourth paragraph (lines 24-32) is to

    (A) explain why hiking the Appalachian Trail is a rare accomplishment.
    (B) detail the steps hikers must take to prepare for the Appalachian Trail.
    (C) describe why it is so difficult for hikers to make it through the Georgia section of the trail.
    (D) create a sense of suspense for the reader.

CONTINUE TO THE NEXT PAGE

Questions #7-12

1   How much difference can one person make in the world? Consider the life of
2   Wangari Maathi – the first African woman to win the Nobel Peace Prize. From fighting
3   for change, to helping others in need, to using words to inspire others, she is one person
4   who left a tremendous impact on the world that will have long-lasting effects beyond
5   her lifetime.
6   Wangari Maathai was born in 1940 in Kenya. Because her family believed in the
7   importance of education, she attended school as a child and then later transferred to a
8   Catholic school, where she learned English. At a time when girls often did not have the
9   same opportunities as boys, it could be difficult for a girl to obtain a higher education.
10   However, Maathai was an exemplary student and was awarded a scholarship to study at
11   Mount St. Scholastica College in Kansas, where she received a degree in biology in 1964.
12   This would be the first of many earned and honorary degrees she would receive during
13   her life. In 1966, she received a master's degree from the University of Pittsburgh and
14   then earned a doctorate in veterinary medicine from the University of Nairobi five years
15   later. This degree in particular was an extraordinary accomplishment. With it, she
16   became the first woman in East or Central Africa to ever receive a doctoral degree.
17   As a leader for the National Council of Women of Kenya, Maathai often fought
18   for women's rights. In addition to her desire to support women's interests, she was also
19   interested in protecting the environment. With these motivations in mind, Maathai
20   ultimately sought to develop a tree-planting program that could help the community
21   while improving the environment.
22   In 1977, she founded the Green Belt Movement. At that time in Kenya, the
23   expanding population created a demand for more homes and other buildings. This
24   increase in development led to an increase in deforestation. With the Green Belt
25   Movement, Maathai encouraged women to go to work planting trees. The mission of
26   the movement was three-fold – it would plant trees to help the environment, create a
27   source of firewood for fuel, and also provide employment for women.
28   After the movement spread across Kenya, Maathai met with people from other
29   African countries to expand the program further. With the support of these additional
30   countries, the Green Belt Movement has planted more than 30 million trees in Africa.
31   Throughout her life, Maathai continued to fight for democracy, women's rights,
32   and environmental protection. Although she passed away in 2011, her work will
33   continue to influence environmental and equality programs in Africa and beyond. And
34   her life will continue to inspire people around the world.

CONTINUE TO THE NEXT PAGE

7. Which statement best expresses the main idea of the passage?

    (A) Wangari Maathai struggled to find educational opportunities.
    (B) Without Wangari Maathai, women in Kenya would not be receiving doctoral degrees today.
    (C) Wangari Maathai fought to improve the lives of others.
    (D) Wangari Maathai helped developers responsibly build houses.

8. The passage implies that the Green Belt movement

    (A) was responsible for deforestation.
    (B) had trouble transitioning to countries outside of Kenya.
    (C) was only interested in increasing the number of trees in Kenya.
    (D) led to a greater number of trees in Africa.

9. It can be inferred from the passage that

    (A) no Kenyan women received doctorates in 1965.
    (B) Wangari Maathai came from a large family.
    (C) Wangari Maathai has not been recognized outside of Africa.
    (D) the number of African women employed has risen.

10. Which word best describes the author's tone concerning Wangari Maathai?

    (A) hesitant
    (B) admiring
    (C) doubtful
    (D) awkward

11. As used in the passage, the term "deforestation" most nearly means

    (A) to plant more trees.
    (B) to expand to other countries.
    (C) to cut down trees.
    (D) providing jobs for women.

12. Information from the passage supports which statement?

    (A) Women are more affected by deforestation than men.
    (B) In 1977 there was a need for more firewood in Kenya.
    (C) There were not other people fighting for women's rights in Kenya during Wangari Maathai's lifetime.
    (D) The Nobel Peace Prize is frequently awarded to Africans.

CONTINUE TO THE NEXT PAGE

Questions #13-18

1   Many students and parents agree that our school district should install solar panels
2 to power some, if not all, of our school buildings. Not only would solar panels be
3 beneficial to our school community for several reasons, they would also help protect the
4 environment in general.
5   First, unlike fossil fuels and other sources of nonrenewable energy, solar energy is
6 a renewable resource. At some time in the possibly near future, nonrenewable energy
7 sources will be completely depleted. Why should our schools create even more
8 pollution and contribute to this destruction of Earth when instead we can do something
9 beneficial for the environment? By using solar energy, we will be drawing from an
10 endless supply of resources that can be renewed. Experts say that it would only take a
11 small fraction of the world's surface to be covered in solar panels to supply enough
12 power for the entire world. People who use solar energy prevent the use of over 70
13 million barrels of oil each year.
14   Solar panels can also help the environment by being a source of educational
15 lessons for children and adults alike. The panels on display are likely to become a talking
16 point for environmental issues. Parents can teach their children about renewable energy
17 sources. They also can show them other ways to minimize their impact on the
18 environment at home and at school. Perhaps the schools' panels will even inspire other
19 people to install panels for their businesses and homes. Like a rock skipping across a
20 pond, our solar panels could create a ripple effect that ultimately benefits the greater
21 community and the world.
22   Likewise, many solar panel programs support this theory. They even offer special
23 initiatives for school districts willing to use their installed panels to educate students and
24 others in their community. We may even be able to apply for a grant from one of these
25 programs and have the panels installed at no cost to our taxpayers.
26   Even if the district has to pay the cost of installation, another major benefit of using
27 solar panels is the money that can be saved on energy costs. One district in California
28 saved almost 300,000 dollars after one year of using a solar system. Based on their best
29 projections, they are hoping that solar energy will save them millions of dollars over 25
30 years. Perhaps our district will benefit from such returns if we install solar panels, too.
31   Overall, with millions of dollars and the fate of the environment at stake, installing
32 solar panels in our school district is one possibility that should not be ignored.

CONTINUE TO THE NEXT PAGE

13. What is the primary purpose of this passage?

    (A) To encourage a particular course of action.
    (B) To inform the reader about the pros and cons of solar energy.
    (C) To disprove a popular theory.
    (D) To discourage the reader from polluting.

14. What does the author mean by "ripple effect" (line 20)?

    (A) An action by one person often influences one other person to do the same action.
    (B) Pollution will lead to more pollution.
    (C) The effect of a single action is often much greater than just the immediate response.
    (D) A little water can lead to flooding.

15. The author's tone when discussing the implementation of solar panels can best be described as

    (A) cynical.
    (B) humorous.
    (C) indifferent.
    (D) passionate.

16. The passage implies that the economic effects of solar panels would be

    (A) potentially significant over the long term.
    (B) disregarded by students.
    (C) hard to determine.
    (D) greater than the educational effects.

17. Which conclusion could be drawn from the evidence presented in the second paragraph?

    (A) Using solar panels for energy production has the potential to reduce oil use by 70 million barrels each year.
    (B) Solar panel use is limited by current technology.
    (C) It is tough to get community support for the installation of solar panels at schools.
    (D) It is necessary for schools to encourage use of alternative energy sources since we could run out fossil fuels in the not too distant future.

18. Which best describes the organization of this passage?

    (A) An argument is presented and then proven wrong.
    (B) An assertion is made and then evidence is provided to support that assertion.
    (C) Several competing theories are presented.
    (D) Events are presented in chronological order.

CONTINUE TO THE NEXT PAGE

Questions #19-24

1   In its over 80-year history, The Seeing Eye in Morristown, New Jersey has placed
2   over 15,000 guide dogs with more than 8,000 visually-impaired people. Due to its long
3   history and reputation for success, along with its influence on the development of
4   similar organizations, The Seeing Eye has familiarized many people with the concept of
5   service dogs for the blind. Yet, few people are aware of how the group began.
6   Thousands of dogs may have passed through training and completed years of service,
7   but as with the start of most things, it all started with one. That one dog's name was
8   Buddy. She was the first Seeing Eye dog.

9   Buddy's human partner was a man named Morris Frank. Although many people
10 often refer to a dog's handler as a "master," the relationship between person and Seeing
11 Eye dog is more a dual partnership than a superior-subordinate match, and Buddy and
12 Morris' relationship exemplified this right from the start.

13   Morris was able to obtain a Seeing Eye dog due to the work of Dorothy Eustis and
14 Jack Humphrey. In 1927, Morris encountered an article in *The Saturday Evening Post*,
15 written by Dorothy Eustis, in which she described a school that trained German
16 Shepherd dogs to lead the blind. Dorothy and the dog-training school were located in
17 Switzerland, but that did little to discourage Morris Frank. Interested in obtaining a
18 guide dog of his own, Morris wrote a letter to Dorothy to inquire about the innovative
19 program discussed in her article. Her encouraging reply led Morris to take a trip to
20 Switzerland. There, he met with Dorothy and Jack Humphrey, the head trainer of the
21 guide dog school.

22   In many ways, this historic meeting was the start of The Seeing Eye's development.
23 Morris was matched with a German Shepherd named Buddy, and together, they
24 completed five long weeks of intensive training. Then Morris and Buddy returned to
25 America. Charged with the task of demonstrating the worthiness of a guide dog, Morris
26 and Buddy walked along a busy New York City street, to the amazement of a group of
27 on-looking reporters. Undoubtedly, both dog and man were proud of what they
28 accomplished in that moment.

29   Shortly afterward, The Seeing Eye was officially formed, with Dorothy Eustis and
30 Jack Humphrey serving as President and Vice President, respectively. Initially
31 operating for two years in Morris' home state of Tennessee, the agency later relocated
32 to its current location in New Jersey. With the help of Buddy, Morris gained a new
33 independence, self-confidence, and sense of purpose. Although Buddy died after 10
34 years of service, every Seeing Eye dog Morris received in successive years was also
35 bestowed with the name Buddy in honor of the original heroine.

CONTINUE TO THE NEXT PAGE

19. The main purpose of this passage is to

    (A) provide background information about the work of Dorothy Eustis.
    (B) describe the importance of working relationships between animals and humans.
    (C) share a story of how one person's perseverance improved the lives of many.
    (D) explain the differences between New York City and Switzerland.

20. According to the passage, Dorothy Eustis

    (A) was Vice President of the Seeing Eye.
    (B) lived in Switzerland.
    (C) trained the original Buddy herself.
    (D) was passionate about bringing seeing eye dogs to America.

21. Why were reporters amazed to see Buddy and Morris Frank walking in New York City?

    (A) Morris Frank was visually-impaired and the reporters had never seen a
        demonstration with a seeing eye dog before.
    (B) It is rare to see a dog on the streets of New York City.
    (C) Morris Frank did not live in New York City.
    (D) Buddy had not yet been trained.

22. What does it mean when the passages states that the relationship between Buddy and
    Morris Frank was "more a dual partnership than a superior-subordinate match"?

    (A) Buddy and Morris were equals in the relationship.
    (B) Morris was clearly the master of Buddy.
    (C) Morris and Buddy made the decision together to come to America.
    (D) Buddy was also visually impaired.

23. According to the passage, how did Morris Frank first find out about seeing eye dogs?

    (A) Dorothy Eustis sent him a letter.
    (B) He read an article in a newspaper.
    (C) On a trip to Switzerland, he was introduced to Dorothy Eustis.
    (D) He was contacted by The Seeing Eye in Tennessee.

24. The statement "charged with the task" (line 25) implies which of the following

    (A) Morris Frank was taking a considerable risk to use only a guide dog to navigate
        New York city streets.
    (B) Dorothy Eustis was disappointed that few people knew about seeing eye dogs.
    (C) Reporters were hesitant to allow a visually-impaired person to walk the streets
        in New York.
    (D) Morris Frank felt responsible for illustrating the usefulness of seeing eye dogs.

CONTINUE TO THE NEXT PAGE

Questions #25-30

1   Seven-year-old Maggie lounged on the porch stoop, trapped in a perpetual state of
2 lethargy brought on by the unbearable heat choking the air around her. A persistent
3 wave of higher than normal temperatures had pounded the region for the past month
4 and only served to worsen the already bad conditions brought on by the severe drought.
5 Whenever Maggie heard her father talking with other farmers in town, this was all they
6 ever discussed – how 1934 was the worst drought year they had ever experienced; how
7 it was sure to be remembered as one of the worst droughts in history.
8   Although Maggie did not know if they were right since her less than decade of life
9 limited her frame of reference, she did know that the conditions were the worst she had
10 ever witnessed. This past season, their crops had withered and slumped over, like fallen
11 soldiers on a battlefield. The dry, hardened ground disintegrated into dust, and then
12 the dust was blown into large, swirling black clouds when harsh winds whipped through
13 the plains.
14   Maggie recalled one day at school when her class became trapped by a sudden
15 storm. As the barreling dust passed over the building, it covered the windows with dirt
16 and debris. In an instant, the bright light of midday turned as dark as night, and the
17 class and teacher were bound to the confines of the room's four walls. In the midst of
18 nature's fury, they huddled together and comforted each other as they waited several
19 hours for the storm to settle down and grant them their freedom.
20   That night at home, Maggie's father referred to the storm as a "black blizzard," and
21 Maggie observed that she would much rather experience a traditional blizzard than this
22 new dusty, dirty variety. At least a white blizzard created an occasion for fun. With any
23 significant accumulation, Maggie and her siblings would take leave from their
24 household duties early and spend the afternoon playing in the snow. In Maggie's view,
25 there was nothing quite as beautiful as a sparkling canvas of fresh snow covering the
26 acreage of their farm. She always paused to admire the untouched landscape before
27 disturbing its newness with her footprints.
28   Now today, in the blistering heat, Maggie looked out onto the cracked layer of dust
29 coating the earth and imagined it covered with a thick layer of snow. She envisioned
30 shimmering hexagonal flakes floating down from the heavens and landing one by one,
31 upon the layer of snow already before her. Slowly she stretched out her hand and
32 pictured the drops softly falling into the curve of her uplifted palm. It was not long
33 before the refreshing thoughts helped to soothe her scorching brain and eased her body
34 into a deep and peaceful sleep.

CONTINUE TO THE NEXT PAGE

25.   The main purpose of this passage is to

(A)   inform the reader of the dire consequences of the drought of 1934.
(B)   compare and contrast dust storms and winter blizzards.
(C)   explain why Maggie left school before finishing elementary school.
(D)   share a childhood experience of a young girl in the 1930s.

26.   According to the passage, a "black blizzard" is

(A)   dirty snow.
(B)   a huge snow storm.
(C)   a giant dust storm.
(D)   extremely common in the area that Maggie lives in.

27.   The mood of the first paragraph (lines 1-7) is best described as

(A)   oppressive misery.
(B)   intellectual curiosity.
(C)   childhood restlessness.
(D)   nostalgic musing.

28.   The passage provides evidence to support which statement about the farmers in the area where Maggie lives?

(A)   Many of them are planning to move away.
(B)   They have had to adopt new farming techniques to deal with drought.
(C)   They can't remember a worse year for their crops.
(D)   Heat stroke has become a major problem for them.

29.   The phrase "they huddled together and comforted each other" (line 18) was included in order to

(A)   inform the reader about a dust storm.
(B)   illustrate how scary it is to be caught in a dust storm.
(C)   explain why Maggie wanted to leave her school.
(D)   show that Maggie was fearless.

30.   The word "lethargy" in line 2 here most nearly means

(A)   lack of energy.
(B)   emotion.
(C)   wonder.
(D)   peace.

CONTINUE TO THE NEXT PAGE

Questions #31-36

1   Did you ever enter an elevator by yourself and stand with your back facing away
2   from the doors? If you are like most people, you probably haven't, and perhaps the
3   thought of facing that way has never even crossed your mind. Perhaps you have never
4   even considered why people in an elevator stand one way versus another. This is
5   because certain practices are social norms – unspoken rules of how people are expected
6   to behave in social situations. This includes facing the door when riding in an elevator,
7   joining an already-formed line by standing at the back of it, and practicing certain
8   manners when dining at a restaurant.
9   Yet, if these customs are not formal rules, why do people follow them so often?
10   Psychologists believe it is because of conformity. Although the term may have a
11   negative connotation for some people, particularly those who desire to be different,
12   conformity is simply a part of our nature as humans. Most people have the desire to be
13   liked, and accepted by, others – at least to some degree.
14   Even people who deny any need to conform may have difficulty resisting
15   conformity when faced with social pressures, and this is especially true when one person
16   stands in opposition to the majority. A majority influence can be very powerful. It can
17   cause people to give an incorrect answer they know to be wrong, to change their views,
18   and even to see things that do not exist.
19   Imagine yourself walking up to a group of people looking up at something in a
20   tree. They all claim to see a snake way up high on one of the branches. You join the
21   group and strain to see the slithering creature that supposedly lies there in plain sight,
22   and yet, you see nothing but a tree. What do you do? Do you report that you honestly
23   cannot see anything, or do you claim that you can see what everyone else is seeing?
24   Surprisingly, when faced with this situation, many people would admit to seeing a
25   snake, just like the rest of the group, even though there is no snake there. This trickery
26   is effective because on some subconscious level, people believe that if the majority says
27   something is true, then it must be so, despite the physical evidence to the contrary.
28   When placed in opposition to the group view, people begin to doubt themselves. Or
29   perhaps they feel confident in their view but do not want to be seen as strange or defiant
30   by other members of the group.
31   In many cases, conformity is harmless, or sometimes even beneficial; but in other
32   situations, it may be dangerous, or harmful to others. One must rely on an independent
33   mind to appropriately discern the difference, though deciding whether to conform is
34   not always a conscious choice.

CONTINUE TO THE NEXT PAGE

31. Which statement about conformity would the author be most likely to agree with?

   (A) Conformity should be avoided at all costs.
   (B) The results of conformity are always harmless.
   (C) People are not always aware that they are even making a choice to conform.
   (D) For the good of society, more people should conform.

32. In line 5, the term "social norms" refers to

   (A) rules that people in a society seem to follow.
   (B) interactions between people.
   (C) large gatherings of people.
   (D) data collected by social scientists.

33. The main purpose of the fourth paragraph (lines 19-23) is to

   (A) introduce a new topic.
   (B) keep the reader's attention with a humorous aside.
   (C) present evidence against a particular theory.
   (D) provide an example to illustrate the main point of the passage.

34. In lines 32-33, relying "on an independent mind" can be interpreted to mean

   (A) completely ignoring the influence of other people.
   (B) evaluating a situation without the input of others.
   (C) not joining social groups.
   (D) weighing the opinions of other people before making a decision.

35. The organization of the passage as a whole can best be described as

   (A) a presentation of conflicting viewpoints.
   (B) a theory is presented and then illustrations are provided.
   (C) several unrelated stories.
   (D) a collection of facts.

36. The passage suggests that a person who faces the door in an elevator most likely does so

   (A) in order to get off the elevator first.
   (B) to limit interaction with other people.
   (C) because other people are facing the door.
   (D) for absolutely no reason.

STOP

IF YOU HAVE TIME LEFT YOU MAY CHECK YOUR ANSWERS IN THIS SECTION ONLY

Mathematics Achievement

47 questions
40 minutes

Each math question has four answer choices after it. Choose the answer choice that best answers the question.

Make sure that you fill in the correct answer on your answer sheet. You may write in the test booklet.

SAMPLE QUESTION:

1. Which number can be divided by 4 with nothing left over?

    (A) 6
    ● 12
    (C) 15
    (D) 22

Since 12 can be divided by 4 with no remainder, circle B is filled in.

STOP

DO NOT MOVE ON TO THE SECTION UNTIL TOLD TO

1. In the coordinate grid below, the area of each square is 4 in².

    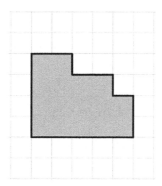

    What is the area of the shaded region?

    (A) 16 in²

    (B) 20 in²

    (C) 64 in²

    (D) 80 in²

2. A bag contains 6 red marbles, 4 green marbles, and 5 yellow marbles. Alexis draws one marble from the bag and then returns it to the bag. She then draws a second marble. What is the probability that both marbles will be green?

    (A) $\dfrac{1}{4}$

    (B) $\dfrac{4}{15}$

    (C) $\dfrac{1}{4} \times \dfrac{1}{4}$

    (D) $\dfrac{4}{15} \times \dfrac{4}{15}$

3. Which of the following is equivalent to $4.3 \times 10^{-3} + 5.6 \times 10^{-5}$?

    (A) 9.9×10^{-8}

    (B) 5.643×10^{-5}

    (C) 4.356×10^{-5}

    (D) 4.356×10^{-3}

CONTINUE TO THE NEXT PAGE

4. Which value is NOT equal to $\frac{1}{3}$?

    (A) $\dfrac{0.5}{1.4}$

    (B) $\dfrac{1.5}{4.5}$

    (C) $0.33333333\overline{3}$

    (D) $0.3\overline{3}$

5. If $\frac{2}{3}x = \frac{3}{2}x$, then what is the value of x?

    (A) $-\dfrac{3}{2}$

    (B) 0

    (C) 1

    (D) $\dfrac{3}{2}$

6. If $\frac{2}{w} \times \frac{w}{2} = 1$, then what value(s) of w makes the equation true?

    (A) 2 only

    (B) all real numbers

    (C) all real numbers except 0

    (D) there are no values for w that would make the equation true

7. Which number is equal to $\sqrt{16 + 9}$?

    (A) 5

    (B) 7

    (C) 12

    (D) 25

CONTINUE TO THE NEXT PAGE

8. Scores for each competitor at a gymnastics competition are shown in the following column graph.

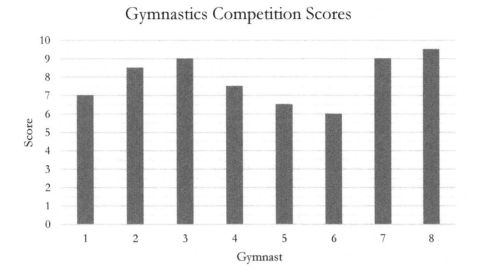

Gymnastics Competition Scores

What was the median score of the competition?

(A) 6.0

(B) 7.0

(C) 8.0

(D) 9.0

9. Annie and Sylvia have a dog walking business. Yesterday, Annie walked twice as many dogs as Sylvia did. If they walked a total of 18 dogs, how many dogs did Annie walk?

(A) 6

(B) 9

(C) 10

(D) 12

CONTINUE TO THE NEXT PAGE

10. Ms. Griffith figured out that the mean test score for her five students on the last test was 85. Now she can only find four of the test papers. The scores on the papers that she can find were 92, 95, 84, and 72. What was the score on the fifth student's test paper?

    (A) 82
    (B) 85
    (C) 88
    (D) 92

11. For her science project, Mona counted the number of butterflies that were in her backyard each day for a month.

    Butterflies Counted Each Day

Number of Butterflies	Number of Days
0	8
1	6
2	4
3	6
4	4
7	1
10	2

    What is the mode of the data?

    (A) 0
    (B) 1
    (C) 6
    (D) 8

12. What is the greatest common factor of $6r^3t$ and $3r^2t^2$?

    (A) $3rt$
    (B) $3r^2t$
    (C) $6r^2t$
    (D) $18r^3t^2$

CONTINUE TO THE NEXT PAGE

13. If $4m - 4 = mz - z$, where $m \neq 1$, then what is the numerical value of z?

(A) -4

(B) 0

(C) 1

(D) 4

14. If b and c are both prime numbers, then what is the least common multiple of $2n^2$, $4nm^2$, and $6m$?

(A) $8nm$

(B) $8n^2m^2$

(C) $12m^2n^2$

(D) $24m^2n^2$

15. Which is equivalent to the expression $3u^3v^2 - 4u^2v^3 - (2u^2v^3 + 4u^3v^2)$?

(A) $7u^3v^2$

(B) $-6u^2v^3$

(C) $7u^3v^2 - 6u^2v^3$

(D) $-6u^2v^3 - u^3v^2$

16. If $\dfrac{x^3-8}{(x-5)(x+3)}$ is undefined, then what are the possible value(s) of x?

(A) $x = 5$ and $x = -3$

(B) $x = -5$ and $x = 3$

(C) $x = 2$, $x = 5$ and $x = -3$

(D) $x = 2$ only

17. Which expression is equivalent to $x^2 - 16$?

(A) $(x - 4)^2$

(B) $(x + 4)(x - 4)$

(C) $(x + 4)^2$

(D) $(x + 2)(x - 8)$

CONTINUE TO THE NEXT PAGE

18.   A line is plotted in the following coordinate grid.

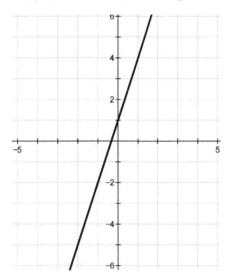

What is the slope of the line?

(A) -3

(B) $-\dfrac{1}{3}$

(C) $\dfrac{1}{3}$

(D) 3

19.   The points $(4, 5)$ and $(8, 7)$ are the endpoints of a diameter of a circle. What are the coordinates of the center of this circle?

(A) $(4, 7)$

(B) $(6, 6)$

(C) $(7, 4)$

(D) $(12, 12)$

CONTINUE TO THE NEXT PAGE

20. A television station wants to predict who will win the next local election. Surveying which group of people would allow the television station to make the most accurate prediction?

    (A) viewers who call in to the television station
    (B) a random sample of all the people who watch that television station
    (C) donors to the television station
    (D) a random sample of registered voters in the local area

21. What is the distance between the points $(3, 8)$ and $(6, 10)$?

    (A) $\sqrt{13}$ grid units

    (B) $\sqrt{26}$ grid units

    (C) 6 grid units

    (D) 8 grid units

22. The following figure shows a quadrilateral with the measures of two of its angles.

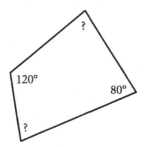

    What is the sum of the measures of the other two angles?

    (A) 70°
    (B) 80°
    (C) 120°
    (D) 160°

CONTINUE TO THE NEXT PAGE

23. There are 5 members of the table tennis team. Only two members may play in an upcoming tournament. How many different two-person combinations can be formed from the 5-member team?

   (A) 2
   (B) 5
   (C) 10
   (D) 20

24. Three vertices of a rhombus are plotted on the following coordinate grid.

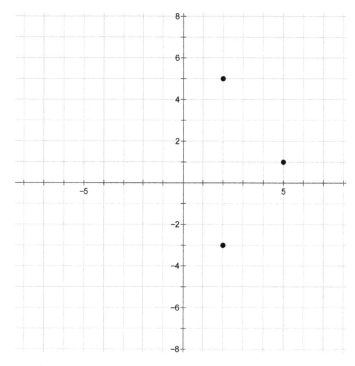

   Which of the following coordinates could be the fourth vertex?

   (A) $(1, 1)$
   (B) $(-1, 1)$
   (C) $(2, 3)$
   (D) $(8, 5)$

CONTINUE TO THE NEXT PAGE

25. What are the values of m that make the inequality $|4m - 2| \leq 10$ true?

   (A) $m \leq 3$
   (B) $m \geq -2$
   (C) $m \leq 3$ or $m \geq -2$
   (D) $-2 \leq m \leq 3$

26. The sum of two irrational numbers could NOT produce what type of number?

   (A) rational number
   (B) integer
   (C) complex number
   (D) irrational number

27. The following column graph shows the number of homes in a neighborhood by the number of bedrooms in each home.

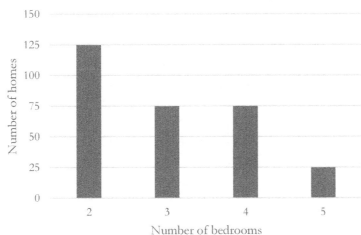

   What is the mean number of bedrooms for homes in the neighborhood?

   (A) 2
   (B) 3
   (C) 3.5
   (D) 5

CONTINUE TO THE NEXT PAGE

28. A solution set is shown on the following number line.

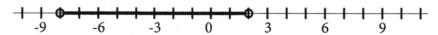

What is the inequality that is represented?

(A) $|n - 5| < 3$

(B) $|n + 5| < 3$

(C) $|n + 3| < 5$

(D) $|n - 5| > 3$

29. Kathryn plans to flip a quarter four times. She created the following table with all of the possible outcomes and the probability of each.

Results of Flipping Quarter

Number of Heads	Probability
0	$\dfrac{1}{16}$
1	$\dfrac{1}{4}$
2	$\dfrac{3}{8}$
3	$\dfrac{1}{4}$
4	$\dfrac{1}{16}$

What is her expected number of heads out of the four coin tosses?

(A) $\dfrac{3}{8}$

(B) 1

(C) 2

(D) 4

CONTINUE TO THE NEXT PAGE

30. There are 60 seconds in a minute and 60 minutes in an hour. There are also 5,280 feet in a mile. If a racecar is traveling at 120 miles per hour, which expression could be used to figure out how fast the car is going in feet per second?

    (A) $\dfrac{120 \times 5,280}{60 \times 60}$

    (B) $\dfrac{120 \times 60 \times 60}{5,280}$

    (C) $\dfrac{120 \times 60}{5,280 \times 60}$

    (D) $\dfrac{60 \times 60}{120 \times 5,280}$

31. Which expression is NOT equal to an integer?

    (A) $\sqrt{6} + \sqrt{6}$

    (B) $\sqrt{6} - \sqrt{6}$

    (C) $\sqrt{6} \times \sqrt{6}$

    (D) $\sqrt{6 \times 6}$

32. The table below shows the results of a student survey. 120 students were asked what their favorite ice cream flavor is.

Favorite Ice Cream Flavor	Number of Students
Vanilla	36
Chocolate	40
Strawberry	24
Other	20

    If a circle graph was made from this data, what would be the measure of the central angle of the section representing students who chose vanilla as their favorite ice cream flavor?

    (A) 36°

    (B) 108°

    (C) 120°

    (D) 240°

CONTINUE TO THE NEXT PAGE

33. Mr. Boyd has a model of a sailboat with a sail that is 6 inches wide and 10 inches tall, as shown in the following figure.

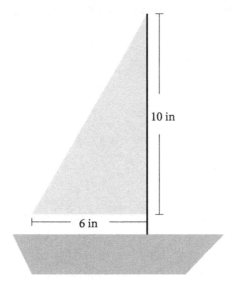

If he wants to build a full-size version of the sailboat with a sail that is 15 feet wide, how tall should the sail be?

(A) 10 feet

(B) 25 feet

(C) 40 feet

(D) 55 feet

34. Which of the following would be the best unit to use when measuring the length of a school bus?

(A) meters
(B) centimeters
(C) kilograms
(D) liters

CONTINUE TO THE NEXT PAGE

35. A square has sides 8m long, and a circle is inscribed in the square as illustrated in the following figure.

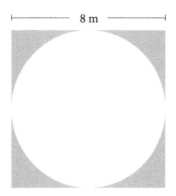

What is the area of the shaded region of the figure, in m²?

(A) $32 - 8\pi$

(B) $32 - 16\pi$

(C) $64 - 16\pi$

(D) $64 - 64\pi$

36. Below are the first four terms of an arithmetic sequence.

$$-2, 2, 6, 10$$

Which expression could be used to figure out the nth term in this sequence?

(A) $n - 3$

(B) $n + 1$

(C) $4n - 4$

(D) $4n - 6$

CONTINUE TO THE NEXT PAGE

37. A cylinder has height, h, equal to half of its diameter. The diameter of the cylinder, shown in the following figure, is 8 cm.

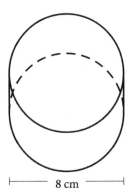

8 cm

Given that the formula for the volume, V, of a cylinder is $V = r^2 h\pi$ (r = the radius), what is the volume of the cylinder shown in cm³?

(A) 64π

(B) 128π

(C) 256π

(D) 512π

38. Penny created the box and whisker plot that follows to summarize the total annual rainfall data in her state from the last 100 years.

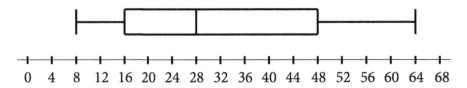

What is the range of the data?

(A) 12

(B) 20

(C) 28

(D) 56

CONTINUE TO THE NEXT PAGE

39. Yesterday, Sally had a collection of 150 pencils. Today, she has twice as many pencils. By what percent did her collection increase?

(A) 50%

(B) 100%

(C) 150%

(D) 200%

40. Two spinners are divided into six equal sections labeled #1-6. Which scenario describes complementary events?

(A) The probability of landing on a 2 and then a 4

(B) The probability of landing on a 3 and then landing on an even number

(C) The probability of landing on a number less than 3 and then landing on a number greater than 3

(D) The probability of landing on an even number and then landing on an odd number

41. Kim surveyed her friends to find out how many times they went swimming over the summer. She put her results into the stem-and-leaf plot below.

```
0 | 3 3 5 6 7
1 | 0 0 2 3 3 3 5 8
2 | 2 4 4 9
3 | 0 3 9
5 | 4
```

What was the mode for this set of data?

(A) 3

(B) 9

(C) 13

(D) there is no mode for this data

CONTINUE TO THE NEXT PAGE

42. Triangle *BCD* is similar to triangle *EFG*.

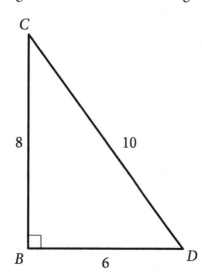
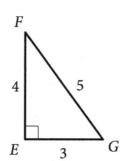

What is the ratio of the length of one side of triangle *BCD* to the corresponding side of triangle *EFG*?

(A)   3 to 1

(B)   2 to 1

(C)   1 to 3

(D)   1 to 2

CONTINUE TO THE NEXT PAGE

43. The figure that follows shows triangle ABC. The length of side BC is 4 inches, and angle BAC measures 65°.

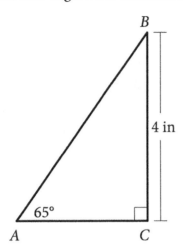

Which of the following expressions is equal to the length of side AB, in inches?

(A) $\dfrac{4}{\sin 65°}$

(B) $4 \times \sin 65°$

(C) $\dfrac{\sin 65°}{4}$

(D) $\dfrac{\sin 65°}{\cos 65°}$

44. Which of the following graphs represents the inequality $37 \leq 3n + 1 \leq 43$?

(A)
```
+  +  +  +  +  +  +  +●—+—●  +
0  5  10 15 20 25 30 35 40 45 50
```

(B)
```
+  +  +●—●  +  +  +  +  +  +  +
0  5  10 15 20 25 30 35 40 45 50
```

(C)
```
+  +  +●●  +  +  +  +  +  +  +
0  5  10 15 20 25 30 35 40 45 50
```

(D)
```
+  +●  +  +  +  +  +  +  +  +  +
0  5  10 15 20 25 30 35 40 45 50
```

CONTINUE TO THE NEXT PAGE

45. The solution set for $m^2 + 36 = 0$ is

    (A) 6

    (B) $6i$

    (C) ± 6

    (D) $\pm 6i$

46. What is the result of the sum $\begin{bmatrix} 4 & 2 \\ 7 & 0 \end{bmatrix} + \begin{bmatrix} 3 & 0 \\ 1 & 4 \end{bmatrix}$?

    (A) $\begin{bmatrix} 7 & 2 \\ 8 & 4 \end{bmatrix}$

    (B) $\begin{bmatrix} 7 & 2 \\ 7 & 4 \end{bmatrix}$

    (C) $\begin{bmatrix} 4 & 0 \\ 7 & 4 \end{bmatrix}$

    (D) $\begin{bmatrix} 4 & 2 \\ 1 & 4 \end{bmatrix}$

47. The formula for the volume of a right cylinder is given by the formula $V = \pi r^2 h$, where r represents the length of the radius and h represents the height. If a cylinder has a height of 8 cm and a volume of 32π cm^2, what is the radius of this cylinder?

    (A) 1 cm

    (B) 2 cm

    (C) 4 cm

    (D) 16 cm

STOP

IF YOU HAVE TIME LEFT YOU MAY CHECK YOUR ANSWERS IN THIS SECTION ONLY

Essay

You will be given 30 minutes to plan and write an essay. The topic is printed on the next page. *Make sure that you write about this topic. Do NOT choose another topic.*

This essay gives you the chance to show your thinking and how well you can express your ideas. Do not worry about filling all of the space provided. The quality is more important than how much you write. You should write more than a brief paragraph, though.

A copy of this essay will be sent to the schools that you apply to. Make sure that you only write in the appropriate area on the answer sheet. Please print so that the admissions officers can understand what you wrote.

On the next page is the topic sheet. There is room on this sheet to make notes and collect your thoughts. The final essay should be written on the two lined sheets provided in the answer sheet, however. Make sure that you copy your topic at the top of the first lined page. Write only in blue or black ink.

(Answer sheets are found at the beginning of the practice test and you can go to www.testprepworks.com/student/download to download additional copies.)

REMINDER: Please remember to write the topic on the top of the first lined page in your answer sheet.

> What is the most important part of the school day?
> Why is it the most important part of the school day?

- Write only about this topic
- Only the lined sheets will be sent to schools
- Use only blue or black ink

Notes

_____

_____

_____

_____

_____

_____

_____

_____

_____

_____

_____

_____

_____

_____

_____

_____

_____

_____

_____

_____

Answers

Verbal Reasoning Answers

Correct answer	Your answer	Put a checkmark here if you answered the question correctly
1. C		
2. A		
3. D		
4. D		
5. B		
6. A		
7. A		
8. C		
9. B		
10. B		
11. D		
12. A		
13. C		
14. C		
15. A		
16. D		
17. B		
18. C		
19. B		
20. A		
21. D		

22.	C		
23.	B		
24.	A		
25.	B		
26.	C		
27.	B		
28.	D		
29.	A		
30.	C		
31.	B		
32.	D		
33.	A		
34.	C		
35.	B		
36.	D		
37.	C		
38.	A		
39.	B		
40.	A		
Total questions answered correctly: _____			

Interpreting Your Verbal Reasoning Score

On the ISEE, your raw score is the number of questions that you answered correctly on each section. Nothing is subtracted for the questions that you answered incorrectly.

Your raw score is then converted into a scaled score. This scaled score is then converted into a percentile score. Remember that it is the percentile score that schools are looking at. Your percentile score compares you just to other students in your grade.

Below is a chart that gives a very rough conversion between your raw score on the practice Verbal Reasoning section and a percentile score.

PLEASE NOTE – The purpose of this chart is to let you see how the scoring works, not to give you an accurate percentile score. You will need to complete the official practice test in *What to Expect on the ISEE*, available for download from ERB at www.erblearn.org, in order to get a more accurate percentile score.

Upper Level Verbal Reasoning

Approximate Raw Scores Needed to Achieve Percentiles

	25th	50th	75th
Applicants to Grade 9	16-17	21-22	27-28
Applicants to Grade 10	17-18	23-24	29-30
Applicants to Grade 11	18-19	24-25	30-31
Applicants to Grade 12	17-18	22-23	29-30

Quantitative Reasoning Answers

Correct answer	Your answer	Put a checkmark here if you answered the question correctly
1. A		
2. C		
3. B		
4. B		
5. A		
6. D		
7. B		
8. D		
9. C		
10. A		
11. B		
12. A		
13. A		
14. C		
15. C		
16. D		
17. A		
18. D		
19. B		
20. D		
21. C		
22. A		
23. A		
24. D		

25. A		
26. B		
27. C		
28. D		
29. C		
30. B		
31. A		
32. C		
33. B		
34. D		
35. B		
36. C		
37. B		
Total questions answered correctly: _____		

Interpreting Your Quantitative Reasoning Score

On the ISEE, your raw score is the number of questions that you answered correctly on each section. Nothing is subtracted for the questions that you answered incorrectly.

Your raw score is then converted into a scaled score. This scaled score is then converted into a percentile score. Remember that it is the percentile score that schools are looking at. Your percentile score compares you just to other students in your grade.

Below is a chart that gives a very rough conversion between your raw score on the practice Quantitative Reasoning section and a percentile score.

PLEASE NOTE – The purpose of this chart is to let you see how the scoring works, not to give you an accurate percentile score. You will need to complete the official practice test in *What to Expect on the ISEE*, available for download from ERB at www.erblearn.org, in order to get a more accurate percentile score.

Upper Level Quantitative Reasoning

Approximate Raw Scores Needed to Achieve Percentiles

	25th	50th	75th
Applicants to Grade 9	15-16	19-20	23-24
Applicants to Grade 10	15-16	20-21	25-26
Applicants to Grade 11	16-17	21-22	27-28
Applicants to Grade 12	17-18	21-22	25-26

Reading Comprehension Answers

Correct answer	Your answer	Put a checkmark here if you answered the question correctly
1. B		
2. B		
3. C		
4. A		
5. D		
6. A		
7. C		
8. D		
9. A		
10. B		
11. C		
12. B		
13. A		
14. C		
15. D		
16. A		
17. D		
18. B		
19. C		
20. B		
21. A		
22. A		
23. B		
24. D		

25.	D		
26.	C		
27.	A		
28.	C		
29.	B		
30.	A		
31.	C		
32.	A		
33.	D		
34.	B		
35.	B		
36.	C		

Total questions answered correctly: _____

Interpreting Your Reading Comprehension Score

On the ISEE, your raw score is the number of questions that you answered correctly on each section. Nothing is subtracted for the questions that you answered incorrectly.

Your raw score is then converted into a scaled score. This scaled score is then converted into a percentile score. Remember that it is the percentile score that schools are looking at. Your percentile score compares you just to other students in your grade.

Below is a chart that gives a very rough conversion between your raw score on the practice Reading Comprehension section and a percentile score.

PLEASE NOTE – The purpose of this chart is to let you see how the scoring works, not to give you an accurate percentile score. You will need to complete the official practice test in *What to Expect on the ISEE*, available for download from ERB at www.erblearn.org, in order to get a more accurate percentile score.

Upper Level Reading Comprehension

Approximate Raw Scores Needed to Achieve Percentiles

	25th	50th	75th
Applicants to Grade 9	17-18	21-22	27-28
Applicants to Grade 10	18-19	23-24	28-29
Applicants to Grade 11	18-19	24-25	29-30
Applicants to Grade 12	16-17	18-19	27-28

Mathematics Achievement Answers

Correct answer	Your answer	Put a checkmark here if you answered the question correctly
1. C		
2. D		
3. D		
4. A		
5. B		
6. C		
7. A		
8. C		
9. D		
10. A		
11. A		
12. B		
13. D		
14. C		
15. D		
16. A		
17. B		
18. D		
19. B		
20. D		
21. A		
22. D		
23. C		
24. B		
25. D		

26.	C		
27.	B		
28.	C		
29.	C		
30.	A		
31.	A		
32.	B		
33.	B		
34.	A		
35.	C		
36.	D		
37.	A		
38.	D		
39.	B		
40.	D		
41.	C		
42.	B		
43.	A		
44.	C		
45.	D		
46.	A		
47.	B		
Total questions answered correctly: _____			

Interpreting Your Mathematics Achievement Score

On the ISEE, your raw score is the number of questions that you answered correctly on each section. Nothing is subtracted for the questions that you answered incorrectly.

Your raw score is then converted into a scaled score. This scaled score is then converted into a percentile score. Remember that it is the percentile score that schools are looking at. Your percentile score compares you just to other students in your grade.

Below is a chart that gives a very rough conversion between your raw score on the practice Mathematics Achievement section and a percentile score.

PLEASE NOTE – The purpose of this chart is to let you see how the scoring works, not to give you an accurate percentile score. You will need to complete the official practice test in *What to Expect on the ISEE*, available for download from ERB at www.erblearn.org, in order to get a more accurate percentile score.

Upper Level Mathematics Achievement

Approximate Raw Scores Needed to Achieve Percentiles

	25th	50th	75th
Applicants to Grade 9	19-20	24-25	29-30
Applicants to Grade 10	20-21	26-27	32-33
Applicants to Grade 11	22-23	28-29	34-35
Applicants to Grade 12	22-23	27-28	33-34

Looking for more practice?

Check out our other book for the Upper Level ISEE:

The Best Unofficial Practice Tests for the Upper Level ISEE

✓ 2 full-length practice tests (different from the practice test in *Success on the Upper Level ISEE*)

TEST PREP WORKS, LLC.

Books by Test Prep Works

	Content instruction	Test-taking strategies	Practice problems	Full-length practice tests
ISEE				
Lower Level (for students applying for admission to grades 5-6)				
Success on the Lower Level ISEE	✓	✓	✓	✓ (1)
30 Days to Acing the Lower Level ISEE		✓	✓	
The Best Unofficial Practice Tests for the Lower Level ISEE				✓ (2)
Middle Level (for students applying for admission to grades 7-8)				
Success on the Middle Level ISEE	✓	✓	✓	✓ (1)
The Best Unofficial Practice Tests for the Middle Level ISEE				✓ (2)
Upper Level (for students applying for admission to grades 9-12)				
Success on the Upper Level ISEE	✓	✓	✓	✓ (1)
The Best Unofficial Practice Tests for the Upper Level ISEE				✓ (2)
SSAT				
Middle Level (for students applying for admission to grades 6-8)				
Success on the Middle Level SSAT	✓	✓	✓	
The Best Unofficial Practice Tests for the Middle Level SSAT (coming soon)				✓ (2)
Upper Level (for students applying for admission to grades 9-12)				
Success on the Upper Level SSAT	✓	✓	✓	✓ (1)
30 Days to Acing the Upper Level SSAT		✓	✓	
The Best Unofficial Practice Tests for the Upper Level SSAT				✓ (2)

TEST PREP WORKS, LLC.

Made in the USA
Monee, IL
07 September 2019